William Heap and his Company

Britannia House, Hoylake.

WILLIAM HEAP

AND HIS COMPANY
1866

by John Millar

'The roads you travel so briskly lead out of dim antiquity, and you study the past chiefly because of its bearing on the living present and its promise for the future.'

Lieutenant General James G. Harboard,
K.C.M.G., D.S.M., LL.D., U.S. Army (Retd.)
Late American Member of Council in London
The Newcomen Society of England

'History is bunk.'
Henry Ford

ISBN 0 9510965 1 6

British Library Cataloguing-in-Publication Data
A catalogue record of this book is available
from the British Library

First Published 15th October 1976
Second Edition April 1977
Third Edition October 1991

Published by John Millar (UK) Ltd, Hoylake,
Wirral, Cheshire, England

Printed by G.M. Business Print, Liverpool

Set in Monophoto 400 Century

CONTENTS

TO MY WIFE DOROTHY

ACKNOWLEDGEMENTS

I have received much help from many people in the preparation of this book and I wish to record my grateful thanks to the following:

The staffs of Birkenhead Reference Library.

Blackpool Corporation Publicity Department.
Blackpool Gazette & Herald, Blackpool.
Blackpool Reference Library.
Brown, Picton & Hornby Libraries, Liverpool.
Burnley Reference Library.
Central Library, Manchester.
Clerk to the Governors, Whalley Old Grammar School.
Cohen Library, University of Liverpool.
Conway Reference Library.
General Registry Office, Somerset House, London.
Hoylake Public Library.
Lancashire County Records Office, Preston.
Liverpool Museum Library.
Mersey Docks & Harbour Board, Liverpool.
Mersey Tunnels Joint Committee, Liverpool.
National Library of Ireland, Dublin.
National Maritime Museum, Greenwich.
Padiham Library.
Radio Times Picture Library, London.
Ulster Museum, Belfast.
UMIST Library, University of Manchester.
Wallasey Reference Library.
Whalley Library.
Widnes Reference Library.

H. E. Bray Esq., Manager of the London Electrotype Agency, London.
J. G. Coté Esq., Research Analyst, Canadian National Railway, Montreal.
C. B. R. Brunswick Esq., Isles House, Padiham.
P. Dawson Esq., Curator of the Newfoundland Museum.
Miss Kathleen Eyre of Lytham St Annes.
Miss M. L. Ellis and Mrs E. M. Roughton.
Liam St John Devlin, Chairman of Coras Iompair Eireann, Heuston Station, Dublin.
J. H. Fell Esq., of Whalley.
G. Forster Esq., Hereford.
T. S. Freeman Esq., Newfoundland.
J. R. Friday Esq., Archivist & Research Fellow, The Royal Institute, London.
Miss Susan Gallagher, Photographic Librarian, Canadian National Railways, Montreal.
I. R. Garnish Esq., Saunders Valve Co., Cwmbran.
M. Holding Esq., Dunham Bush, Portsmouth.
Dr Quentin Hughes, The School of Architecture, University of Liverpool.

F. J. E. Hurst Esq., Librarian, New University of Coleraine, County Londonderry, Northern Ireland.

P. McAteer Esq., KSB Northfleet.

A. P. Miller Esq., Ingham & Yorke, Padiham.

K. A. Murray Esq., Dun Laoghaire, Eire.

Q. W. Parkin Esq., Brede, Nr. Rye, Sussex.

J. Potter Esq., Dunham Bush, Portsmouth.

B. Quinlan Esq., Powerflex Division of Senior TIFT.

D. Morgan Rees Esq., Keeper of Industry, National Museum of Wales, Cardiff.

Mrs B. Robertson, Newfoundland Historical Society, St Johns'.

P. Robinson Esq., KSB Northfleet.

G. F. Singleton Esq., Lytham St Annes.

F. Roscoe Esq., Dunham Bush Ltd., Toronto, Canada.

D. Simpson Esq., Hindle Cockburns Ltd., Leeds.

D. Smith Esq., Hindle Cockburns Ltd., Leeds.

J. Smith Esq., Principal, Adult Education Centre, Old Grammar School, Whalley.

G. P. Le Gendre Starkie Esq., Huntroyde Hall, Padiham.

E. A. L. Sulley Esq., CED Projects Ltd., Marlow, Bucks.

Miss Lloyd Thomas, Assistant Librarian, The Royal Institute, London.

G. R. Tolliday Esq., Oxton, Birkenhead.

W. Shanzenbecher Esq., K. S. B. Manufacturing Co., London.

A. I. Smith Esq., National Engineering Laboratory, East Kilbride.

R. Unsworth Esq., Bowden, Cheshire.

B. Varley Esq., Hindle Cockburns Ltd., Leeds.

J. Waite Esq., Tomoe Saunders Ltd., Newport, Gwent.

H. K. Bale Williams Esq., Stewart Bale Ltd., Liverpool.

R. P. Williams Esq., Aform Ltd., Thatcham, Berkshire.

My special thanks to, Janet Swanson, May Garrity, Helen Williams and Susan Lunt for their valuable assistance; to N. A. Jones and John Thompson of Photographics Ltd., Birkenhead; J. A. Latter of Carl Fox Photography, Liverpool and R. Sanders of Roger Sanders Photography, Hoylake, for the excellent photographs they have taken; to Mr J. Pendlebury of E. Wrigley & Sons, Rochdale and Mr R. B. Elliott of G. M. Business Print & Systems Ltd., printers of Liverpool, for much help and advice regarding the printing; to my wife Dorothy for reading and correcting the manuscript and for constructive suggestions; to my daughter Ann for designing the title layout; to my son John for reading through the proofs and compiling the index and to my son David for words of wisdom.

J.M.

PREFACE TO FIRST EDITION

This book has been written to celebrate the one hundred and tenth anniversary of the founding of this company in the hope that the story of the life and times of William Heap and his company may prove to be of interest to some at least.

Although we have been in continuous business for over a century we still only employ about forty people and yet we have always been a successful company in our own field and we think we play, and have played, a useful part in the industrial and commercial life of this country.

William Heap was not one of the giants of the Victorian Age, but there are plenty of books about the giants and not many about the men who backed them up and frequently did the work for which their masters are rightly remembered. Similarly there are many books written about the large companies but not many about small firms.

The writer was fortunate to be a partner of A. H. Atkins and worked with him for sixteen years until A.H.A. died in harness in 1968. In turn A. H. Atkins was a partner of William Heap and worked with him from 1906 until William Heap retired in 1910; so our lineage, going back to the Industrial Revolution, is perhaps surprisingly short.

Although this is the story of a small engineering company the technical content has been kept as simple as possible as this is the story of people, and their times.

J. Millar
West Kirby
April 1976.

PREFACE TO THIRD EDITION

Fifteen years have passed since this book was first published and in that time the country, and this company, have faced many difficulties and have undergone great changes.

When the book was first published in 1976 small companies were under very real threats from the then Labour Government which did not understand the value of small companies. One of the objectives in first publishing the book was to tell of the important part played by small firms in increasing the prosperity of the nation.

Within a few weeks of the book being published in1976 the magazine "Cheshire Life", asked permission to print an extract from the book about one of the problems we had suffered at the hands of the Labour Government (The Robots of Whitehall, see page 168). We gave permission, but unknown to us, they sent a copy of the article to every Member of Parliament and then the National Press took up the story and there was some laughter about our little difficulty.

Within a year, or so, the attitude of the Labour Government towards small companies started to change for the better and when the Conservatives came to power in 1979, the transformation was complete. It is possible that this book encouraged the change of attitude towards small firms.

In spite of the great difficulties we have had to face since 1979 we have continued to make progress and whereas we only employed about 40 people in 1976 we now have over 70 employees, all very busy.

We are very interested in our past and admire our forbearers enormously but we know that we cannot survive by continuously looking back, but must look ahead and be ready for adventure and change at all times. For the moment however let us look back at our story.

John Millar
"Roseneath"
West Kirby
September 1991

William Heap J.P. M.I.Mech.E. Born 23rd September 1826—Padiham, Lancashire. Died 10th March 1912—Wallasey, Cheshire.

CHAPTER I

Early Days

HEAP FAMILY TREE

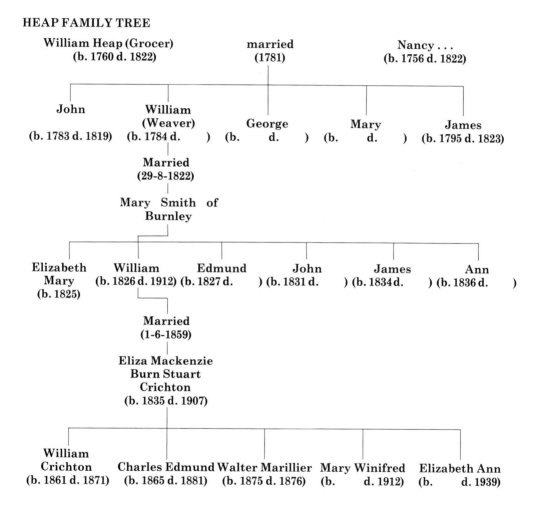

PADIHAM 1760–1800, RIPE FOR REVOLUTION

In the north of Lancashire lies the small town of Padiham, built on a hill rising from the banks of the River Calder with Pendle Hill to the north, home of witches and warlocks. The town is industrial but has a certain charm because it is on the edge of some beautiful country and the older houses are all built of the grey local stone, weathered, strong and enduring like the people of Lancashire.

In 1760, when the first William Heap was born, Padiham was a little village in a lovely setting with rolling hills on all sides. The quiet rhythm of life of its inhabitants had not changed for centuries but elsewhere in England men were working on new inventions that were to change the life of the Heap family, Padiham and eventually the whole world. The old pastoral way of life was about to be changed by a revolution.

When the first William Heap was seven years old not many miles away James Hargreaves invented the Spinning Jenny; the year after Arkwright made his water frame in Preston, the following year in 1769 James Watt patented the separate condenser for steam engines, which vastly improved the clumsy, inefficient engine first built by Thomas Newcomen in the early part of the century. When the first William was fifteen, two events occurred which primed the bomb of the industrial revolution, in Bolton, Samuel Compton invented the spinning mule and James Watt teamed up with Matthew Boulton and they started to produce more efficient engines at their Soho Manufacturings near Birmingham.

Padiham like other towns in Lancashire had coal for fuel, stone for building, the right climate for spinning cotton but, most important, had a hard working, enterprising people. It was ripe for the revolution which shook, and is still shaking the world, which enabled our small country to build the greatest empire the world has known, which opened up dark continents and changed society all over the world. It brought great benefits and great destruction and eventually enabled man to reach out to the stars and beyond.

WILLIAM HEAP (I) 1760–1822

Until the railways opened up the country, almost everybody with the surname Heap lived in Lancashire and the Public Records Office at Somerset House in London show that in 1832 they were not only almost all in Lancashire, but in general they nearly all lived within ten miles of Burnley.

Our founder's grandfather was a grocer and when he was twenty one he married a twenty-five year old girl called Nancy. They had five children, John, William (father of our founder), Mary, George and James.

The grocery business was a small family shop and it served the quiet, modest needs of the small country village, supplying flour, local cheese, black puddings, tripe, smoked ham and other local produce.

WILLIAM HEAP (II) 1784

It seems likely that the first William Heap's eldest son John was intended to carry on the family business because William initially decided to go into the new industry which was just starting up—cotton, and he became a weaver in one of the local mills.

On the 29th August 1822 William married Mary Smith of Burnley and they set up house in one of the stone built cottages in Padiham. Shortly afterwards, William's father died and as William's brother John had died three years earlier William left the mill and took over the family grocery business. William and Mary had six children between 1825 and 1836, Eliza, William (our founder), Edmund, John, James and Ann.

The coming of the cotton industry to Padiham and the growth of other industries, such as mining and quarrying in the area made a great impact on the village. The new industries attracted workers from the surrounding countryside and even as far away as Ireland. In 1800 the population of Padiham was 250 but by 1822 it had grown to 6,000 because of the new influx.

The rapid growth of population increased the demand for supplies of all kinds including groceries and the growth of the Heap business kept pace with the increasing demand. Within a matter of months William started to mill his own flour to keep up with the demand and then he started as a corn dealer as well so that he was able to buy corn from the farmers, mill it into flour and then retail. By the time our founder William Heap (III) was born the Heap family business had grown so much that his father was no longer a grocer but a prosperous merchant.

Isles House, Padiham. The childhood home of William Heap

The increase in the family fortune must have been as rapid as the progress of the Industrial Revolution itself because our William was born in Isles House, Padiham, a large, if not pretty, house and within ten years his father also owned half a dozen cottages in Padiham and rented an estate of 75 acres of lovely rolling parkland which was owned by the local Lord of the Manor, Le Gendre Pierce Starkie who lived in nearby Huntroyde Hall.

Isles House formed part of the Starkie estate Huntroyde Demesne and in the 1820's the Heap family lived in some style with their own coach, horses in the stables at the back of the house and several servants.

William Heap Senior must have been on friendly terms with Pierce Starkie because the 75 acres that Mr Heap rented swept down quite close to the front of the magnificent country mansion Huntroyde Hall, the home of the Starkie family. Although it may seem surprising that a weaver turned grocer, turned merchant in the short time of five years should be on good terms with an ancient family it should be remembered that for centuries Padiham had been quite isolated in the hills and everybody knew each other in such a small village and there was mutual respect between the classes in this country in spite of what the apostles of class hatred would have us believe.

HUNTROYDE DEMESNE

The Starkie family originated in Cheshire in Norman times and there were branches of the family in Stretton and Barnton. In 1464 Edmund Starkie of Cheshire had the good sense to marry Elizabeth de Symonstone and through her gained possession of considerable estates in the Padiham area at Simonstone and Huntroyde Demesne.

Huntroyde Hall is a gracious building set in a natural bowl, the surrounding parkland is like

The 75 acre estate that William Heap's father rented from Le Gendre Pierce Starkie who lived in Huntroyde Hall, seen in the background, with Pendle Hill beyond.

The entrance gates from the land at the back of Isles House leading to the Huntroyde Demesne land rented by the Heap family.

so many other English country estates, a little gem with well positioned groups of elm and other trees. The estate is still in excellent order and the Starkie family still live there, although they have had to reduce the size of the Hall and have had to sell off part of the estate presumably to meet death duties. (Sadly in 1982 the Starkie family had to sell Huntroyde Hall after 500 years continuous occupation by the same family.)

WILLIAM HEAP (III) 1826–1912

Such was the background of the founder of our company, a large house with prosperous middle class parents, servants, horses and 75 acres of beautiful parkland to roam in with his brothers and sisters and other children of the village. The industrial revolution might be under way outside their grounds but that was unimportant to a child when there was Huntroyde Brook to fish in and horses to ride like the wind over lovely parkland.

SCHOOL DAYS

When William was old enough it was decided that he should go way to school and he was sent as a boarder to the best school in the area, Whalley Grammar School, situated some four miles from his home in Padiham.

The school was founded in 1549 by Edward VI the boy King son of Henry VIII and Jane Seymour. Edward was born in Hampton Court and succeeded his father to the thone in 1547 when he was only nine years old and was crowned in Westminster Abbey by Archbishop Cranmer. He was a sickly boy and the country was ruled by his Guardians, but one of the lasting monuments to his memory is the enormous number of schools he founded. The best

Whalley Grammar School painted in 1840 by a twelve year old pupil, J. G. Booth, who attended the school at the same time as William Heap.

Royal Grammar School.
WHALLEY.
N.E. LANCASHIRE.

known is Christ's Hospital, the Bluecoat School in London, founded four years after Padiham Grammar School and where the boys still wear the same uniform designed in Edward's day.

Edward VI granted Letters Patent to Whalley Grammar School in the second year of his reign and like many other splendid schools founded by Edward it gave a sound education to pupils for over four centuries. The school is still standing but although it has a Board of Governors it ceased to function as a school in the early days of the first war, but there are still one or two elderly residents living in Whalley who attended the school before it stopped taking pupils and now the school is used as the local Community Centre and Adult Education Centre.

These schools are part of our heritage handed down to us over four centuries and how any community can allow these schools to be destroyed by petty minded politicians, as they are in some areas, is beyond comprehension.

When the day came for William to leave Isles House for Whalley, his trunk was put in the family carriage and the horse trotted through the leafy road to the ancient village of Whalley and there he was left in the care of Mr and Mrs George Preston, the schoolmaster and his wife. Judging by letters sent by Joshua Ashworth, a pupil at the school, to his parents in 1853, the Prestons seemed to be quite reasonable people, but rumour has it that not all the schoolmasters at Whalley Grammar School were so inclined.

Even though Mr and Mrs George Preston were not unkind, William felt lonely in his first few days at the school and he missed his parents, brothers and sisters, but they were worked quite hard and he soon settled down.

The school was small by today's standards and like most of our best and most expensive boarding schools today, the emphasis was more on education than creature comforts, whereas in State schools the opposite is true and the country suffers accordingly. The floors in the school were flagged, the heating was by open coal fires and lighting was by oil lamps and candles. In the yard there was a hand water-pump and a stone trough and it must have been

William Heap's classroom. The concentration was on education not comfort. The gas lights were installed after William Heap had left.

The woodwork room at Whalley Grammar School. Here William Heap first learned to handle tools.

invigorating, to say the least, to go out into the cobbled yard on an icy winter's morning to draw water for washing from the well.

There were two classes of boarder's, those who stayed for the whole term and weekly boarders and it is likely that William Heap returned home to Isles House each weekend. The fees were £32 a term for the weekly boarders under ten, and £38 a term for those over ten. The extra for those boarders for the whole term was £4 a term.

There was no nonsense about the curriculum and William studied Holy Scripture, Reading, Writing, Arithmetic, Geography, History, Grammar, Composition, Literature, Euclid, Algebra, Trigonometry, Mensuration, Land Surveying, Latin, French, German, Greek, Natural Science, Chemistry, Mechanics and Drawing (Freehand, Model, Mechanical and Shading), Elocution, Book-keeping, Drill and Vocal Music and there were a number of optional extras—Woodwork, Dancing, etc. The excellent education William received at Whalley Grammar School stood him in good stead in his later life.

Whalley is a pleasant village, and William enjoyed the walks in the surrounding countryside and over the ruins of the beautiful Whalley Abbey. On those Sundays when he did not go home, William went with the other boys in a "crocodile" to Whalley Parish Church to worship. There the boys occupied certain pews reserved for the pupils of the Grammar School and he was able to see the Starkie family in their special pew at the front of the congregation.

So William spent his schooldays, working hard, but enjoying life as well. Towards the end of his school days the question of his future career was raised by his father and as William was the eldest boy, it was hoped that he would go into the prosperous family grocery business, but William told his parents that he wanted to become an Engineer, a decision he never regretted. He would undoubtedly have made a larger fortune if he had entered the family business, but he would not have led such an interesting life.

The Royal Grammar School, Whalley, as it is now.

APPRENTICESHIP

After leaving school, William Heap served an engineering apprenticeship but at this time we do not know the name of the firm, and we may never know. His subsequent career leads one to think that it may have been at a works similar to William Fairbairn's famous Canal Street Works, Ancoats, Manchester, but there are no early records of Fairbairn's apprentice's available apart from the more famous ones such as Albert Escher son of the founder of the Zurich factory.

We do know that after serving his apprenticeship William Heap saw an advertisement by William Evans of Cambridge who had secured the contract to build the tubular bridge at Conway and that William Heap was offered a position as a junior engineer with Evans and moved to the lovely little Welsh town of Conway in 1846 when he was just twenty years old, and where he was to meet some of the great giants of the Industrial Revolution, Robert Stephenson, Robert's father George, Brunel, Fairbairn and others

CHAPTER 2

The Conway, Britannia and Drogheda Bridges

Three masterpieces side by side. Edward the First's Conway Castle, Telford's Suspension Bridge and Robert Stephenson's Tubular Bridge—the world's first great tubular bridge.

CONWAY

The small Welsh coastal town of Conway is remarkable in having three great masterpieces side by side, all perfect jewels in their own right. Edward the First's castle, Thomas Telford's suspension bridge and Robert Stephenson's railway bridge, the first great tubular bridge ever built.

CONWAY CASTLE

Conway Castle was one of the chain of castles built by Edward I in Wales, but it is uncomparably the most magnificent. It was designed by James of St George, Master of the King's Works in Wales who was the greatest military architect of the age and was built by the greatest builder in the country, Richard of Chester.

Conway Castle is one of the most outstanding achievements of medieval military architecture in all Europe and men came from all over England and Wales to build it. In 1285 the labour

18

force was 1,500 men and the chief joiner was Robert of Frankby who came from the small village of Frankby in Wirral about two miles from our Hoylake office.

TELFORD'S SUSPENSION BRIDGE

When Thomas Telford was given the task of building the A5 to improve the links between London and Holyhead, and hence Ireland, he built the graceful suspension bridge over the Menai Straits, but the Government also commissioned him to build a similar bridge over the river Conway, because a few years earlier a mail boat had capsized in the river and several local people had drowned.

Telford chose to build suspension bridges and the beauty of the wrought iron masterpieces are a joy to behold to this day.

ROBERT STEPHENSON'S RAILWAY BRIDGE

Robert Stephenson was retained as the Engineer for the Chester to Holyhead Railway which was started in 1845 and the greatest engineering problems were crossing the River Conway and the Menai Straits between Caernarvonshire and the Isle of Anglesey.

After surveying the land, Stephenson decided to build his railway bridge close to Telford's bridge at Conway, which meant that it would have to pass very close to the Castle.

The official guidebook to Conway Castle states "Where there might have been indiscriminate destruction, posterity can be grateful to the railway builders of a century ago for their skilfull and considerate handling of the problem which the presence of the Castle and walls at that particular spot posed for them".

Robert Stephenson's railway bridge is not pretty but it was a great step forward in engineering and accelerated the science of strength of materials, as well as being a triumph of man's ability to overcome great and novel engineering problems, in the same way as some of their descendants are tackling the great engineering problems posed by the North Sea Oilfields today.

THE RAILWAY BUILDERS

It must have been quite an experience for the middle class William Heap to join a firm in the railway business, because the navvies were the roughest, toughest, drunken, hardworking group of men ever seen.

The Victorian middle class engineers were usually men of integrity, with strict standards and usually of gentle upbringing, yet they controlled the toughest workforce the world has ever known. Surprisingly enough, there was mutual respect on both sides and they worked very well together.

At this time Thomas Carlyle wrote of the railway builders: "The country is greatly in a state of derangement, the harvest with its black potato fields, no great things, and all roads and lanes overrun with drunken navvies; for our great Caledonian Railway passes in this direction and all the world here, as elsewhere, calculates on getting to heaven by steam. I have not in all my travels seen anything uglier than that disorganic mass of labourers, sunk threefold in brutality by the threefold wages they are getting. The Yorkshire and Lancashire men, I hear, are reckoned to be the worst; and not without glad surprise I find the Irish are the best in point of behaviour. The Postman tells me that several of the poor Irish do regularly apply to him for money drafts, send their earnings home. The English, who eat twice as much beef, consume their residue on whisky, and do not trouble the postman."

When the Chester–Holyhead line reached Penmaenmawr in May 1846, three hundred Welshmen fought a pitched battle with the Irish navvies, the Riot Act was read by Magistrates and the military were called out—a not unusual occurrence.

Terry Coleman's book "The Railway Navvies", deals in depth with this splendid army of roughnecks who could outdrink, outfight and outwork anybody, and frequently did all over the world. Some idea of their drinking habits can be gauged by the fact that when Sir Morton Peto decided that heavy drinking had to stop during working hours he issued instructions to this effect but added, "A man has a right to bring a gallon with him if he likes in the morning". The English navvies ate two pounds of beef a day and drank gallons of beer and whisky, but they regularly shifted 20 tons of rock and earth and they built the world's railways with pick, shovel and wheelbarrow.

CONWAY RAILWAY BRIDGE

The Conway and Britannia bridges are landmarks in the history of engineering, not only were they the first large tubular bridges ever made, but for the first time the engineering problems posed were solved by a completely new science called "Strength of Materials", which first saw the light of day in William Fairbairn's famous Canal Street Works, Ancoats, Manchester.

The development of bridge design was given a great impetus by the railways because before the Liverpool to Manchester line was opened in 1830, there were only 20,000 bridges in the United Kingdom, but in the next twenty-five years there were no less than 25,000 bridges built by the railway engineers and William Heap played an important part in the building of the most famous of all.

When George Stephenson first started building the Liverpool to Manchester line, cast iron was used instead of stone, the traditional material, and the early iron bridges were arched following traditional bridge design, for example the best known of all those early bridges, that at Ironbridge in Shropshire, imitated the traditional designs.

It was during the building of the Liverpool–Manchester railway that Stephenson decided to break away from the arched design and he consulted Eaton Hodgkinson, a brilliant engineer who was born in the small country town of Anderton, near Northwich, Cheshire. Later, Hodgkinson worked with Sir William Fairbairn in establishing the principals of structural design which were the foundation of modern strength of materials.

Eaton Hodgkinson worked out the design of a cast iron beam and one of the first of these bridges ever made was over Water Street, Manchester, carrying the railway lines out of Liverpool Road Station.

George and Robert Stephenson were forceful and extremely good at solving problems by improvisation but they were working at the frontiers of engineering knowledge and the risks they took in accepting contracts before they had any inkling as to how they were going to solve the engineering difficulties are astonishing. Just as the great Victorian explorers marched off into the unknown, not knowing what they would find, so did the Victorian engineers. The result was a rapid acceleration in engineering knowledge, and a few mistakes.

The Chester to Holyhead railway was a typical example, because Robert Stephenson accepted the commission to build the railway before he had any idea as to how he was going to solve the two greatest engineering problems on the line, how to bridge the notorious, fast flowing, Menai Straits and the river Conway.

Stephenson's first thought was to build a wrought iron arch over the Straits but the Admiralty would not allow this because of the obstruction to shipping. He had designed a small tubular bridge by rule of thumb methods, which spanned the river Lea at Ware on the North East Coast in 1841, but he did not seriously consider this design until fate stepped in with one of those extraordinary co-incidences that it sometimes favours the brave and courageous.

At the Blackwall yard of Miller & Ravenhill on the river Thames, an iron steamship 180′ long by the name of "Prince of Wales", was being built. As she was being launched a bolt holding a cleat sheared and the bilge of the "Prince of Wales" came down on the wharf and the stern tipped downwards. She could not be freed for some hours and by then the tide had ebbed and this left the ship suspended for over 110′ at an angle with one end on the wharf and the other in the water. The onlookers expected that at any time the vessel would crack up but to their amazement when she was eventually freed by screw jacks and floated off on the next tide she had not suffered any structural damage apart from one or two damaged plates where she had hit the wharf.

* The Prince of Wales iron steam-vessel.

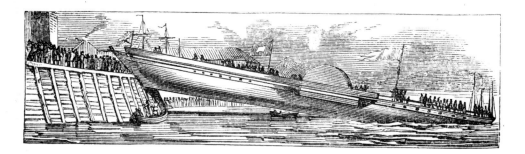

The accident to the "Prince of Wales". When Robert Stephenson was told that the vessel has not cracked up even though she was only supported at the two ends, it solved his problem of how to build the bridges over the Conway and Menai Straits. He would build iron "ships", float them in position, lift them and use them as tubular bridges.

This accident was related to Robert Stephenson and he immediately saw this as the answer to his problem, if the "Prince of Wales" could be suspended for 110' and suffer no damage, then he would build his bridges as tubes on land and then float them in position. In fact that is what he did, he built iron "ships", lifted them in position and used them as bridges: but engineering knowledge and science had to be developed by others before his dream could be accomplished.

Although fate had given him the idea, he was still not clear about the precise design; his first thought was to have a circular tube, then he changed this to an elliptical shape, but it was obvious that further studies were needed and so he went to see William Fairbairn in Manchester.

SIR WILLIAM FAIRBAIRN'S CANAL STREET WORKS, ANCOATS, MANCHESTER

William Fairbairn (1789–1874) was born in Roxboroughshire, Scotland, but settled in Manchester in 1812 when he was twenty-three years of age and five years later he set up his own business with a workmate, Mr James Lillie. They rapidly built up Canal Street works into one of the most important in the country and not only did they manufacture water wheels, bridges and locomotives, but William Fairbairn set out to test engineering materials and structures in a most methodical way and developed the science of testing in a way never known before. Fairbairn tested rivetted joints and devised the tables still used today for this type of joint, he tested iron beams, trellis girders, devised creep tests, worked out and tested materials used in pressure vessels, worked on the properties of steam and for the first time determined directly the density of steam over a wide range of pressure and temperature.

Such was the quality of work done in the Canal Street works that engineers from all over Europe flocked there for training, one was Albert Escher son of the founder of the Zurich factory, another was the brother of Lord Kelvin who became Professor of Engineering at Glasgow University.

FINAL DESIGN OF TUBES

After carrying out tests William Fairbairn rejected Stephenson's ideas for a circular or elliptical tube and calculated that the most suitable structure would be a rectangular tube with a cellular base and roof for added strength.

For Stephenson's convenience they built at Fairbairn's Millwall works a one sixth scale model 80′ long, 4′–6′ deep and 2′ 8″ wide with supports 75′ apart. This was then loaded with weights and the deflection measured. It was found that the tubular construction enabled the bridge to support eleven times its own weight. Other tests were then carried out at Canal Street.

William Fairbairn and his men did their work well, for in those days trains were similar to "The Rocket" and yet today, one hundred and twenty eight years later, the "Irish Mail" and other great express trains thunder across the original bridges whistling their salute to the Victorian Engineers.

WILLIAM EVANS OF CAMBRIDGE

The contract for the masonry for Conway Bridge was let to William Evans of Cambridge, and the first stone was laid in the N.E. corner of the Conway tower on the 12th May 1846 by A. M. Ross the Superintendant Engineer for the Chester–Holyhead Railway.

The enquiry for the wrought iron work was sent to a number of companies in England and Scotland including William Fairbairn who also wanted to build the bridge, Hick & Co of Bolton (now Hick Hargreaves), Rothwell & Co of Bolton (still in existence) and Fairbairn's old partner James Lillie of Manchester.

None of the tenders were satisfactory and to some surprise William Evans offered to do the iron work as well as the masonry for the bridge. Objections were raised because he did not have a workshop for ironwork, but he said that he thought it was preferable to have the workshop there on the site in Conway and that if appointed he would do just that.

Robert Stephenson and Edwin Clark the Resident Engineer were both impressed with William Evans and so they gave him the enquiry and he was awarded the contract in October 1846 for the ironwork, for £145,190 and that price was to include for the fabrication of the six pontoons that were to be needed for floating the tubes in position and also for lifting the tubes in position.

Obviously, William Evans was not a man lacking in courage and enterprise.

As soon as his tender was accepted William Evans advertised for engineers and one of those taken on was William Heap then a young man twenty years old. He moved into lodgings in Conway and stayed there until the bridge was finished, taking part in the fabrication and lifting of a bridge that is a milestone in engineering history, where he met Robert Stephenson, Isambard Kingdom Brunel, Sir William Fairbairn, George Stephenson and for the first time, Thomas Brassey who was building 35 miles of the railway, but not the bridges.

PLANS FOR LIFTING THE TUBES

Stephenson instructed Edwin Clark to build the tubes partly on dry land 600′ from the site of the bridge, and partly on the pontoons which were in the river, but when the tubes were finished they would be floated off on the high tide, positioned, and then lifted bodily by "some means or other" into their final position. Stephenson was still very vague as to how they would carry out the daunting prospect of lifting the tubes weighing 1,300 tons and he made one or two suggestions which Edwin Clark dismissed as being impractical; and off he went back to London leaving Clark to work things out.

The method of lifting such enormous loads troubled Edwin Clark and Fairbairn but one day fate again came to the rescue, because on the 14th July 1846 Stephenson sent Clark to Manchester, and he had to change trains at Crewe. While he was waiting for his connection he saw some workmen lifting a very heavy cast iron water tank into position by means of a screw jack and to prevent accidents they packed up underneath as they lifted. This gave Clark the idea of lifting the tubes by means of hydraulic power through high pressure pumps driven by steam engines and, as with the water tank, they would pack up underneath as they lifted in case anything went wrong with the engine pumps or lifting "chains".

This was three months after work had started on the masonry towers which are higher than they need to have been because at one time they thought they would have to carry chains over the top of the towers to hoist the tubes.

The Roberts Jacquard Press, the world's first punched card controlled machine tool. It could automatically punch ▶ up to thirteen holes $1\frac{1}{8}$″ diameter in $\frac{3}{4}$″ plate at one time and the punches in operation were controlled by the punched card. William Heap had charge of this machine from its invention in 1847 until he set up on his own in 1866. The problem with this magnificent machine tool, at least a century ahead of its time, was to find enough work for it to do.

PREPARING THE PLATES

Two platforms were built part on land, part on piers just above high water mark and on these platforms the tubes were constructed. The tubes were fabricated from $\frac{3}{4}''$ thick wrought iron plates 4' to 8' long and 2' wide. The plates were rolled in Staffordshire and were transported to Runcorn by rail and then by road and sea to Conway. When they were delivered the plates were bowed and the first job was to straighten them. This was done by teams of blacksmiths with sledge hammers and a six inch thick flat bedplate on which the plates were hammered. The noise of this hammering was deafening and under the terrific hammering the flat bedplate eventually became concave so it was turned over and the hammering started again; this had to be done several times.

WORKSHOPS AT CONWAY

William Evans built a complete workshop at Conway equipped as follows:

A drawing office with two draughtsmen
1—20-hp steam engine with shafting to drive the machinery
3—Punching and shearing machines
1—Vertical drill
1—Lathe
3—Flypresses for punching holes
2—Travelling cranes and several fan blowers for the rivet furnaces. Air was carried from these blowers to furnaces in all parts of the works by square wooden ducting.

As well as the workshop machinery there were the steam engines and hydraulic pumps that were to be used to lift the bridge in position.

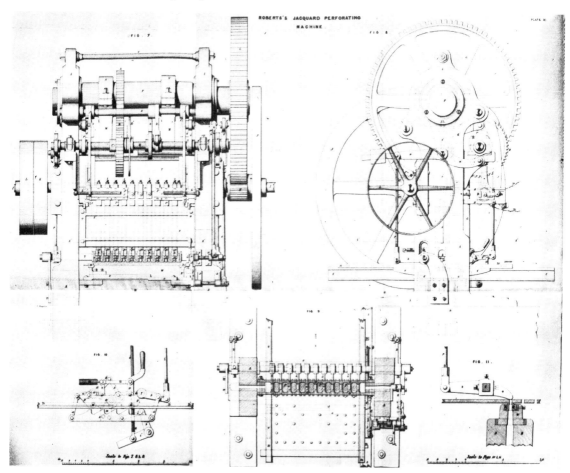

ROBERTS' JACQUARD PRESS

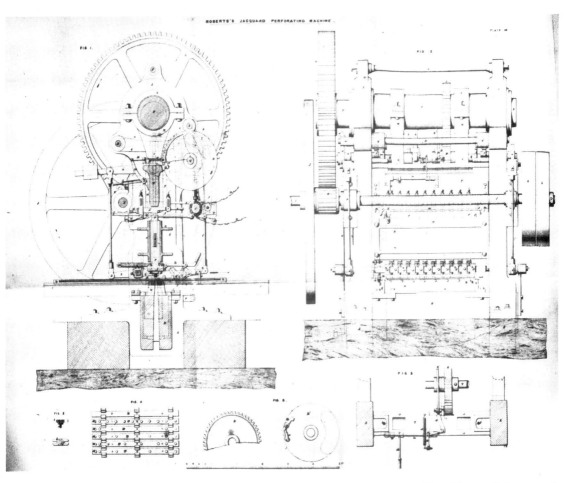

Roberts's Jacquard Perforating machine. The worlds first automatic punched "card" controlled press tool built in a matter of months by Richard Roberts of Manchester.

William Evans was an imaginative, enterprising man and he thought that they could speed up the punching of the plates if the Roberts' presses could be automated. The fly presses could punch one, two or three holes in the $\frac{3}{4}$ inch plate and a good punch lasted three days, and punched some 8,500 holes. However, Mr Evans was more ambitious and so he went to Manchester to see Richard Roberts, the famous engineer, to put to him some sketches for a multi-punch press. He went to the right man because Mr Roberts was also interested in cotton machinery as well as machine tools.

William Evans proposed that the new press should be automated by using the Jacquard card control which was being used in weaving machinery — the Jacquard loom, for lifting the warp and weft in a predetermined manner. The idea was to control the number of punches being used at any one time by the card control, and those punches not required were lifted, so that they did not touch the plates. Richard Roberts and his men set to work and in a remarkably short space of time, they had designed a completely new machine, 16′ high, 12′ wide and 12′ long with a flywheel 10′ diameter and main gear 12′ diameter with a 12″ diameter shaft, and this could punch up to thirteen holes $1\frac{1}{8}″$ diameter in $\frac{3}{4}″$ thick plate at one time and where the punch selection was by card exactly as proposed by William Evans.

This was the first time that an engineering machine tool was controlled by punched card and it worked superbly well.

Two men were employed in adjusting the plate to the sliding table which passed underneath the punches and then after all the holes had been punched two other men lifted the heavy plates off the machine. In this manner, the bottom plates of the tube which needed 144 holes, $1\frac{1}{8}″$ diameter punching in them were punched in under three minutes and this remarkable machine operated for long periods at the rate of 3,168 holes (twenty-two punched plates) an hour.

One can only marvel at the speed with which this sophisticated machine, even by modern standards, was developed and made in a matter of weeks by Mr Roberts and his men in Manchester.

William Heap had a long association with this machine because after the Conway bridge was finished he took it over to Drogheda in Ireland but due to problems dealt with later it was bought by Thomas Brassey and installed at Canada Works, Birkenhead, where it punched the holes in the plates for the Boyne Viaduct, the Victoria Bridge, the longest bridge in the world at that time, and later the Jumna River bridge in India. It was so good that the problem in later years was to find enough large jobs to use it on, because it operated so rapidly.

Surely the banks of the River Conway is the most improbable setting for the worlds first punched card, or tape, operated automatic multi-head press.

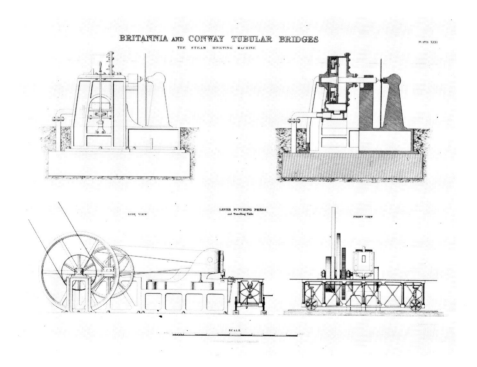

Riveting Machine used on Conway Tubular Bridge.

RIVETTING

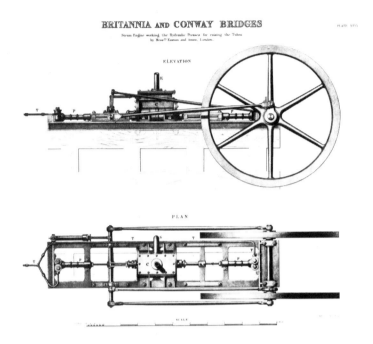

Combined Steam Engine and Pump, Conway Bridge.

A rivetting team comprised two rivetters, one "holder up" and two boys who were usually eleven or twelve years old. One boy worked on the portable forge which was fitted with a bellows, or he used a reverberating furnace to heat the rivets which varied from 2·25″ to 5″ long and they weighed $\frac{3}{4}$lb. When the rivets were red hot the boy would pick them up in his tongs and throw them in a curved arc some thirty or forty feet where they would be caught by the tongs of the second boy. He then put the rivet 1·5″ or 2″ into the hole. The "holder" would be inside with a heavy hammer and the two rivetters outside. After rivetting the rivets were then the finished off with the familiar dome shaped head.

Initially the rivetters started off with $2\frac{1}{2}$ lb to 4 lb hammers such as were used in boiler work but it was found that these were too light and they were changed to 7 lb hammers. The hammers used by the "holders" weighed between 30 lbs to 60 lbs. There was some difficulty in persuading the rivetters to change to the heavier hammers but once they started to use them they encountered no difficulties.

An eye witness described how people came from miles around to see the rivetters at work and the precision with which the eleven and twelve year old boys threw the rivets excited great admiration.

"By night red hot rivets ascending in graceful curves to a height of thirty or forty feet formed an interesting sight."

A steam rivetting machine made by Garforth of Dukinfield near Manchester, proved to be most successful and it was used wherever possible. Later this was taken to the Britannia Bridge over the Menai Straits, but there the contractors used London rivetters and they would not allow the machine to be used because they felt it would rob them of their craft.

The platform where the tubes were fabricated were made of wood and fire was a constant hazard, because of the presence of the furnaces and the red hot rivets flying through the air. To overcome this problem two fire engines were in constant attendance and cast iron fire mains were laid to every point of the platform and flexible hoses were available for the fire fighters. This system was later used on the Britannia platforms.

SIZE OF EACH TUBE

Each tube measures 412' long, 14' wide, 25' high in the middle and 22'–3" high at each end and the weight of each of the Conway tubes is 1,300 tons.

The expansion of the tubes due to temperature changes, was accommodated by twenty-four pairs of rollers and twelve 6" diameter gun metal balls. Mr Clark suggested that they should attach to the end of one tube a system of levers and a dial, so that the relationship between temperature and movement could be measured, providing a means whereby they could learn more about the movement of large masses.

Eventually in February 1848, the first tube was finished and was ready to be towed into position, an eye witness recorded:

"When completed and resting on its massive platform, with crowds of busy workmen, the fuming chimney, the vast pontoons, all contributed to make the scene one of the most interesting and anamalous that was ever witnessed; especially when the peculiarity of the situation is remembered: the calm river floating idly by and the old castle, the work of hands long since crumbled to dust and of instruments long since eaten to rust, looking as it were in astonishment on the whole, while a crowd of Welsh country folk incessantly gaped with amazement at the idea of putting a long iron chest over their ancient river."

METHOD OF LIFTING THE BRIDGE

As we have already seen the idea of positioning the tubes was to float them into position and then to slowly hoist them into place. Robert Stephenson was not very happy about floating the tubes into position but Edwin Clark was very persuasive and finally convinced Stephenson

Conway 1848— Working on the second tube.

that it could be done with proper planning and with the right man in charge of the marine operation. The man chosen for this task was Captain Claxon R.N., who had achieved fame by refloating Brunel's superb ship "The Great Britain", the mightiest ship ever built at that time, when she ran aground in Dundrum Bay, Ireland two years earlier on a voyage from Liverpool to New York.

The hydraulic machinery for lifting the bridge was made by Easton & Amos of Grove Iron Works, Southwark, London, and they positioned at the top of each tower two large hydraulic rams, 18" inside diameter and 36" outside diameter, giving a wall-thickness of 9". To the top of each ram a cross-head was secured two square feet thick, with two square holes through which the chain passed. These "chains" were made of flat wrought iron bars $1\frac{1}{2}$" thick, 7" wide and 6' long. Each ram lifted two chains comprised of nine links, containing eight bars in the upper links, but only four in the lower. The stroke of the ram was 6' and at the end of each stroke the bridge was to be supported, the chains disconnected, one link taken out to shorten it, the ram lowered and the chain reconnected, and then the lift started again.

HYDRAULIC PUMP

In the recesses where the bridge was to be finally positioned were two steam pumps or in the words of an eye witness "steam engines of a peculiar construction". The engines were horizontal, high pressure (for those days) engines, and the piston rod ran through the cylinder at both ends. The drive end was connected to a con-rod and flywheels and the other end formed the piston of the hydraulic pump.

From the pump ran a $\frac{3}{8}$" bore wrought iron tube and this conveyed the hydraulic pressure to the lifting cylinders.

Details of the pumps and hydraulic rams are:

Steam pressure	50 p.s.i.g.
Engine bore	12"
Stroke	16"
Pump Piston diameter	$1\frac{1}{16}$"
Pump speed	40 strokes/minute
Pump discharge pressure	8,556 p.s.i.g. (3 ton/sq in)
Hydraulic ram O.D.	36"
Hydraulic ram I.D.	20" (after modification)

Great difficulty was experienced when the rams were being constructed because such high pressures had never been used before. When the ram was first tested it was found that despite the 9"-thick walls the bore increased to such an extent that power was lost. A new larger piston was made but the same thing happened, a third piston was then made with the same result and the engineers were despairing when somebody noticed that although the bore was still increasing, the rate of increase was dropping and that furthermore, the outside diameter of the cylinder had not increased. This indicated that the wrought iron was being compressed under high pressure and so they carried on until compression was completed and the cylinder bore did not change under pressure.

When finished the rams were capable of exerting a lift of 900 tons each which was adequate for Conway as well as the heavier Britannia tubes.

POSITIONING THE TUBES

On Monday 6th March 1848, twelve months after construction of the tubes had started the great experiment was made. Some of the greatest engineers in the world at that time journeyed to North Wales to witness the lifting of the tubes. Robert Stephenson, the engineer for the Chester–Holyhead line, his father George, Isambard Kingdom Brunel, William Fairbairn of Manchester, Eaton Hodgkinson and all the gentry for miles around came with a great crowd of locals.

Conway 1848—Preparing for the second lift.

*Conway. Floating the second tube into position
12th October 1848.*

The first tube with its ends blanked off to make it watertight rested on the platforms with the pontoons under them; as the tide started to rise, the six immense pontoons each 100′ long were floated underneath by sailors from Liverpool under the command of Captain Claxon; as the tide continued to rise the pontoons lifted the bridge and it was ready to be floated into position. There were seventy men on the pumps, valves and crabs and two hundred sailors on the capstans and pontoons with several rescue boats in attendance. Captain Claxon with his megaphone and a system of signals directed the bridge across the river towards the estuary until eventually it was in position, resting on two temporary stone piers. This was a very tricky operation because this was by far the largest iron "vessel" ever to float at that time, and to manoeuver such an ungainly craft into position on the fast flowing Conway was no easy task. As soon as it was accomplished, great cheers rang out from the onlookers and workmen and in his exuberance Captain Claxon smashed his megaphone and threw it into the river.

When the first tube was in position ready for the great lift, a restless Robert Stephenson, a concerned Edwin Clark, a cigar smoking Brunel and a cadavorous William Fairbairn, climbed on to the top of the tube and witnessed the chains being secured to each end of the monster structure. The boilers were then fired up to full pressure, the engines and lifting rams were manned and the excitement was intense—many wondered if it would be possible to lift such a gigantic load by means of the tiny $\frac{3}{8}''$ bore pipes and even Edwin Clark was extremely tense and concerned. An eye witness reported:

"Regarded in itself this little $\frac{3}{8}''$ bore tube was the least imposing portion of the whole mechanism and no one who looked at it by the side of the vastly proportional instrument it was attached to would have believed that this tiny cylinder was the channel of a force equalling 700 or 800 tons. Could it be possible that this vast work was to be lifted by the direct instrumentality of two tubes the size of a quill barrel?"

Conway Tubular Bridge.

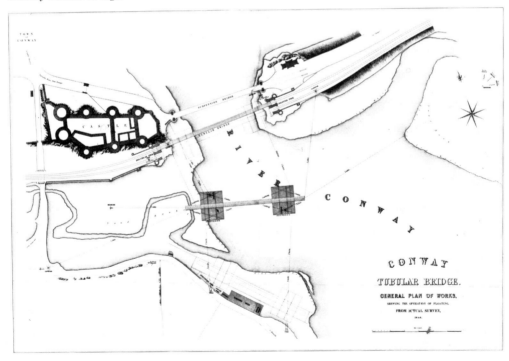

When all was ready Edwin Clark gave the signal and the engines at both ends of the bridge started work and slowly the mighty structure started to lift, but the bridge started a tremulous motion like a wave running along its length. The lift was stopped and the engineers consulted together and concluded that the motion was being created by both engines working together at the same time. The lift was started again but this time with each engine working alternatively.

Under the bridge were slung two platforms at both ends and on these were teams of men who put timber packings under the tube every inch, so that if any of the lifting gear failed, the tube could not fall. Following this team came the stonemasons who built the final stone supports of white limestone from Penmaemawr and the Great Orme. The stone used for the interior of the columns was sandstone from Runcorn.

An eye witness wrote:

"Amid the buzz of voices, the muffled sound of clacking valves and the hurrying too and fro of swarthy mechanics, the Tubular Bridge rose majestically but with great slowness, into the air. At every rise of six feet the engines were stopped and the chains readjusted to the head of the ram and the top links removed. By a succession of such rises the tubes finally reached its desired elevation of about 24 ft, and there dangled in the air as though a mere plaything in the hands of two hydraulic giants."

The masonry was built up underneath and then the bridge was allowed to take up its final position. The anxiety of William Evans, his men, Stephenson, Clark and the other great engineers present, was at an end and the tubular bridge lay across the river Conway, a great and lasting monument to the skill and courage of the Victorian engineers who had worked so hard to build it.

Railway lines were then laid through the tunnel and a locomotive and carriages loaded with 300 tons of ballast were rolled on to the bridge and left for three days, but the maximum deflection did not exceed $1\frac{1}{2}''$ and on removal of the load the deflection disappeared.

So a new type of scientifically designed and tested bridge was born and a novel method of lifting had been invented and proved, the sceptics were confounded and another link in the nation's network of railways was forged by sweat and genius.

The "London Illustrated News" later reported:

"Since its erection the bridge has been continuously used and the vast hollow, which a few months ago resounded with the deafening clatter of the rivetters' hammers, now roars with the rush of carriages and re-echoes in a voice like thunder the hoarse and impetuous expectations of the flying locomotive. The mathematicians still nurse their forebodings; but may God forbid that a work of so much skill and ingenuity, and the destruction of which would inevitably involve so fearful a loss of life, should become a mass of ruins! We do not share these fears, experiment has long since settled the question; and we believe that nothing but some anomalous and unforseen class of circumstances could injure the security of the Tube Bridge. The Tube Bridge is pre-eminently a work of our own era; it is one of those vast and complicated efforts of skill which no previous period of the world's history could command."

The young William Heap had to work extremely hard from very early in the morning until late at night, but they were heady days for a young engineer and he knew that he was taking part in a great and exciting adventure.

The second tube was floated on the 12th October 1848 and was raised on the 30th October 1848, this tube was loaded with 235 tons–14 cwt–2 qrs and it deflected 1.86″ and again this disappeared when the load was removed. When a normal train was run over the deflection was less than $\frac{1}{8}''$.

William Fairbairn patented the tubular bridge and there were some hard feelings between him and Stephenson because Fairbairn felt that Stephenson had not given him due credit for the work he had done in perfecting the design, this was a pity but understandable.

PUBLIC DINNER

On the 17th May 1848 a public dinner was given by the Gentry of Conway to Mr Robert Stephenson to celebrate the successful erection of the tubular bridge. This dinner was held in a temporary pavilion at the back of the Castle Hotel, Conway. The tent was 70' long by 25' wide and at each end of the pavilion were the gigantic initials "R. S." in a blaze of variegated lamps and the whole was festooned with flowers and evergreen. The interior of the tent was lined with crimson and white drapes and formed a splendid setting for the celebration.

One hundred and thirty tickets were sold at one guinea each and young William Heap found himself in exalted company because the guests included:

Hon. Edward Mostyn
Lloyd Mostyn M.P.
Robert Stephenson
George Stephenson
Captain Claxon
Wm. Evans

Mr Fairbairn and Mr Brunel sent letters of apology.

At the head table sat the Hon. Edward Mostyn, Lloyd Mostyn M.P., Robert Stephenson sat on his right and George on his left. The food was superb and the vintage wine flowed freely.

Robert Stephenson spoke about the bridge and one speaker marvelled at the speed of the railway "We are now whirled along at a speed exceeding that of the fastest horse".

Messrs Ryalls, G. Holden Jnr., Roberts and G. Holden of Liverpool were the Glee Singers and the latter gentleman officiated as conductor of the piano-forte, and they entertained the distinguished guests with renderings of:

"The Winds Whistle Cold"
"The Huge, Huge, Globe"
"Mynheer Van Dunk"

There was great pride in the skill of British engineers in building Conway Bridge and "Chambers Journal" reported:

"There are men who are in raptures with the engineering skill which reared the Pyramids, built Baalbec and adorned Petra, but turn with a smile of pity to the 'puny efforts', as they call them of modern times. If the eye of such persons rests on this page let them accompany us while we describe one of the most surprising and stupendous efforts of modern engineering enterprise—the Tubular Bridge—and they will become acquainted with a work which Egypt and the ancient might have been proud of, but could never have excelled."

The Conway Tubular Bridge today. Although it was only built for locomotives similar to the Rocket, it now carries modern trains such as the one leaving the bridge. The depression in the foreshore on the right is where the first tube was made.

THE BRITANNIA BRIDGE, MENAI STRAITS, NORTH WALES

CONSTRUCTION OF TUBES ON THE CARNARVON SHORE.

Construction of tubes on the Carnarvon Shore.

Following the successful construction and lifting of the Conway Bridge came the building of the Britannia Bridge across the Menai Straits. It was a great consolation to the engineers to know that they now had a tried and proven method of making and positioning the tubes, but although the problems were the same as Conway they were of a greater magnitude. There were four spans each of two tubes, not one double, as at Conway; the Straits are very difficult waters to navigate as any yachtsman will tell; the lift of the tubes was one hundred feet not 24' and each tube was 472' long—72' longer than Conway and weighed 1,600 tons as against Conway's 1,300 tons.

William Evans was not the Contractor for the Britannia Bridge but in view of the experience that the Evans' men had gained at Conway, they were frequently consulted and their lifting gear and pontoons were used as the two sites are only 17 miles apart. William Heap was one of those who periodically visited and worked at Menai and he was able to see the progress of the Britannia Bridge.

Two complete villages were built on either side of the Straits near to the site for the bridge, including huts for the men, shops, schools for the children and a chapel of worship. There were some complaints about the prices of the goods in the shops but in general the villages were almost self supporting.

At Conway, Stephenson built his bridge alongside Telford's suspension bridge and similarly at Menai the tubular bridge can be seen from Telford's delicate and elegant road bridge.

33

*Apparatus for lifting the
tube of the Britannia bridge.*

The Britannia tubes were constructed on the bank some 600′ from the permanent site and as well as the Conway pontoons the contractors built several large ones 98′ long by 5′ wide and 11′ deep drawing 5′ when fully loaded. In the bottom of the pontoons were large valves which were normally open to admit the tide, but when they were ready to lift, the valves were closed and the water pumped out.

Captain Claxon was again in charge of the floating of the tubes, each tube was 472′ long and 98′ high and some idea of the navigational problems may be gained by noting that each tube was three times as long as the largest ship then afloat anywhere in the world at that time—the "Great Britain".

Large pontoons with giant capstans bolted to them were towed out into mid-stream and anchored there. Each capstan was worked by fifty men, hawsers passed around the capstans from the shore and the masonry tower. There were no less than 600 men employed in the floating and positioning of the tubes and of this number, three hundred and eighty six were sailors from Liverpool.

Because of the distances involved between the various teams of men Captain Claxon evolved a system of signalling by means of boards with numbers and letters painted on.

The towers were built of Anglesey marble with an interior of Runcorn sandstone as are those at Conway. The blocks of Anglesey marble are gigantic and each block weighs between 10 and 12 tons and conveying them and lifting them into position to build the towers in mid-stream was no mean feat. At the top of the piers there are rectangular slots which were built in in case it was necessary to have chain supports for the tubes at a later date, but of course these were not needed.

STEAM ENGINES AND LIFTING TACKLE

There were two horizontal steam engines, made of a similar design to those used at Conway, each of 40-hp with cylinders 17″ I.D. × 16″ stroke. The pump piston was $1\frac{1}{16}''$ diameter and the wrought iron pipe used at Menai was 0.5″ internal diameter and 1″ outside diameter.

The hydraulic presses used for lifting were 20′ I.D. × 42″ O.D. and were made at the Bank Quay Foundry in Warrington. In his report on the Britannia Bridge Edwin Clark calculated that the pressure generated by the pump was 5,040 lb/circular inch, that is 6,400 p.s.i. which was 2,150 p.s.i. less than the Conway pumps.

ENGINEERS AND CONTRACTORS

Engineer—Robert Stephenson
Resident Engineer—Edwin Clark
Consultants—William Fairbairn
Masonry and scaffolding—Messrs Nowell, Hemmingway and Pearson
Fabrication of one tube—Messrs Garforth of Dukinfield
Remaining seven tubes – Messrs Ditchburn & C. Mare of Blackwall, London
Hydraulic presses—Easton & Amos of Southwark, London

Most of the platers were from London, the stonemasons and labourers were Welsh and the sailors were from Liverpool.

LIFT OF THE FIRST TUBE

On the 27th June 1849 the first tube was floated and prepared for lifting. The correspondent of the "Illustrated London News" gave this eyewitness account on the 30th June 1849:

"Mr Stephenson and other Engineers gathered to witness and direct the operation, as with Conway, Captain Claxon R.N. was in charge of the floating and positioning of the tubes and he

Britannia Bridge, Menai Straits.

Britannia Bridge, Meani Straits (Entrance to the Tubular Bridge).

used his speaking trumpet and he had a number of men with cards on which were printed different letters which indicated to the various capstans, so that no mistake could occur as to which capstan should be worked, and flags red, blue or white, signalled what particular movement should be made with each.

'About 7-30 in the evening the first perceptible motion which indicated that the tide was lifting the mass was observed, at Mr Stephenson's desire the depth of water was ascertained and the exact time noted. In a few minutes the motion was plainly visible; the tube being fairly moved forward some inches. This movement was one of intense interest; the huge bulk gliding as gently and easily forward as if she had been a small boat. The spectators seemed spellbound for no shouts or exclamations were heard, as all watched silently the silent course of the heavily freighted pontoons. The only sounds heared were the shouts from Captain Claxon as he gave directions to "let go ropes', to 'haul in faster' etc and broadside on the tube floated majestically into the centre of the stream.

'I then left my station and ran to the entrance to the works, where I got into a boat and bade the men to pull out as fast as they could into the middle of the Straits. This was no easy task as the tide was running strong; but it afforded me several splendid views of the floating mass and one was especially fine; the tube coming directly on down stream; the distant hills covered with trees; two or three small vessels and a steamer—its smoke blending well with the scene— forms a capital background; whilst on one side, in long stretching perspective stood the three unfinished tubes destined, ere long, to form with the one then speeding on its journey one grand and unique roadway.

"It was impossible to see this imposing sight and not feel its singleness, if we may so speak. Anything so mighty of its kind had never been seen before; again it would assuredly be; but it was like the first voyage made by the first steam vessel—something till then unique."

When the tube was eventually positioned it was lifted into its place in the same way as at Conway being lifted at the rate of 2″ per minute and again men worked on platforms slung under the tube following the tube up with wooden packing pieces, and they in turn were followed by the Welsh stonemasons.

ACCIDENT

On Friday 17th August 1849, after three of its lifts had been successfully accomplished on the previous days; the lift was proceeding and 2′-6″ of an individual lift of 6′ attained when between 11 am and noon the bottom of one of the cylinders of one of the long presses "burst out" and the 1·5 ton piece fell 70′ to 80′ on to the top of the tube below.

As already related Stephenson and Clark had insisted that the wooden packings, 1″ thick, should be inserted as rapidly as possible as the tube rose. These packings were then carefully removed piece by piece and the spaces filled in with brick work in cement so as to be nearly flush with the outer wall of the tower.

As it was the fall of the tube was only one inch but even so the 1,600 ton tube caused quite a shock. The bottom of the cylinder in falling unfortunately struck a sailor who was ascending a rope ladder from the tube to the hydraulic ram and killed him.

A new cylinder was made in six weeks by Bank Quay Foundry in Warrington and when it went into service this worked very well, all the other tubes were lifted successfully.

The Britannia Bridge took four years from work first starting on the masonry, the first stone was laid in May 1846, the first rivet was hammered in on the 10th August 1847 and the last 2,000,000 rivet was hammered in by Robert Stephenson himself and to this day this rivet is painted white; the first train went through in March 1850.

The cost of the Britannia Bridge was £601,865 and as Edwin Clark commented in his book on the Conway and Britannia Bridges only twenty years earlier these bridges could not have been built because "not only was there no machinery nor tools for the manufacture and working of such heavy plates, but that intelligent and valuable class of men who carry out such operations with an energy and skill in the practical detail and a sound mechanical appreciation of what is required, which it is a delight to witness was not then in existance: they are the peculiar offspring of railway enterprise and among the most valuable fruits of its harvest." One such man was William Heap.

After the bridge was finished the great hydraulic cylinders that had been used for lifting the tubes were exhibited at the Great Exhibition of 1851 held in the Crystal Palace, Hyde Park, to take stock of the products of the Industrial Revolution and of Victorian achievement.

THE FIRE IN 1970

A modern sequel to the story of the Britannia Bridge is that on the 23rd May 1970 two young boys entered the tube on the Anglesey side looking for bats, and they accidentally set fire to the timber lining of the tube. This badly damaged some of the plates before the fire was discovered such that the bridge had to be closed.

After studying the consultants reports it was decided that a new supporting arched structure should be built under the tubes and sometime in the future a road bridge is going to be built across the stone towers. While the Britannia Bridge was out of action, the island of Anglesey suffered great difficulties indicating the continuing importance of this great Victorian Bridge, one hundred and twenty-five years after it was built.

THE BOYNE VIADUCT, DROGHEDA, IRELAND

The next large contract William Heap worked on was also an historic bridge because it was one of the first large lattice bridges to be built of wrought iron and where the problem would prove to be so great that his employer William Evans would be forced into liquidation.

The lattice work bridge had been widely used in America because this design was ideal for building with timber which was found in abundance all over America. Sir John MacNeill was the Consultant Engineer for the Dublin and Drogheda Railway and in the early 1840's he had built the first ever lattice bridge in wrought iron to carry a private road across the line and having proved the design he used the lattice design to build a bridge across the Royal Canal.

In 1845 it was decided to join up the Dublin to Drogheda line to the Ulster Railway and so make a continuous line from Dublin to Belfast and the new system was to be re-christened the Dublin and Belfast Junction Railway.

The main engineering problem was to build a bridge across the Boyne at Drogheda and as at Menai the Admiralty insisted that the bridge must have adequate headroom for shipping and specified that the headroom should be 90' and that there should be a clearway of 250'. Again as at Menai this ruled out an arched bridge and the choice lay between a lattice bridge and a tubular model. Sir John MacNeill sent out a general enquiry asking for suggested designs to several ironworks and he received tenders for two or three lattice work viaducts and a very comprehensive and detailed proposal from William Fairbairn in Manchester for a tubular bridge. Sir John had also made a very sketchy design of a lattice bridge himself and he showed this and Fairbairn's proposals to the Board.

The Boyne Viaduct, Drogheda, Ireland.

About this time (1849) James Barton joined the D. & B. J. R. as Engineer and when he saw Sir John's plans he was critical because they were incomplete and far too vague; so he seconded one of his own men, Mr A. Schaw, to work in Sir John MacNeill's Dublin office in order to complete the design. James Barton was a most thorough man and he checked and re-checked the lattice bridge design. Then he had a 60′ span made in Belfast and tested this to destruction. This revealed weaknesses in the original design so they started again and Barton and Schaw worked fifteen to twenty hours a day to complete the revised design.

In May 1851 the plans were sent out again for re-tender, and William Evans was awarded the contract at a price of £68,000 and William Heap moved to Drogheda to prepare for the production of the wrought iron which it was expected would be needed within a few months because the bridge had to be finished by 1853.

William Evans in his customary energetic style set to work and recruited labourers and stonemasons locally paying enhanced wages to the men preparing the foundations. Unhappily they ran into considerable trouble with the alluvial soil, particularly with the foundation for pier 14 which was to be positioned in the water and was to carry one of the iron spans across the Boyne.

The coffer dams were built and day after day the men worked hard digging out the subsoil but all they found were unstable clay, loose fragments of rock and small boulders. William Heap was kept occupied by building a temporary wooden arch across the Boyne which was to be the support for the latticed iron structure during construction, but month after month went by and still the men digging in the coffer dams did not hit a solid foundation.

Trouble was looming ahead for William Evans because the bridge had to be finished in time to carry traffic from the North down to Dublin for the Irish Great Industrial Exhibition of 1853 and daily it grew more and more obvious that in view of the problems with the foundation that the viaduct would not be finished in time.

The long delays were now creating financial problems for William Evans but he was determined not to let the Railway company down and so he mortgaged all his plant and tackle, offering to convert the sturdy, but temporary, wooden arch into a temporary railway bridge so that the trains could cross the river. His offer was greatfully accepted and £2,000 was spent on strengthening the wooden arch. A track was laid across it and the Dublin to Belfast line was complete, albeit temporarily.

On 11th May 1853 a test train of a locomotive with four wagons of ballast was steamed on to the temporary arch and Captain Wynne of the Board of Trade tested for deflection and found this was only $\frac{3}{8}''$ and so he gave permission for trains to cross the bridge at a speed of 4 m.p.h.

Work continued in the coffer dam and they were 30′ down but still had not found bottom, so William Evan's financial problems were now enormous. Although he fought on as long as he could, desparately hoping to gain enough time for his men to find the foundation he was seeking, he was within a few weeks of finishing the temporary structure when he was forced into liquidation and William Heap at the age of thiry-three found himself out of work—but not for long.

At the same time over the other side of the Irish Sea work had just started on a new works to make bridges, locomotives and other railway equipment. The man behind the new venture was Thomas Brassey, a contractor, whom William Heap had first met at Conway and a man with an excellent reputation as a contractor and employer. The prime reason for building the new works, called "Canada Works" was to build the equipment for the Grand Trunk Railway in Canada and Robert Stephenson was the engineer. The most difficult part of the contract was the building of the "Victoria Bridge", the largest bridge in the world and to this day the longest tubular bridge ever built.

Robert Stephenson had been very impressed with the work of William Evans and it is possible that he suggested to Thomas Brassey that William Evans and William Heap would be ideal for running the Bridge Department, but whatever the reason William Evans joined Thomas Brassey in 1853 as Manager of the Bridge Department and William Heap became sub-Manager.

Back in Ireland the Dublin and Belfast Junction Railway decided that they would finish the bridge themselves, because once they reached a firm foundation for Pier 14, the rest would be easy because of the wooden arch already spanning the Boyne.

James Barton set his men to work again in the coffer dam for pier 14 and in October 1853 they were rewarded by finding sure foundations at a depth 45 feet below the low water level of the river. William Evans had been so near success, had gambled, and had lost everything. After his splendid work on the Conway Bridge he deserved a kinder fate.

Thomas Brassey had bought the magnificent Roberts-Jacquard press from William Evans and this produced all the iron work for the Boyne Bridge and James Barton's men rivetted it together to form the first great wrought iron lattice work bridge. The punched cards for the Boyne, the Conway and the Victoria bridges were kept at Canada Works for many years as a reminder of the three great historic bridges that the machine helped to build.

William Evans did not stay long at Canada Works and in 1856 William Heap took over as Manager of the Bridge Department, a post he was to hold for ten years.

CHAPTER 3

Thomas Brassey and Canada Works

Thomas Brassey in 1862.

THOMAS BRASSEY—RAILWAY CONTRACTOR

William Heap's new employer was a man who was to exert a great influence on him and through William Heap on this company. After Thomas Brassey had died and his company went into liquidation we took over many of his connections and to this day we benefit from the work and influence of this Victorian giant.

Today Thomas Brassey is one of the great unsung heroes of the Victorian Age, a gentle, kindly man he nevertheless was the World's first great Contractor employing 85,000 men, he was respected by his competitors, loved by his men, a man of great integrity.

Thomas Brassey was born to John and Elizabeth Brassey on the 7th November 1805 at Buerton which is about five miles south east of Chester on his father's farm; and as well as their own farm they rented another neighbouring farm from the Marquis of Westminster. The family originated from Bulkeley which is near Malpas, which in turn is about fifteen miles south east of Chester, and although at the time Thomas was born they were living on the Buerton farm they owned, and the family still own, Bulkley Manor House and 400 acres of good Cheshire farmland which have been in the Brassey family for over six hundred years.

In 1805 the population of Buerton was only thirty-nine and the community comprised the Brassey farm and about fourteen scattered cottages. In those days there was no school in the village and so Thomas must have had some private tuition from his mother or a governess.

In 1817 when he was twelve, Thomas was sent to school in Chester and his parents chose that run by Mr Harling known as The Boarding School, St John's Rectory, Vicar's Lane, Chester. There were at that time about fifteen boarding schools in Chester patronised by families living on farms or country estates in the surrounding area. Although the Brassey farm was only five miles from the city the roads were poor and it was out of the question to expect a child to do this journey twice a day, so Thomas Brassey became a boarder.

Mr William Harling gave Thomas a sound basic education and although the young Brassey was not a brilliant scholar he was a hard worker, intelligent and showed a certain aptitude for mathematics. He was such a balanced, happy man that he no doubt enjoyed life in the busy little city, which must be one of the most perfect towns in Europe with its Roman road layout, virtually unchanged for 2,000 years, its unique "Rows"—the elevated covered pavement, its lovely black and white timbered buildings all encircled by the ancient city walls; the only complete city walls in Britain.

Such was the background of Thomas Brassey, Yeoman stock, with roots going back deep in the soil of Cheshire since the Norman Conquest. Some may scoff, but it matters this question of roots and soil—England has been particularly fortunate in the number of men who came from this sort of background to play an honourable part in our history.

In 1821, when Thomas Brassey was sixteen, he took his farewell of Mr Harling and was articled to Mr Lawton who was a Land Agent and Surveyor. Mr Lawton was agent for several people including Francis Richard Price of Overton near Wrexham. Mr Price was a landowner of considerable standing and part of his estate included the township of Birkenhead which at that time only comprised a few straggling houses on a bleak and sterile coast.

In 1824 Thomas Telford was building the A5 from Shrewsbury to Holyhead and he employed a surveyor from Oswestry called Mr Penson to do some of the surveying, but he had so much work to do that he asked Mr Lawton if he could borrow Thomas Brassey to help in the surveying. For two years young Brassey worked surveying the land for the A5 and he gained invaluable experience which was to stand him in good stead in later life.

In 1826 two events occurred which later had a considerable influence on us, firstly Mr Lawton realising that Birkenhead had considerable development potential sent Thomas Brassey there to open an office and almost fifty miles away, in Isles House in the shadow of Pendle Hill, a baby, later christened William, was born to Mary Heap on the 23rd September 1826.

In 1801 the population of Birkenhead was 110 people but by 1826 the town had grown to about 4,000 and in the next decade the size increased to 6,000. They were busy days for Thomas Brassey and in a short time Mr Lawton made him a partner.

Thomas Brassey then borrowed some money from his father and bought some clay bearing land in the dock area of Birkenhead and set up a brick works. One of his first large contracts was the supply of some millions of bricks for the new Customs House that was then being built over the river. In 1839 he took advantage of his work with Telford and he tendered for, and won, the contract for building the New Chester Road from Tranmere to Bromborough. It is a wide, well surfaced road and was built to accommodate the increased coach and carriage traffic from Birkenhead to Chester and it included a large bridge needed to span Bromborough Pool.

One of the first residents of Birkenhead was Joseph Harrison, who lived in a pretty cottage called Mersey Cottage right on the banks of the Mersey shore close to Monk's Ferry. He had two sons Henry and George and a daughter Maria, and Thomas was very friendly with the Harrison boys and they used to invite him home where he got to know Maria and found her a very pleasant young lady. Eventually he and Maria were married and they lived in a large house in Park Road South, Claughton, Birkenhead, which Thomas built himself.

Mr and Mrs Brassey were well liked in Birkenhead, as indeed they were later elsewhere, and the owner of the Birkenhead Brewery Company, Henry Kelsall Aspinall, knew Thomas Brassey very well and he described him as "a gentleman in the fullest sense of the word; quiet, simple living and simple hearted, amiable and kind to a degree." Every person who knew him, including William Heap, had the same opinion.

For the next few years Thomas Brassey carried on as Agent for Mr Price and he also carried out one or two more building contracts including the building of Holy Trinity Church, Birkenhead; he opened a lime works and a builders merchants' yard and gradually prospered.

On fine summer weekends Mr and Mrs Brassey enjoyed taking a pony and trap and going to West Kirby to sit on the beach and then have a simple, but excellent tea of shrimps and home made bread and butter. Years later when he was a millionaire several times over and was living in a fine house in Lowndes Square, London, he still remembered those teas. He had been given a magnificent banquet by the Emperor and Empress Louis Napoleon of France in the splendour of the Tuileries, he had been wined and dined by the Emperor of Austria, and was eagerly sought by half the nobility in London; but when one day he had to visit Canada Works in Birkenhead he wrote to Mr Aspinall saying that he would like to visit the Aspinalls in their summer residence in West Kirby as he had not been to West Kirby for years. When Henry Aspinall asked him if he would like a dinner party or tea Brassey wrote back; "Certainly, tea, shrimps and bread and butter, nothing else. We can get plenty of dinners in London." He came up and after he had finished his business in Canada Works and had seen his brother in law George Harrison, he spent the whole afternoon on the beach with the Aspinalls and then they retired for their shrimp tea.

In the early days of Birkenhead there was no bank and as late as 1850 the only one was that of the North and South Wales Bank in Hamilton Square, and so one day when Mr Brassey decided that he needed a bank account he travelled to Chester and walked into the Chester branch of Dixon & Wardle's Bank, Northgate Street, and asked to see the Manager. When he was interviewing the well mannered, soft spoken, young man did the manager, one wonders, realise that the young fellow sitting opposite him would within a few years command the largest industrial army in the world and that he would be responsible for more gold flowing through the bank in a year than passed through many European treasuries and yet he was so loved by his navvies that when he lay on his deathbed many of them travelled great distances to see him and to weep?

T. BRASSEY'S FIRST RAILWAY CONTRACT

In 1827 George Stephenson was building the world's first commercial passenger railway between Liverpool and Manchester. The Liverpool terminus has long since gone but the Manchester Station, Liverpool Road, still stands, forlorne and neglected, the oldest passenger railway station in Europe left to rot by British Railways. Only a nationalised undertaking could be so uncaring abut part of our heritage.*

Stephenson was building the Sankey Viaduct and went to see Brassey in Birkenhead in search of load bearing stone. He had been told of the hard Kyper sandstone being cut in Storeton Quarries and Brassey was looking after these quarries. George Stephenson was impressed by Thomas Brassey and so he suggested that Brassey should try his hand at railway building and so fired his imagination that Brassey started preparations and made a bid for the contract to build the Ditton Viaduct on the Grand Junction Railway.

The Ditton tender was unsuccessful but in 1834 Brassey was invited by Joseph Locke to tender for the Penkridge Viaduct between Stafford and Wolverhampton on the Grand Junction Railway. Brassey put in a price of £26,000 but Locke thought this was too high so he visited Brassey in Birkenhead and went over an ammended specification which reduced Brassey's price to just over £20,000. On the strength of this the contract was awarded to Thomas Brassey and he was in the railway building business.

The Penkridge Viaduct still stands a superb example of Brassey's workmanship and it was the beginning of a very fruitful partnership between Locke and Brassey. Brassey once said that what he built was not intended to last ninety-nine years, but after that period it should be as good as when it was built. There can scarcely be a reader of these notes who has not travelled on a Brassey built railway line and almost all of his work still stands after one hundred and forty years apart from those lines closed by British Rail.

*1988 Note. Happily since this was first written in 1976 British Rail have sold the station to a trust who have restored the station to its original splendour.

In 1835 Locke again invited Brassey to tender for 36 miles of the London and Southampton Railway from Basingstoke to Winchester and again Brassey was successful. The cuttings on this line are amongst the most immense of any railway, but again the contract was carried out to the entire satisfaction of Joseph Locke and more and more he became impressed with Brassey's vigor, energy, ability, honesty and integrity.

Thomas Brassey's energy was fantastic, at the peak of his career he employed 85,000 men all over the world and yet he did not have an office organisation as such. He did not employ a secretary and wrote his own correspondence by hand. Wherever he went he carried a bag containing letter and writing material and all letters were answered immediately. At one time he shared a shoot in Scotland with Joseph Locke and one day while they were out shooting there was a lull in the sport and after a short time Locke missed Brassey and then found him sitting on an old box in a delapidated shepherd's hut quietly writing letters. A Dr Burnell who travelled with him in Italy recalled that one evening they had dinner and at 9 o'clock Dr Burnell went to bed and when he came down in the morning found thirty one letters in Brassey's handwriting to agents and sub-contractors all over the world.

Henry Harrison, Thomas Brassey's brother-in-law recorded that "I have known him come direct from France to Rugby, having left Havre the night before, he would have been engaged in the office in London all day; he would then come down to Rugby by the midnight mail train and it was his common practice to be on the works by six o'clock the next morning. He would frequently walk from Rugby to Nuneaton in the afternoon, a distance of sixteen miles. Having arrived at Nuneaton he would attend to his work and the same night would go to Tamworth by road. The next morning he would be up early and would walk the line they were building from Tamworth to Stafford; that evening he would take the train from Stafford to Lancaster to inspect the line from Lancaster to Carlisle which he was building. This route was one he frequently followed."

The railway contracts followed thick and fast and in 1841 he started the first railway that he built abroad. He was awarded the 82 mile Paris to Rouen railroad, the first in France, this is a story in itself, but sufficient to say that by 1848, seven years later Thomas Brassey had built three quarters of the entire French railway system.

Brassey built thousands of miles of railways in Britain, France, Spain, Norway, Austria, Germany, Denmark, Italy, India, Mauritius, Australia, Canada, Poland, Russia and South America. All his work was to a very high standard of workmanship and if he made a mistake he put it right at his own expense; his reputation for honesty and integrity spread all over the world and he became a national figure.

CANADA WORKS, BIRKENHEAD

In 1852 Thomas Brassey teamed up with Sir Morton Peto and Edward Betts. Peto's brother in law and formed Peto, Brassey and Betts. They were awarded nine contracts that year one of which was for the construction of the 540 mile Grand Trunk Railway of Canada. This line was to be the longest railway to be built at that time and was to run from Quebec to Lake Huron through virgin forests and across the mighty one and three quarter mile St Lawrence River at Montreal.

Thomas Brassey decided that they would have to build a new works to make the vast amount of railway equipment needed for this enormous undertaking and he decided to build his works in Birkenhead because the Mersey was excellent for shipping goods out to Canada; it was in an area where there was excellent labour—still true—and he knew it well because it was his, and his wife's, old home town.

The way Thomas Brassey and his men set about building a large and sophisticated engineering works in a matter of months is an object lesson for modern industry.

Brassey recalled his brother-in-law George Harrison who was working for him in Canada and told him what he wanted and put him in charge of the new works which was to be called Canada Works in honour of their biggest contract.

George Harrison returned to England late in May 1853 and on the 29th May he toured the

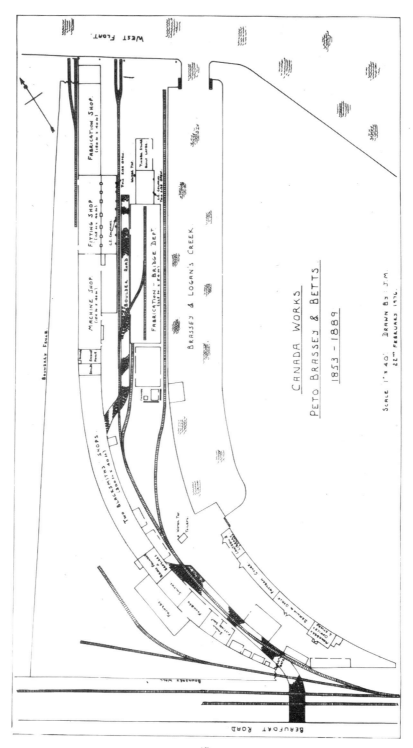

CANADA WORKS

PETO BRASSEY & BETTS

1853 – 1889

SCALE 1" = 40'   DRAWN BY J.M.
22ND FEBRUARY 1976

dock area of Birkenhead with a building contractor, Mr Meakin, looking for a suitable piece of land. Late in the morning they found a piece of land which, although not ideal in all respects, would meet their needs. It was excellent in that it fronted on the Great Float and sea-going vessels could moor against the quay and that there was another dock running the length of the land, but it was banana shaped which is not ideal for an engineering works, but it was the best they had seen. The land covered about nine acres and although there was no access road there was a railway line nearby, built by Brassey in 1849.

In the afternoon Mr Harrison spent one and a half hours doing sketch drawings for the new works and was given a budget price by Mr Meakin. That evening he travelled to London by train and saw Thomas Brassey early the next morning, they went over the plans and he returned to Liverpool the same afternoon by the express train.

The next day George Harrison bought the land and placed a verbal order with Mr Meakin, who started work immediately and the first brick was laid on the 4th June 1853, exactly a week after they had first found the land. Work was pressed on and the new factory was virtually finished by October of the same year. The whole project from finding the land to taking over, occupying only 5 months. It would take longer than that now to obtain planning permission.

The new works were an absolute model of what an engineering works of that era should be, the 13″ walls were made of red pressed brick, the roof was lined slates, the floors were flagged and illumination by day was by generous windows and rooflights, and at night by gas lights.

The main shop was 900′ long and 40′ wide and the works comprised iron and brass foundries, blacksmiths shops, copper smiths, machine shops, fitting out bay, fabrication shop, woodwork and pattern shop, engine house, stores and drawing office. The very latest machines were bought and because, at that time, American woodworking machines were in advance of ours— because the shortage of skilled labour in America had encouraged the development of machinery—Brassey sent two men to America to buy the latest machines and they brought back morticing and planing machines.

The machine shop was equipped with a number of Whitworth lathes, including one which could turn a wheel 7′ diameter without any adjustment of the bed. Planing machines, slotters, drills, etc, were all driven by two 40-hp steam engines.

The fabrication shop where the bridges were made and boiler work was done and which was run by William Evans and William Heap, was equipped with three furnaces for heating rivets, one furnace for angle and "T" iron, eight punching and shearing machines, two sets of bending and plate rollers, two rivet making machines, two automatic rivetting machines and power was provided by a 35-hp steam engine. Later the number of machines was doubled. One of the presses was the immense Roberts Jacquard press already referred to and this probably had a separate drive. The great problem with this machine as already mentioned, was to find enough long runs to keep it fully occupied, but on the Victoria Bridge, the Jumna and other great bridges it was ideal and its accuracy in punching holes is remarked on by James Hodges, the Resident Engineer on the Victoria Bridge in the extract from his report which we print later.

The fitting shop for locomotive production was 150′ long and comprised ten engine building pits and was designed to produce forty locomotives a year; this capacity was to be fully employed over the next few years because the Canadian railway alone needed three hundred engines over the next eight years.

There were two well equipped blacksmiths' shops. The main shop was equipped with forty furnaces, each with its own anvils, blacksmith's tools and all were fully manned; there were also two small, but efficient, steam hammers. The smaller smithy was quite interesting because that was where the wrought iron locomotive wheels were forged. The wheels were made by heating up individual bars and then welding together two bars to form a "V"; then another "V" was made and then welded to the first and so on until all the spokes were welded by the smith into position. At the end of each spoke was a knob of metal and these were welded together and then the rim was forged. The rough forging was then taken to the machine shop and the wheel was turned up by one of the many wheel lathes.

Down the centre of the works was a cobbled road made up of rounded boulders, probably brought to Liverpool by sailing ships that left these shores loaded with manufactured goods

Excavating the cobbled road at Canada Works 1971.

Relaying the boulder road from Canada Works at Britannia House, Hoylake. The water fountain stood for over a century in Pall Mall, Liverpool.

and sailed back with the stones as ballast. These stones were beautifully laid and when in 1971 we bought a stretch of the road from Mersey Docks & Harbour Board, so we could relay them in the garden in front of our offices at Hoylake, we had great difficulty in lifting them, because although they were rounded, they had been cleverly interlocked. In the end we were making such little headway with picks and crowbars that we brought in a bulldozer, but even so they did not give up easily.

On the right of the works was the drawing office and stores and adjoining them two houses and in one of them lived Andrew Alexander M.A., who was a sub-manager with William Heap,

The site of Canada Works from the West Float. Brassey and Logan's creek is on the left. Today only the quay and two buildings remain of that remarkable engineering works.*

*1988 Note. Since 1976 Logan's Creek has been filled in.

under the Manager, George Harrison. Later William Heap was made Manager of the bridge department which was a most important section of the works.

Canada Works was well in advance of its time because they also had a test and inspection department where the plate, bar, rod and other raw materials were tested for tensile strength, impact and compression.

BRASSEY'S TREATMENT OF HIS MEN

When Canada Works opened in October 1853 there were about four hundred men in the machine shop and one hundred and twenty-three men under William Heap in the bridge department but later these numbers were increased to about one thousand two hundred men, evenly split between the two sections. The average wage paid was £1 a week and considering that there were a considerable number of young apprentices the skilled men were taking home much more than a pound a week which was a very good wage for the day. There was little wrong with the food that they ate because as previously mentioned Brassey's navvies ate two pounds of beef a day for a start.

Thomas Brassey and his Managers differed from some of the other prominent engineers of the time, such as George and Robert Stephenson and Isambard Kingdom Brunel, in their attitude towards the education of their workmen and they were not alone in this respect because many employers in Victorian times provided their own schools or subsidised British Schools. In Turton, Lancashire as early as 1825 it was reported that five hundred and twenty-five out of five hundred and thirty-two employees could read and that there was a library at the mill.

The Stephensons however and Brunel (even great men have some failings) did not think it necessary for mechanics to be educated beyond their immediate work, but Thomas Brassey, George Harrison, William Heap and Andrew Alexander took the opposite view and at the very outset they built at Canada Works a canteen and a library for the workmen.

The Management gave £75 to start the library and provided 600 well selected volumes, the men gave a concert and ball in one of the large halls of Birkenhead for five hundred of the men and their wives and they raised a further £12. On the 20th October 1853, the reading room was opened and the men found available a wide selection of books as well as a selection of local and national newspapers. In those days advertising revenue had not reduced the price of a newspaper to the fantastic bargain of today and for example the "Liverpool Courier" cost 5d which in those days was a tremendous sum.

The men paid a penny a week towards the reading room, which was open every meal time and was run by a committee of workmen. Books were given out twice a week and at the same time those that had been borrowed could be returned. It is of interest to note that with the exception of the Waverley Novels, most of the books borrowed were of an educational nature, particularly those dealing with engineering and mechanics.

"THE LADY ELGIN"

The speed of Canada Works was breathtaking to a modern observer because the first locomotive was tested in May 1854 exactly a year after George Harrison and Mr Meakin walked on to the barren, banana shaped field which they transformed into Canada Works.

Engine No. 1 was called "The Lady Elgin" after the wife of the Governor General of Canada and it passed its tests with flying colours, every part of the engine except the tubes and plates had been made in Canada Works and that included the wheels and even the rivets.

"The Lady Elgin" was a bogy chassis passenger locomotive built for the "Grand Trunk" and if one is permitted to talk about such intimate details of a lady, her vital statistics were:

Cylinder	15″ bore
Piston Stroke	20″
Tube Size	$1\frac{1}{4}$″ diameter

No. Tubes	175 in the smoke box
Total Heating Surface	948 square feet (872 sq. ft. in the smoke box + 76 sq. ft. in fire box)
Wheel Gauge	5'–6"
Leading Wheels	3'–6" diameter
Trailing Wheels	6'–0" diameter
Load	22/23 passenger per carriage
Speed	40 m.p.h.
Fuel	Wood burning

After the highly successful trials on the specially laid 5'–6" track, "The Lady Elgin" gave a mighty shriek of triumph on her whistle and she was decorated with oak branches by the workmen and there was loud cheering. That Monday evening George Harrison took Andrew Alexander, William Evans, William Heap and the Foremen to a dinner at the Woodside Hotel, Birkenhead and the following Saturday they gave a celebration dinner for all the men at an hotel in Birkenhead.

At the same time, engine Number 2, "The Lord Elgin", was almost finished and there were five other passenger and five goods locos in the course of erection. The goods engines differed from the passenger engines, only in the cylinder bore, which was 16" and the driving wheels, which were 5' in diameter.

By the end of 1854, ten locomotives had been shipped to Canada, eight more goods engines were ready for shipment, there were sixteen others being made and No. 35 was being started.

"The Lady Elgin". The first engine to be built by Canada Works, successfully completed her trials in May 1854 exactly a year after the site for Canada Works was found.

THE VICTORIA BRIDGE, MONTREAL

Constructing the Victoria Bridge, Montreal 1853–1858.

In the bridge department William Evans and William Heap had not been idle, because they had been given several jobs to do and one of them was the construction of the Victoria Bridge, which was to be almost two miles long—by far the longest bridge in the world and even now, one hundred and twenty-five years later, is in the top five longest bridges ever built and will stand as an all time record as the longest tubular bridge ever built.

The site problems were immense as we shall see later, but William's task was gigantic because over three million holes had to be punched and drilled in hundreds of thousands of components and shipped to a site thousands of miles away in such a way that they arrived on site on time, in the correct order and somehow they had to be readily identified by the men working on the bridge.

Mr Heap's first task was to set up a system for marking and tagging the hundreds of thousands of plates and girders, each piece was laid out on the floor together with its companion pieces and then properly marked so that it could be located quickly on the other side of the Atlantic.

Mechanical digger built at Canada Works, Birkenhead, working on the foundations for the Victoria Bridge 1853.

50

Victoria Bridge 1853–1858.

The plates were ordered from Staffordshire and when they arrived they were then rolled flat and wherever possible they were punched on the Roberts Jacquard press, which had been programmed for this immense task. Wherever possible they built up small assemblies at Canada Works to save site work.

By the time "The Lady Elgin" had been tested in May 1854, William Heap had already shipped out one span of 155′ and they were busily engaged on the next span. But it should be remembered that this was not the only work they were doing because they had made and shipped by December 1854 a 120-hp winding engine and a large boiler for a works in Derbyshire, as well as working on a number of other smaller bridges for the Grand Trunk.

CONSTRUCTION ON SITE

William Heap visited Canada during the construction of the Victoria Bridge and saw at first hand the tremendous difficulties that had to be overcome by Brassey's engineers and navvies, he was also able to see that the system he had devised was working splendidly.

The winter ice in the St. Lawrence poses a threat to any bridge because it piles up to a height of twenty feet or more and in the spring with the thaw, these tremendous weights of ice are carried forward by the fast current and form a ferocious battering ram. Stephenson designed his masonry piers so that they are of the most robust construction and facing upstream; the piers are wedge-shaped to cut the ice and guide it around the piers.

Tremendous problems were encountered in building the piers because before construction

51

Emigrants' Stone, Montreal.

was started it was thought that the bottom of the river was rocky and firm, but in many places they found it was comprised of loose boulders, some of immense size and these had to be cleared away before the coffer dams could start. Some idea of the difficulties can be gained from a report in the "Engineer" dated 9th September 1859 in which it is mentioned that one boulder alone weighed 24·5 tons and this had to be moved from the bottom of an icy, fast flowing, river.

The workmen used one of the boulders they had taken from the bottom of the river as a memorial stone to the 6,000 emigrants who lost their lives of "ship fever" or typhoid in 1847. on the voyage to the New World, and they mounted this on a plinth near to the railway. In the early days it was known as "The Emigrants' Stone", but now is known as the "Irish Emigrants' Stone".

Before the piers could be made, coffer dams had to be constructed in the river and great difficulties were experienced in their building, because even in summer there were dangers such as the occasion when logs swept down the river destroyed the coffer dam made for pier 13. Once the dams had been constructed around the area where the piers were to be built, then the water had to be pumped out and "The Engineer" of 18th March 1859 reported that the pump used was: a portable centrifugal pump, light enough for a man to carry over his shoulder. Astonishingly enough this pump had a capacity of 800 g.p.m. and "could pass stones up to 6″ square". This pump lowered the levels of the coffer dam at the rate of 2′ an hour and in 10 hours the first coffer dam was pumped dry. Regrettably "The Engineer" did not give the manufacturer of this pump, otherwise we should now be writing for the Agency.

The Victorian Engineers needed little excuse to give a party; on reflection times have not

Log jamb damages Coffer Dam on Pier 13.

changed all that much; but they were unusual in the way that they linked the celebration with an engineering achievement. After the heartbreaking struggle by Sir Marc Brunel to build the Thames Tunnel, which was eventually finished by his son, Isambard Kingdom Brunel (we are sorry to keep on repeating his full name, but it sounds like a roll of thunder worthy of the Victorian engineers), they gave a magnificent dinner in the tunnel itself, with an enormous table laid with a white cloth, gleaming silver and decanters.

When Thomas Brassey finished the Paris to Rouen railway in May 1843, there was a ceremonial opening of the line by a Bishop, but Brassey gave his men an open air banquet where 600 men sat down. A whole ox was roasted by three French chefs but one of Brassey's men turned the spit and in a contemporary drawing he is shown drinking wine from a bottle. The French became so agitated at the prospect of six hundred British navvies going on the rampage that they ringed the field with their cavalry.

The men of Peto, Brassey and Betts were not to be outdone because they gave a party at the bottom of one of the pumped out coffer dams, and as "The Engineer" commented at the time, "It was an unusual setting, with the mighty St Lawrence swirling outside to a height of thirty feet."

It is a pity that this direct linking of an engineering achievement with a celebration has gone out of fashion, because one can think of dozens of good excuses for a banquet for those who have achieved much in recent times that has passed by with nothing to mark the event. For example when man first landed on the moon—incidentally an engineering rather than a scientific achievement—would it not have been glorious if the Astronaut had climbed down the steps and set out a table for a celebration dinner, instead of mumbling those embarrassing words dreamed up by some hack in the State Department months earlier about "A small step for man . . .".

53

Please do not write to us as we do appreciate the problems, but engineers are not too bad at solving them, particularly if they think that a party is at stake!

Having overcome the problems of the coffer dams James Hodges the Resident Engineer for Peto, Brassey and Betts, then had to find the stone to build the piers and after a long search he found a hard limestone about sixteen miles upstream of the bridge, but it was on land owned by the Red Indians.

Mr Hodges arranged a meeting with the thirteen chiefs involved and disappointingly enough for the writer, he found that the most convenient time to meet them all together was on Sunday morning after church! If you wonder why we find this remarkable remember that this was twenty-three years before General Custer made his last stand before the Sioux Indians, but then the British have always been better Colonisers than the Americans, or the Russians come to that.

Instead of the proud befeathered Chiefs of the writer's most loved films, the Red Indians turned out to be miserable, dirty looking old men, smoking short clay pipes, no doubt made in England. On their side, the Chiefs were not at all impressed with James Hodges; they complained that he was far too young to negotiate with them—"Why, he has not even grown whiskers!" Mr Hodges gravely assured them that he was over forty years of age. Thus assured the Chiefs then agreed to negotiate and eventually agreement was reached and after the Red Indians had been paid, the stone was cut and transported to the site of the bridge.

The volume of stone cut for the piers of the Victoria Bridge was 2,713,000 cubic feet, or

Invitation to the Opening of the Victoria Bridge.

54

enough to cover a six acre field to a height of eleven feet, and all this was done without our modern means of transport.

After the piers were built, work started on the first spans and Brassey's men built temporary wooden lattice bridges, supported in winter by the frozen river, and on this they built up the world's biggest "Mechano Set" sent out with full instructions by William Heap in faraway Birkenhead. To facilitate the assembly of the parts they had a number of quite advanced mechanical devices built for them by their colleagues on the Great Float, one of these was a travelling crane which ran on tracks run on the temporary wooden structure and the plate layers and rivetters could move this by operating two cranked operating handles. They also had the advantage of the first mechanical shovel ever made by a British Contractor, this was improved on site and the men found it was excellent for digging out very hard material, but in light sand and gravel it was easier, and cheaper, to use manual labour.

These grand Victorians were building the longest bridge in the world and as well as overcoming the engineering problems they had to combat a climate which in winter was to say the least, inhospitable. The temperature dropped so low that if a man touched the steel with his bare hands the flesh stuck to the frozen metal; icy winds caused frost bite and they suffered from dysentry and cholera. At one time over a third of the men working on the bridge were sick with cholera and many died, but Brassey's men had guts and they built their bridge well and on time.

Great Tubular Bridge at Montreal, Canada.

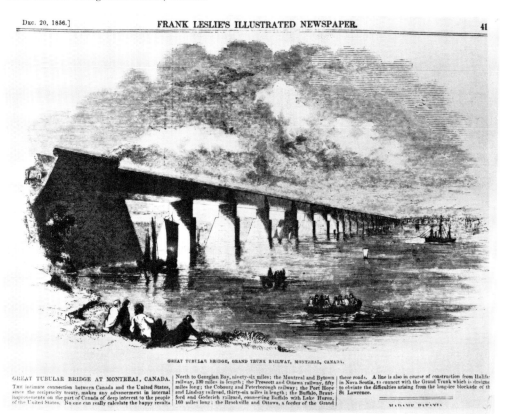

DEC. 20, 1856.]   FRANK LESLIE'S ILLUSTRATED NEWSPAPER.   41

GREAT TUBULAR BRIDGE, GRAND TRUNK RAILWAY, MONTREAL, CANADA.

GREAT TUBULAR BRIDGE AT MONTREAL, CANADA.

THE intimate connection between Canada and the United States, since the reciprocity treaty, makes any advancement in internal improvements on the part of Canada of deep interest to the people of the United States. No one can really calculate the happy results North to Georgian Bay, ninety-six miles; the Montreal and Bytown railway, 130 miles in length; the Prescott and Ottawa railway, fifty miles long; the Cobourg and Peterborough railway; the Port Hope and Lindsay railroad, thirty-six miles in length; the Buffalo, Brantford and Goderich railroad, connecting Buffalo with Lake Huron, 160 miles long; the Brockville and Ottawa, a feeder of the Grand these roads. A line is also in course of construction from Halifax in Nova Scotia, to connect with the Grand Trunk which is designed to obviate the difficulties arising from the long-ice blockade of the St Lawrence.

MADAME RATAZZI

Report by James Hodges

James Hodges wrote a report of the building of the "Great Victoria Bridge" and we give the following extract:

CONSTRUCTION
OF THE
GREAT
VICTORIA BRIDGE
IN
CANADA.
BY
JAMES HODGES,
ENGINEER
TO
MESSRS. PETO, BRASSEY, AND BETTS,
Contractors.

London
JOHN WEALE, 59, High Holborn.
1860

The whole of the iron-work for the tubes was prepared at the Canada Works, Birkenhead, where a plan or map of each tube was made, upon which was shown every plate, T bar, angle iron, keelson, and cover plate, in the tube, the position of each being stamped and marked upon it by a distinctive figure, letter, or character. As the work progressed at Birkenhead, every piece of iron, as it was punched and finished for shipment, was stamped with the identical mark corresponding with that on the plan; so that, when being erected in Canada, although each tube was composed of 4,926 pieces, or 9,852 for a pair, the workmen, being provided with a plan of the work, were enabled to lay down piece by piece with unerring certainty till the tube was complete. To an uninitiated spectator this proceeding would appear as complicated and hopeless a task as the fitting together of a Chinese puzzle; but to such perfection did they arrive at Birkenhead in making the plans, in preparing and punching the iron, and in shipping it, that when it arrived in Canada (where the iron for each tube was, as it arrived, sorted and stacked separately for use), the workman being provided with the plan would proceed with his work throughout, and never put a piece in the wrong place, nor have to alter a single plate. It was not uninteresting to watch the gradual diminution of the pile of iron on the platform as the work progressed, and eventually to see the last piece taken to fill up some out-of-the-way hole or corner, and then to hear for certain that the tube was completed.

As soon as it became evident that the centre piers, 12 and 13, would be finished in time to receive the centre tube if erected during winter, two temporary piers were commenced in the centre opening, the intention being to carry up these erections in cribwork till they were high enough to support a continuous Howe-truss extending across the opening, the ends of which were to rest upon large stone corbels left for that purpose on the face of the piers.

At this period the sectional area of the river was so much diminished by the temporary works now in the deep water, that the current was increased greatly, and it was almost impossible to hold a crib of any dimensions in such a current till it was sunk in position. The plan pursued in this instance was to build the crib in the eddy on the south side of No. 12 (the stream which set partially across the piers being favourable to such an operation), and then to strut it off into the current from the dam, and sink it as speedily as possible. Of course heavy moorings were laid out ahead to hold the crib in place against the stream, and chains were likewise made fast to the bow.

I have before noticed that the whole of the iron work for the tubes was prepared at the Canada Works, Birkenhead (an establishment erected by Messrs, Peto, Brassey, and Betts expressly for the manufacture of the bridge work and rolling stock for their Canadian contracts). At these works every plate, &c., was finished ready for putting in place. I have likewise endeavoured to show with what care and accuracy the whole of this was done; but I trust I may be excused for again drawing attention to the extraordinary perfection attained in the preparation of this ironwork. In the centre tube, consisting of 10,309 pieces, in which were punched nearly half a million of holes, not one piece required alteration, neither was there a hole punched wrong! The importance of this accuracy may be estimated by considering that had any portion been carelessly prepared, or even wrongly marked, a failure might have been the result, involving the delay of a year in the opening of the bridge, and a loss of many thousands of pounds. Therefore, to Mr. George Harrison, the manager of the Birkenhead works, &c., and to his able assistants, Messrs. Alexander and Heap, is due as great credit for the successful completion of this work as to those engaged in its erection. For details of tubes, see Plates 24 and 24a.

The bridge was first opened for the passage of trains on the 19th of December, 1859. The formal inauguration by his Royal Highness the Prince of Wales, who visits Canada for the purpose, is appointed for the 25th of August, 1860, when, under God's blessing, this work, of such great social and international importance, will be duly dedicated to the great purposes for which it is designed.

The following are the inscriptions at the entrance of the Bridge:—

[ON THE OUTER LINTEL.]
ERECTED A. D. MDCCCLIX.
ROBERT STEPHENSON AND ALEX. M. ROSS,
ENGINEERS.
[ON THE INTERIOR LINTEL.]
BUILT
BY
JAMES HODGES,
FOR
SIR S. MORTON PETO, BART., THOMAS BRASSEY,
AND
EDWARD LADD BETTS,
CONTRACTORS.

DATES.

First part of north abutment coffer-dam towed into place 24th May, 1854.

First stone of bridge laid 20th July, 1854.
First train passed over the bridge 17th December, 1859.

DIMENSIONS, WEIGHTS, &c.

Total length of tubes, 6592 feet.
Total length of bridge, 9144 feet.
Height of bottom of centre tube above surface of water, 60 feet.
Height of bottom of tubes at abutment, 36 feet.
Rise of tubes to centre, 1 in 130.
Weight of iron in tubes, 9044 tons.
Number of rivets in tubes, 1,540,000.
Painting—number of coats, 4; number of acres in each coat, 32. Total acres, 128.
Number of piers, 24.

Number of spans, 25; twenty-four from 242 to 247 feet each; one, 330 feet.
Quantity of masonry in piers and abutments, 2,713,095 cubic feet.
Greatest depth of water, 22 feet.
Average rate of current, seven miles an hour.
Quantity of timber in temporary works, 2,280,000 cubic feet.
Quantity of clay puddle used in dams, 146,000 cubic yards.

Number of steam-boats, 6.
Number of barges, 75.
Tonnage of ditto, 12,000.
Power of steamers, 450 H.P.

Number of men employed, 3040.
Number of horses, 144.
Locomotive engines, 4.

The Grand Trunk Railway was not well conceived by the promoters and it was one of the most difficult contracts that Thomas Brassey ever tackled. Financially the building of the Victoria Bridge nearly broke Brassey, and incidentally, the backers of the railway, but as a piece of engineering it was a masterpiece and as such it was widely acclaimed.

"The Engineer" in an editorial to mark the opening described it as "The greatest example of engineering construction in the world". When the Prince of Wales opened the bridge on the 19th December 1859 he said of Peto, Brassey & Betts of Birkenhead, "They left behind an imperishable monument of British skill, pluck, science and perseverance".

The final word must be given to Robert Stephenson who at a dinner given for him later in Toronto by the Engineering Profession of Canada said of Peto, Brassey and Betts' work on the Victoria Bridge "The Contractors left even the Engineers themselves little more than the poetry of engineering".

The original Victoria Bridge gave good service for over forty years and was only converted in 1892 to a lattice girder bridge on the original piers because the original specification called for a single line track and this was later converted to a double track with a subsequent speeding up of traffic, and also the two mile line tubular bridge caused smoke problems in the days of steam.

The links that William Heap forged in Canada whilst working on the Victoria Bridge remain with us to this day.

CANADA WORKS AND THE CRIMEAN WAR

The Crimean War has stayed alive in public memory largely because of Alfred, Lord Tennyson's poem "The Charge of the Light Brigade" and for the work done by Florence Nightingale in setting up hospitals to nurse the sick and the wounded; but few know that the British Army might well have been defeated but for the organising ability of Canada Works and the stupendous efforts of Thomas Brassey's engineers and navvies. At the time Brassey and his men were national heroes but now their deeds are almost forgotten.

In 1854 a British Army of 30,000 men, together with a French Army, were fighting the Russian Army in the Crimea and at the end of the year were beseiging Sevastapol. All the supplies for the army had to be dragged, sometimes axle deep in mud, over a single road from Balaclava, the nearest part in British hands.

Unlike our modern army, the British Army of 1854 was badly led, ill clad and equipped and the casualty lists grew alarmingly as men died of wounds, frostbite, cholera and starvation. It was plain to all that the British Army was about to be defeated by the same factors that had beaten Napoleon earlier, and Hitler later—the Russian winter and overstretched supply lines.

The British Army had not fought a major battle since Waterloo, thirty-nine years before and although its Officers were brave enough they had become incompetent. Cecil Woodham Smith summed up the officers who fought in the Crimea as follows: "They affected elegant boredom, yawned a great deal, spoke a jargon of their own, pronouncing 'r' as 'w', saying 'vewwy', 'howwid' and 'sowwy' and interlarded their sentences with loud and meaningless exclamations of 'Haw, Haw!'. Their sweeping whiskers, languid voices, tiny waists, laced in by corsets and their large cigars were irresistable; frantically admired and as frantically envied. Magnificently mounted, horses were their passion, they rode like the devil himself, and their confidence in their ability to defeat any enemy single handed was complete. Cavalry officers were saying in London drawing rooms that to take infantry on such a campaign was superfluous; the infantry would merely be a drag on them and had better be left at home."

A French Commander after praising British horses and their riders said: "The British cavalry officer seems to be impressed by the conviction that he can dash or ride over everything as if the art of war were precisely the same as that of fox hunting." How right he was.

We can question their competence but not their bravery. Lord Cardigan who commanded the Light Brigade during the famous charge knew it was madness to charge into the "valley of death", but after receiving the mistaken order he saluted and said to himself "Well here goes the last of the Brundenells"—his family name; prepared to charge in perfect drill book order "The Brigade will advance, walk, march, trot."

Beautifully dressed, stiffly upright, never turning his head, Lord Cardigan charged down the mile and a half of murderous Russian shot and shell right to the Russian guns. Out of seven hundred horsemen only one hundred and ninety-five returned and five hundred horses were killed. Miraculously, Lord Cardigan was not hit and charged right through the astonished Russian gunners.

After returning to his own lines he rode back to his private yacht moored in the harbour, had a bath and drank a bottle of champagne.

The immortal words of the French General who watched the charge from the heights summed up the waging of the Crimean War 'C'est Magnifique, mais ce'nes pas la Guerre", it was magnificent but it was not war and the public were stirred into action by the reports of William Howard Russell to "The Times" and the photographs taken by one of the earliest war photographers Robert Fenton.

The value of a free press to a Nation was clearly illustrated by Mr Russell, because he exposed the criminal incompetence of Government and Army and people in many walks of life started to take action.

One of the many difficulties encountered by the British Army was that our troops still had to fend for themselves, whereas in the French Army one soldier cooked for twelve. Our methods worked well enough in kinder climates, but not in the depths of a Russian winter and the outcry in the Press prompted Alexis Soyer the chief cook at the Reform Club in London to volunteer to go to Scutari and there he devised the field kitchen and new methods of cooking for an army. Florence Nightingale went out to organise Field Hospitals, and incidentally to start out on a path which was to revolutionise nursing. Another group of men who thought they could help were Thomas Brassey, Morton Peto M.P., and his brother-in-law Edward Betts who were trading as Peto, Brassey and Betts of Canada Works.

On the 30th November, 1854 Morton Peto told the Government that Peto, Brassey and Betts could overcome the supply problem by building a thirty-nine mile long railway from Balaclava to all parts of the front and to cut delay to the minimum they would do this at no profit, would provide men and materials and would run the line when it was finished. News had reached the Government a little earlier that the plight of the Army was desperate. On 14th November there had been a dreadful blizzard; the troops before Sevastapol only had thin clothing, no tents and no fuel. The icy winds had blown the blankets off the wounded and many froze to death, there was little food for the men or fodder for the horses and soon there were 8,000 men in hospital and replacements from England often died before they reached the front.

Although many doubted if it would be possible to build a railway quickly enough to save the situation in the depth of a Russian winter, the Government were absolutely desperate and they gratefully accepted the offer. Thomas Brassey then set his superb organisation to work and what a difference between the criminal incompetence of the Government employees and those of the Birkenhead firm.

On the 30th November, 1854 when Brassey's offer was made the rails and sleepers didn't exist, but as soon as Brassey gave the order his men spent the first day drawing up a list of the materials they would need and where they could be produced. To save time they chartered, or bought, vessels near to the location of the materials they were to carry. For example some of the rails were to be produced at Walker on Tyne and so they bought the screw steamer "Hesperus" which was just being completed by Messers Mitchell in the next yard on the Tyne and the rails were loaded warm from the furnances into the hold of the "Hesperus".

In three days Peto, Brassey and Betts had bought, or chartered, a fleet of ships, all on verbal order and without any security. All the shipowners and shipyards worked night and day to convert the ships to their new use. and cabins and bunks for Brassey's engineers and navvies were built in a few days. The first ship bought by Canada Works was the clipper "Wildfire". She was bought from Tonge, Curry & Co. of Liverpool for £4,500 and was sailed over to the Great Float, Birkenhead for conversion and loading. Needless to say, she was the first vessel ready to sail, but she was closely followed by others and the fleet comprised:

"Wildfire"	Clipper sailing ship	457 tons	
"Mohawk"	Clipper sailing ship	800 tons	
"Lady Alice Lamberton"	Screw steamer	511 tons	90-hp
"Great Northern"	Screw steamer	578 tons	90-hp
"Earl of Durham"	Screw steamer	554 tons	90-hp
"Baron von Humboldt"	Screw steamer	420 tons	60-hp
"Hesperus"	Screw steamer	800 tons	150-hp
"Prince of Wales"	Paddle steamer	627 tons	120-hp
"Levant"	Paddle steamer	694 tons	500-hp

The "Prince of Wales" was the same vessel that had suffered the fortuitous accident at Millwall that had given Robert Stevenson the idea of the tubular bridges at Conway and Menai.

In three days verbal orders were placed for vast quantities of material and where there was not sufficient time to make the large items of plant or rolling stock they were found and bought. For example the steam machinery was at work on the Victoria Docks, London, which Brassey had built, and as it was needed for the Crimea it was bought.

The loading of the ships was so organised and the material was distributed such that if one vessel was delayed, or lost, then it would not endanger the whole operation.

An initial labour force of five hundred navvies and engineers was organised, many of whom

The Clipper "Wildfire" about to sail from Birkenhead for the Crimea 21st December 1854.

had worked on the Victoria Bridge and the Grand Trunk Railway in Canada and were used to working in extremely low temperatures. On Wednesday 13th December, only four days after the order was given, the first party of fifty-four navvies left Euston Station, London, bound for Birkenhead, to embark on the "Wildfire" and by Friday 15th December she was ready to sail loaded with equipment built by Canada Works. She was unable to sail however, because of fierce gales that raged in the Mersey for the next six days.

Thomas Brassey's navvies were the elite, they were paid £2-16s a week plus clothing, food and tobacco, which was a very high wage indeed for the day. Before they sailed they all signed allotment papers making over a weekly sum to be paid to their families and this averaged £1 per man.

Unlike the Government, Harrison, Heap and Alexander saw to it that Brassey's men were properly clothed, housed and fed and each man was issued with:

1 Painted bag (waterproof)
1 Painted suit
3 Coloured cotton shirts
1 Red flannel shirt
1 White flannel shirt
1 Flannel belt
1 Pair Moleskin trousers
1 Moleskin vest lined with serge
1 Fearnought slop
1 Linsey drawers
1 Blue cravat
1 Blue worsted cravat
1 Pair leggings
1 Pair boots
1 Strap and buckle
1 Bed and pillow
1 Pair mitts
1 Rug and blanket
1 Pair of blankets
1 Woollen coat
1 Pair of long waterproof boots
1 Pair of fisherman's boots
1 Pair of grey stockings
1 Pair of strong nailed boots
2 lbs tobacco for present use
and a portable stove for every ten men

The bag was to contain his kit and three days rations, and to facilitate storage no boxes—nor lumber, were allowed. For those working in water there were one hundred pairs of hip boots available.

To house the men, they provided ten portable, weatherproof huts, which were made such that they would not easily catch fire and each hut had a stove for heating together with vast quantities of coal, coke and firewood. Each hut was large enough to accommodate forty men and after they saw how successful the huts were, the Government later provided a number for the Army.

There was a plentiful supply of food and one of the new field kitchens was provided for every ten men, these were portable, but very efficient and could boil, bake or fry, in the open air.

On Thursday 19th December, "Wildfire" was still moored by Canada Works held up by the weather and so George Harrison, William Heap and Andrew Alexander gave a dinner at Gough's Hotel, Woodside Ferry to take leave of one of their colleagues, Mr Shaw who was to be in charge of the first party.

The men who had travelled up from London were accommodated in various inns in

Birkenhead and one of them wrote to the editor of the "Liverpool Mercury" just before he sailed in "Wildfire":

"Gentlemen,

You would greatly oblige the thirty miners engaged by Messrs Brassey, Peto and Betts to proceed to the Crimea, and now staying at the Sun Inn, Birkenhead in making known the excellent treatment we have received under the management of our worthy landlord, Mr Pear, The Sun Inn, Bridge Street, Birkenhead. We have likewise to return our most hearty thanks to our employers and all our supporters for the most gentlemanly manner in which we have been treated, not forgetting Mr Harkdus.

I remain your humble servant,

Evelin Flinn.
Miner.

Birkenhead
20th December 1854.

On Thursday 21st, four days before Christmas, the winds had dropped enough for embarkation to start. Mr Shaw, Mr George Arkle, a relative of William Heap's future partner T. W. Arkle, and a party of miners and navvies left the Sun Inn and walked down Bridge Street to the docks. The pavements were crowded and every window had a crowd of spectators all cheering Brassey's men on their way.

So at 11 am on Thursday 21st December, only twelve days after the order had been given, the first of the fleet, the Clipper "Wildfire", Captain Downward in command, set sail and by the 30th December, the other ships had left, or were about to leave Birkenhead, Liverpool, Hull, Sunderland and London loaded with:

50 horses.
1,800 tons of rails and fastenings.
6,000 sleepers.
600 loads of timber for bridges etc.
3,000 tons of machinery.
Fixed engines.
Cranes.
Pile drivers.
Trucks.
Wagons.
Barrows.
Blocks.
Chainfalls.
Wire rope.
Picks.
Bars.
Capstans.
Crabs.
Plant and tools.
Sawing machines.
Forges.
Carpentors tools.
100 railway tarpaulins.
A number of Dean and Adam's revolvers.

Each ship carried a surgeon and a clerk to attend to the victualling and care for the stores. The labour force comprised:

One chief engineer.
500 navvies—eventually raised to 900.
3—Assistant Engineers.

1—Chief Agent.
3—Assistants.
1—Accountant and Clerk.
Foreman and timekeepers.
30—Miners.
1—Chief Surgeon.
4—Assistant Surgeons.
4—Nurses from London's leading hospital.
Medical stocks and stores.
Borehole sinkers.
2—Railway missionaries.
A selection of books.

Balaclava 1855. Brassey's navvies at work. Note the initials P.B. & B. on the winding drum to the right of the lithograph.

Balaclava 1855. Unloading the railway equipment. Photograph by Robert Fenton—developed in his mobile caravan/darkroom. One of the first war photographs ever taken.

Balaclava 1855. Moving supplies on the railway. Photograph by Robert Fenton.

On arrival one ship was to become a stores and hospital ship and the others to be used as expedient.

This outstanding event was not reported in the Liverpool papers but "The Illustrated London News" wrote on 30th December 1854:

"The immense resources of Peto, Brassey and Betts have enabled them with very little exertion to collect, organise and ship off in an almost incredibly short space of time this important expedition for which the order was only given on 9th December.

At that time the rails were not rolled, the sleepers were uncut and the steam machinery was performing its daily function at the Victoria Docks and several of the ships were not finished."

The revolvers that were taken raised some doubts because it was felt that they might endanger Brassey's navvies and again the "Illustrated London News" wrote:

"It has been stated that the Crimean navvies are to be armed—this is a mistake—they are two valuable and expensive to be put in the way of shot if it can be avoided.

"A few arms have been sent for special cases and a few of the candidates enquired if they might have the chance of a shot at the Russians."

The ships made calls at Gibralta and Malta and the navvies went ashore, became fighting drunk and then showed the locals what they were going to do with the Russians.

Eventually the fleet arrived off Balaclava early in February 1855 and their first task was to erect their huts to protect them from the icy, howling blizzards. This was done and in no time they had heated, weatherproof accommodation. Compare this with the thin tents the poor soldiers had to live in at Balaclava.

Balaclava February 1855. Brassey's men at work building the railway. Compare the heated huts provided by Brassey for his navvies with the thin tents of the soldiers in the depths of a Russian winter.

The men named the huts "Peto Terrace", "Brassey Terrace", "Preston Hall", "Napoleon", "Victoria", "Blackwall", "Suffolk" and "Lancashire".

The man in charge of building the line was Mr Beattie, a colleague of William Heap who had worked on the "Grand Trunk". He split the labour force into two, half working by day levelling the ground, laying the sleepers and lines, and the other half worked by night, banking up and filling in between the sleepers with stones and earth. Within the first two weeks of landing they had built their encampment, several bridges and seven miles of line!

As an example of their speed of working one correspondent of the "Illustrated London News" noted that the line had to cross a small, but very marshy stream that ran into the harbour. A piledriver was landed one evening and carried piecemeal to where it was to sink piles for the bridge. The machine was erected early the next morning and all the piles were driven, the machine removed, a stout wooden bridge was constructed and the rails were laid across the bridge and one hundred yards beyond before evening!

The same publication carried a story of a "wild dog" hunt that the Army organised near the front line in similar fashion to a foxhunt. Facing them were the Cossacks and when they saw all the activity in the British lines they became very agitated, assuming, reasonably enough, that the British were about to attack. After a while however, it dawned on their incredulous

The railway works at Balaclava, by night.

Progress of the Balaclava railway to the church of Kadikol (March 24, 1855).

Cossack minds, what was going on and they watched with bewildered fascination the progress of the hunt.

A little while after the British noticed two riders from the Cossack lines galloping towards them, so they detained them and found they were two deserters who had tired of fighting. The British officers found out that the two horses did not belong to the deserters so they took them back towards the Russian lines and pointing them towards the Cossacks, gave them a smack on their rump, and sent them back. Gentlemen did not steal horses.

Something similar occurred when a Russian deserter offered military information about the Russian defences. Lord Raglan flatly refused to listen to him because he was so appalled at the man's treason and sent him away with a flea in his ear.

Perhaps it was not the ideal way to win a war, but they have a certain appeal and incompetent though they were they were infinitely more likeable than some of the more efficient but cruel officers of other armies at that time.

We do not know what Brassey's navvies thought of the soldiers but a Captain Henry Clifford,

Balaclava 1855. Work on the railway is finished and supplies are unloaded from the ships in the harbour direct into the railway wagons and taken to the front at Sevastopol.

later Major General Sir Henry Clifford, wrote that the navvies looked "unutterable things" but did more work in a day than a regiment of soldiers did in a week. Not surprising since Beattie had not included "wild dog" hunting in the programme.

In just over six weeks the railway was finished and by the 7th April 1855 there were seventeen engines busy pulling the desperately needed supplies to the front, but from the very start of building the railway it was in use shortening the lines of supply and enabled the Army to survive that terrible winter. By the end of March they had carried 1,000 tons of shot and shell, 3,600 tons of clothing, blankets medical supplies and other goods.

In September 1855 Sevastopol fell and the great Russian naval base was destroyed by the victorious British Army still being supplied by the men of Peto, Brassey and Betts running the Crimean Railway.

Beattie, the engineer, had hardly any sleep for the three weeks before the convoy arrived, because he had to survey the route and do the prior planning and he worked continuously throughout the building of the railway. When it was finished, he was completely exhausted and worn out and although he was sent back to England he died shortly after his return. He gave his own life but he saved the lives of thousands of his fellow countrymen.

A correspondent wrote that the railway was expected to be finished by the end of April but was completed by mid March and commented, "the skill of the men entrusted with the building of the railway appears to have overcome all obstacles in a manner which few could have anticipated, even though accustomed to the celerity of workmanship in England and which to our soldiers in the Crimea, worn out by the failure of so many fine schemes, appeared an idle dream.

"It has once more proved that the men who have made England great by their skill and enterprise and powers of organisation, are of a far different calibre from the officials whom Government employs. While months have been spent in getting warm clothing and the barest necessities for hospital practice a few weeks only has been required for the conception and execution of a novel and most difficult enterprise."

Such was the power and skills of the Birkenhead firm of Peto, Brassey and Betts, Thomas Brassey and his men, they became national heroes and received acclaim in the Press and the Government heaped praise on them in the House of Commons, but unlike Florence Nightingale and others they are now almost forgotten—even in Birkenhead.

CANADA WORKS AND INDIA

For many years William Heap and Company did a considerable trade with India, supplying iron, steel, pumps and machinery and as in Canada, this business sprang from friendships forged while Mr Heap was working for Thomas Brassey on railway contracts in that country.

In 1855 the Governor General of India, Lord Dalhoussie made a minute in which this remarkable man planned the whole integrated network of railways to cover India and he even specified a uniform gauge of 5'–6", the same as the Grand Trunk Railway, which was midway between the standard British Gauge of 4'–8½" and the Great Western broad gauge of 7'–0". The Indian Mutiny of 1857 accelerated the building of the railway as it encouraged the British Government to press ahead.

Victorian Imperialism is not fashionable in certain miserable quarters, but whilst agreeing that a people should rule themselves, Imperialism was inevitable with large masses of the earth backward and unexplored and given the need for Imperialism then history will show that it was fortunate that it was Britain that was cast in the role of chief Empire builder. By and large British rule was enlightened, and just as we benefitted from the Roman occupation, so India and other countries of the Empire benefitted from British rule. Even while the Indian Mutiny was in progress, the Universities of Calcutta, Madras and Bombay were founded, Grant in Aid helped the rapid expansion of private colleges, western style education was promoted on a large scale and the foundations of modern Indian medicine and science were laid.

Not all these measures were welcomed by the Indian ruling classes, the Hindus in particular did not like the suppression of suttee and infanticide. Even though the British stopped the widow being burned on her husband's funeral pyre, her family then treated her like a dog and she was made to wear sackcloth and ashes for the remainder of her life and was only allowed to do the most menial tasks in the household she had controlled up to the time of her husband's death.

Another great problem which had plagued India since time began was famine and this was one of the reasons why Lord Dalhousie wanted a railway network, because then foodstuffs could be rushed into famine areas. He also wanted to encourage new industries such as jute and cotton and good transport was needed to enable this to be done, but the Hindus were not enthusiastic because they felt that it would break down the Caste system.

It is true that the Mutiny also illustrated the need to move troops about quickly, but Lord Dalhousie had drawn up his plans two years earlier. It is fashionable in some quarters to draw a picture of a subjected people held down by brutal British force of arms, but this is quite untrue. There were occasions when there were only 20,000 British soldiers in the whole vast endless land mass of India with its teeming millions. Last year there were more troops in Northern Ireland than we had in the whole of India during our Imperial reign and we could not have ruled for so long without the consent of the people.

The Indian Civil Service was undoubtedly the most efficient, dedicated and uncorrupt in the East and this small band of 1,200 men gave wise Government to 300 millions. Today the Department of Industry alone employs in just a couple of its office blocks more people than were in the whole of the I.C.S. and they could not run a fish and chip shop. The I.C.S. laid down the legal and ruling system which the British bequeathed to India and in our day they had freedom of speech and if we had to imprison a comparative few, compare this with the situation now where the Socialist Mrs Gandhi is reported to have no less than 80,000 political opponents in jail including 30 M.P.s and freedom of speech is forbidden.*

It was not possible for Lord Dalhousie to obtain the capital to build the railways from the Indians and so all the cash was raised in Britain and the British Government guaranteed every mile of railway that was built. Eight firms were approached to build sections of the network and one of them was the greatest contractor of them all, Thomas Brassey and his men of Canada Works, Birkenhead.

EASTERN BENGAL RAILWAYS

In 1858 a year after the Mutiny, Thomas Brassey in partnership with Sir Joseph Paxton and Mr Wythes was awarded the contract for the 112 miles of the Eastern Bengal Railway. The engineer was Isambard Kingdom Brunel who not only built remarkable ships but engineered the splendid "Great Western Railway" known as Brunel's billiard table because the gradient was 1 in 1,380.

As usual, much was left to Thomas Brassey's men because while the Eastern Bengal was being built, Brunel was struggling with the immense problem of building the largest ship in the world the "Great Eastern". Indeed a year after work started Brunel died on Thursday, 15th September 1859, heartbroken when he learned that the feedwater heaters on the "Great Eastern" had blown up on the 9th September. He had pushed out, way beyond the then frontiers of engineering knowledge and it is sad that he died despairing with a feeling of failure.

The Eastern Bengal Railway ran from Calcutta to the village of Kushtia, further up the River Ganges and all the materials were made and despatched from England, much of it from Canada Works. On this contract lattice bridges were used rather than tubular, because it was easier to despatch material for a lattice design and William Heap was responsible for the bridges built on this railway.

The Eastern Bengal was not a financial success for Thomas Brassey but his appetite was whetted and he then tendered for the much larger Delhi Railway.

DELHI RAILWAY

The Delhi Railway was part of the East Indian Railway and runs 304 miles from Delhi to

*Written in 1976.

Umritsir in the Punjab. Brassey's contract included all the civil engineering work, the permanent way, station, locomotives, wagons, carriages and signalling equipment for the fixed price of £14,630 per mile. This was higher than the tender price for the Eastern Bengal, but Brassey had no intention of losing money twice.

Canada Works again made much of the equipment and the logistics were tremendous. Remember there were no roads, nor railways in this area at that time to carry the materials for the new railroad in India and the total weight of the material shipped out from England came to the staggering total of 100,000 tons and this had to be carried by a variety of transport, including ox carts, camels and elephants, over 1,000 miles from the landing point in India to the site of the railway.

BRIDGES OVER THE JUMNA RIVER

William Heap was given the job of building all the bridges on the Delhi line and there were many that were major engineering feats in themselves, including those over the River Sutley and the River Beeas, but the greatest of all the Indian bridges and one to rival the Victoria Bridge was the bridge over the Jumna River. Years later when William Heap was a Director of Canada Works Engineering Company and they invited subscriptions for the shares in the company, out of all the magnificent achievements of this superb works the prospectus gave as examples of the work that had been done there, the Victoria Bridge and the Jumna River Bridge.

The Indian rivers posed different problems to the St Lawrence because the width of the rivers varied tremendously from season to season and were quite unpredictable as to the course they would take. For example, the Jumna River at the end of the hot dry season is a placid stream but at the beginning of the spring when the Himalayan sun starts to melt the snow on the mountain ranges, small torrents start way up in the mountain, then join together to form tumbling rivers and finally these rivers join forces to become great belts of foaming, swirling, raging torrents where the railway had to cross the river.

The position chosen for the crossing was at Allahabad, about one and a quarter miles from its junction with the River Ganges and at that spot the depth of the river was only 15', but three quarters of a mile away, up stream downstream, the depths increased to 65' and 72' respectively. Like all Indian rivers, the Jumna winds about a great deal in its course to the sea and the torrential flow of water when the snow starts to melt cut away the sand from the banks and scour out the bed of the river. The Ganges under the influence of the cutting power of the torrents has moved in places, one and three quarter miles east in the last forty-five years at the rate of 200 ft per year.

Great difficulties were experienced in preparing the foundations for the piers which were to support the fifteen spans and although Brassey's men went down to 80' only encountered sand with a few loose stones and so they made artificial islands of sand with sand bags and loose sand and on the islands they positioned ten iron curbs 13'–6" outside diameter and 8'–6" inside diameter and these were lowered into the sand by scooping out the sand from under, then another curb was set down on top and so on until they had a firm foundation. The masonry for the piers was then cemented to iron bars projecting up from the curbs.

The bridge was 3,278' between abutments and consisted of fifteen openings of 205' clear span, each crossed by wrought iron lattice girders thus giving a total waterway of 3,075', the height to the top of the pier was 58'–6" and the top of the rails is 80' above low water level. At the last minute the River Jumna changed course again, so much so that a cable was sent to Canada Works saying that the length of the main viaduct would have to be increased to 6,600' or one and a quarter miles long not counting the approach viaducts.

Eventually the bridges and the lines were finished and a report in "The Engineer" of 1862 on the opening of the railway stated "A Brahmin looking at the locomotive at Umritsir remarked 'All the incarnations of the Gods in India, never produced such a thing as that'. By this time the news had been carried by the trading caravans into Cabul and Central Asia and so our prestige increases."

THE CHORD LINE

The last railway line that William Heap worked on in India was also Brassey's last Indian contract; this was the Chord Line which ran 147 miles on the Delhi to Calcutta, East Indian Railway. It was called the Chord because it cut off a great semi-circular loop on this line.

THE HERITAGE OF THE INDIAN RAILWAYS

The nervous system of modern India is the railway network, it has done everything that Lord Dalhousie, that man of vision, planned. It reduced the pestilance of famine, it enabled the Indian cotton, jute and tea industries to be set up and prosper and, as the Hindus feared, it did help to break down the caste system. Of this the people of Birkenhead have much to be proud, because of the important part played by Canada Works.

As well as having a long term economic benefit the building of the railway system in India brought some immediate benefit to the Indian workers employed in building the railway. Much of the British capital spent on the railway was paid to the Indian workers, labouring under the supervision of the British navvies. This was referred to by Mr Henfrey, Thomas Brassey's partner in the Delhi Railway at the opening of the Meerut and Umballa section of the Delhi Line, when he said "How greatly the working classes of this country (India) have profitted by the construction of the railways may be judged by the fact that out of seventy-five to eighty million pounds sterling expended to this present time on Indian railways nearly two thirds, or between forty to fifty million pounds has passed, I cannot say into the pockets, but into the hands of the working classes."

When George V came to the throne in 1910 as Emperor of India he was able to see a railway network in India comprising 31,500 miles of track and every mile of track had been financed by British capital and built by British firms. This may be compared with the railway network in present day Germany which totals 18,000 miles and which is about to be reduced to 10,000 miles or with the total motorway mileage built in the U.K. which is 1,312 miles to date. In the whole of the vast sub-continent of India there was fast transport and in the vast, densely populated, band of country from Calcutta to Peshawe it was hard to find a town that was more than 25 miles from the railway.

When our splendid Imperial past is under attack, compare the British achievements in India with the state of a similar country facing the same sort of problems, enormous population, no birth control, poor economy, large land mass—China.

In that country whole densely populated provinces 400 miles across had no railway system, nor metalled roads and in that gigantic, endless, country there was only 3,000 miles of railway.

CALCUTTA WATERWORKS

Another of Lord Dalhousie's schemes was to improve irrigation and water supply throughout India and the British built irrigation canals and piped water into the teeming cities just as two thousand years earlier the Romans laid wooden pipes from the wells at Boughton into the centre of Chester. When in 1820 water flowed into the centre of Delhi the population went wild with excitement, donned gala dress and there were great celebrations in the streets.

Another city with enormous water problems was Calcutta and in 1865 it was decided to build a completely new water works system. The overall plan was done by the Chief Engineer for Calcutta, William Clark. He designed the three large pumping stations, the filter beds, settling tanks and distribution network.

Thomas Brassey was awarded this contract, but ill health forced William Clark to return temporarily to England before the scheme started. William Heap was given this contract to handle because the Bridge Department at Canada Works were specialists in pumping because of the numerous coffer dams they had to pump out. William Heap became very friendly with William Clark and in 1872, Mr Clark seconded Mr Heap's application for Membership of the Institution of Mechanical Engineers.

William Clark was formerly a resident engineer with the East Indian Railway Company and when later he became Engineer to the Municipality of Calcutta he carried out another very important scheme by designing a completely new sewerage scheme for the city, but there was very strong local objections and he had to fight hard to push the scheme through.

William Clark remained as Chief Engineer for the City of Calcutta until 1874 when he finally retired to England and entered into Partnership with W. F. Batho who proposed William Heap's application for the Institute of Mechanical Engineers. Together they designed a number of machines including the invention of the first steam driven road roller.

The friendships William Heap formed in India during the building of the railways and Calcutta Waterworks stood him in good stead when he set up on his own and for many years we supplied pumps, machinery and wrought iron pontoons to Calcutta Municipal Authority, steel for bridges, railway equipment and high grade iron and steel to Jessops of Calcutta who were the Purchasing Agents for the Indian Government.

AUSTRIAN RAILWAY AND CANADA WORKS

At the same time as the Indian Railways were being built Thomas Brassey was building in many other countries. In 1863 Thomas Brassey was awarded the 165 mile Lemberg and Czernowitz Railway in Austria and its story illustrates the sort of man that worked for Thomas Brassey.

Apart from the technical and logistical problems to be overcome, Mr Brassey had great financial problems; the skies were darkening and the sound of distant thunder heralded the build up to the financial storms of 1866. Another small difficulty his men had to contend with was that Austria and Prussia were at war and their armies were fighting fiercely on the sector of the Crocow and Lemberg railway line which Peto, Brassey and Betts had recently finished.

At one point money was running out for the firm in Austria and it was necessary to get cash up the line which was closed because of the battle. Mr Ofenheim, Thomas Brassey's agent decided that if they waited until the battle was finished it might be too late for the firm and so he decided that he must do something about it. He found one of the Birkenhead-built locomotives in a shed and then fired it up and built up a head of steam and set off down the line. A medieval fight was about to be interrupted by the Industrial Revolution.

As Mr Ofenheim looked out of the locomotive he could see that he was approaching the battlefield, there were wounded stragglers dragging themselves along and wild, fear crazed, horses galloping away. A fierce fight was taking place with cavalry engaged in bloody hand to hand fighting, cannons were booming and men and horse screamed as fragments of iron tore into their bodies. Mr Ofenheim gave a mighty blast on the locomotives whistle which startled men and horses on both sides. The cavalry struggled to control their horses, the gunners with lighted tapers in their hands stood open mouthed at the astonishing sight of such a monster as they had never seen before charging towards them, smoke belching from its chimney, at the unprecedented speed of 50 m.p.h. They all stood motionless for a few seconds and then realising that the monster was not going to stop they scattered away from the railway line and stood watching the progress of the locomotive with awe and perhaps a little admiration. It took more than a battle to stop Thomas Brassey's men going about their business.

This feat was relayed by the Austrian officers present to their Emperor, Franz Joseph of Austria who was so impressed that he sent for Victor Ofenheim, and after congratulating him asked: 'Who is this Mr Brassey, this English contractor, for whom men are to be found who will work with such zeal and risk their lives?"

For his work in Austria the Emperor awarded Thomas Brassey the Cross of the Iron Crown, but one suspects that Mr Brassey valued Mr Ofenheim's loyalty and bravery more than medals.

THE CRASH OF 1866

The year 1866 saw the culmination of a crisis for Thomas Brassey and the other railway contractors which was to lead directly to the formation of our company. The crisis had been gathering momentum for some time and was eventually triggered off by the failure of the London private bank of Overend & Gurney, for forty years one of the World's greatest financial houses.

A year earlier in 1865, the Indian cotton market built up under Lord Dalhousie's guidance, collapsed and a number of small failures occurred which were symptomatic of the underlying financial weakness, so that when Overend & Gurney went under with financial liabilities of nineteen million pounds, it caused a shock wave of bankruptcies all over the country. One of the first to fail was Sir Morton Peto, Thomas Brassey's old partner became almost all his wealth had been tied up with Overend & Gurney. There was a run on the banks and on Friday, 11th May 1866, Mr Gladstone, the Chancellor of the Exchequer raised Bank Rate to 10% and credit became unobtainable. The shock waves then spread out from this country and companies all over the world collapsed and only the strongest survived.

Thomas Brassey rode out the storm because he finished the Lemberg and Czernowitz Railway just in time and this released one million pounds, he used part of his own private fortune and although credit was almost unobtainable his standing was so high that he managed to borrow another quarter of a million pounds.

It became apparent to William Heap that although Peto, Brassey and Betts had survived the crisis, the great heyday of railway building was passing, he had been with Thomas Brassey for almost fourteen years, ten of those as the Manager of the Bridge Department of Canada Works and during that time had taken part in some of the greatest engineering adventures ever undertaken. He had met, and worked with, Robert Stephenson, Isambard Kingdom Brunel, Thomas Brassey, Sir William Fairbairn, Eaton Hodgkinson, Joseph Locke and others, but now he felt that at the age of forty-years, he should start up his own business.

William Heap's parting with Thomas Brassey and George Harrison was very friendly and indeed until the firm finally went under after the death of Mr Brassey we were favoured with a considerable volume of business with Peto, Brassey and Betts and later when Canada Works became a public company, William Heap was invited to be a Director.

THE END OF THOMAS BRASSEY

William Heap's judgement proved sound because after he had left his old firm they only built another 550 miles of railway and in the spring of 1870 Thomas Brassey was told that he had cancer. He refused to stop working and continued to visit sites in Britain checking that the work was being done well and looking to the welfare of his men.

In the late summer of 1870, Mr Brassey was forced to take to his bed and in those days suffering was more intense than today because there were no pain killing drugs. Right up to the end his engineers and navvies used to visit him, some of them walking great distances, so they could quietly pay their last respects.

Finally on 8th December 1870, Thomas Brassey, the first great contractor in the world died, a gentle, soft spoken, kind man, a brilliant engineer and an organising genius. He had built 1 out of every 20 miles of the world's railways, even as early as 1850 he had built 3 out of every 4 miles of French railways, he had helped to open up continents and changed social pattern all over the world.

Thomas Brassey left £3,200,000 and he deserved every penny of it, he left £2,000,000 on trust for his children, but more important he left a heritage of railways all over the world and to this day he is remembered with love, affection and admiration by the few who know of him.

In the Birkenhead News of 21st August 1886 there was a letter from John Wilson of Congleton who wrote about the granting of a Peerage to Thomas Brassey's son Thomas, Lord Brassey "Whilst Thomas Brassey cared for no distinction for himself he would have been proud of his son's well deserved Peerage, but he would have been most proud of his son's words the other day; 'In being allowed to choose my future title I wish for no name but that of my father to whom I owe everything'".

In his lifetime Thomas Brassey gently, but firmly, refused all honours offered in this country, but he accepted those offered by foreign countries because he thought that a refusal might cause offence. Having lost the Legion of Honour bestowed on him by the Emperor Napoleon III of France and the Order of St Maurice and St Lazarus bestowed on him by King Victor Emanuel of Italy, he sent out for duplicates to please his wife and as he remarked "Mrs Brassey will be glad to possess all these crosses".

Today the Brassey family live in Apthorne Hall near Oundle in Northamptonshire; the first Lord and Lady Brassey were remarkable in their own way because they sailed around the world in their, Mersey built, yacht "Sunbeam" and Lord Brassey wrote a book about the classical doctrine of supply and demand, and the present members of the family are also not without distinction.

In 1966 the late Lord Brassey bought a small circular hover machine to raise money for the local church and he became so interested in hovercraft that he founded a firm "Hoverair" to make this type of vehicle. Lord Brassey died in the Autumn of 1966 but the amazing Lady Brassey carried on with the work and by the end of 1968 had produced a magnificent little Hovercraft, one of which was used in 1969 by the young adventurer Captain Sir Ranulph Twisleton-Wykeham-Fiennes in his expedition to the source of the White Nile.

BIOGRAPHY OF THOMAS BRASSEY

In 1872 Sir Arthur Helps, Clerk of the Privy Council, wrote "The Life and Labours of Mr Brassey (1805–1870) and he wrote the following dedication to Queen Victoria:
"To the Queen.
Madame,

I am very grateful for the permission given me to dedicate this work to your Majesty.

I desire so to dedicate it, because I do not know of any one who has a deeper sympathy with the labouring classes than Your Majesty, or anyone who takes a more heartfelt interest in everything that concerns their habits, their education and their general welfare. Moreover this sympathy, and this interest are not confined to those classes in Your Majesty's Dominions only, but are extended to them wherever they are to be found.

I think also that it cannot but be very gratifying to Your Majesty to have full evidence that, in a special kind of labour of a very important character, namely the construction of railways, your own subjects have hitherto borne the palm, and have introduced their excellent modes of working into various Foreign countries.

Your Majesty will find that the late Mr Brassey was an employer of labour after Your Majesty's own heart, always solicitous for the wellbeing of those who served under him, never keeping aloof from them, but using the powerful position of Master in such a manner as to win their affection and to diminish the distance which is often too great between the employer and the employed.

I venture, therefore, to think that the volume will be of interest to Your Majesty on its own account; and that you will be disposed to view with favour the merits, if any, and to deal gently with the faults of a work written by one who, with all respect, is ever Your Majesty's.

Faithful and devoted
Subject and servant
Arthur Helps.

London, June 1872.

Sir Arthur Helps gave a list of Thomas Brasseys contracts to which we have added one or two others as follows:

TABLE
OF
RAILWAY AND OTHER CONTRACTS

COMPLETED BY MR BRASSEY BETWEEN THE YEARS 1834 AND 1870

Year	Contract	Partner	Engineer	Agent	Mileage
1834	Branborough Road				4
1835	Grand Junction Railway		Mr Locke, M.P., F.R.S.		10
1837	London and Southampton Railway (Branches and Maintenance)		Mr. Locke, M.P., F.R.S., Mr Neuman	Mr Ogilvie and others	36
1839	Chester and Crewe Railway		Mr R. Stephenson, M.P., F.R.S.	Mr G. Meakin	11
	Glasgow, Paisley, and Greenock Railway		Mr Locke, M.P., F.R.S.	Mr Strapp and others	7
	Sheffield and Manchester Railway		Mr Locke, M.P., F.R.S.	Mr Dent and others	19
1841	Paris and Rouen Railway	Mr Mackenzie	Mr Locke, M.P., F.R.S., Mr Neuman	Mr E. Mackenzie, Mr J. Jones, Mr Goodfellow, Mr Day and others	82
1842	Orleans and Bordeaux Railway	Messrs. W. & E. Mackenzie	M. Pepin Lehalleur	Mr E. Mackenzie	294
1843	Rouen and Havre Railway	Mr Mackenzie	Mr Locke, M.P., F.R.S., Mr Neuman	Mr Day, Mr C. Smith, Mr J. Jones, Mr Swanson, Mr Goodfellow	58
1844	Lancashire and Carlisle Railway	Mr Mackenzie, Mr Stephenson	Mr Locke, M.P., F.R.S.	Mr G. Mould	70
	Colchester and Ipswich Railway	Mr Ogilvie	Mr Locke, M.P., F.R.S., Mr Bruff	Mr Ogilvie	16
	Amiens and Boulogne Railway	Mr W. Mackenzie, Mr E. Mackenzie	M. Bazaine, Sir W. Cubitt, F.R.S.	Mr E. Mackenzie	53
1843	Trent Valley Railway	Mr Makenzie, Mr Stephenson	Mr R. Stephenson, M.P., F.R.S., Mr Bidder, Mr Gooch	Mr J. Jones, Mr S. Horn	50
	Chester and Holyhead Railway	Mr Mackenzie, Mr Stephenson	Mr R. Stephenson, M.P., F.R.S., Mr Ross, Mr F. Forster	Mr Woodhouse	31
	Ipswich and Bury Railway	Mr Ogilvie	Mr Locke, M.P., F.R.S., Mr Brutt	Mr Ogilvie	24½
	Kendal and Windermere Railway	Mr Mackenzie, Mr Stephenson	Mr Locke, M.P., F.R.S.	Mr G. Mould	12
	North Wales Mineral Extension Railway	Mr Mackenzie, Mr Stephenson	Mr Robertson	Mr Meakin	5
1845	Caledonian Railway (1st Contract)	Mr Mackenzie, Mr Stephenson	Mr Locke, M.P., F.R.S.	Mr G. Mould, Mr Woodhouse	125
	Clydesdale Junction Railway	Mr Mackenzie, Mr Stephenson	Mr Locke, M.P., F.R.S.	Mr Woodhouse	15
	Greenock Harbour	Mr Mackenzie, Mr Stephenson	Mr Locke, M.P., F.R.S.	Mr Goodfellow, Mr Barnard	—
	Scottish Midland Junction Railway	Mr Mackenzie, Mr Stephenson	Mr Locke, M.P., F.R.S.	Mr G. Mould	33
	Scottish Central Railway	Mr Mackenzie, Mr Stephenson	Mr Locke, M.P., F.R.S.	Mr Falshaw	46
1846	Lancashire and Yorkshire Railway (Maintenance)	Mr Field	Mr Hawkshaw, F.R.S.	Mr Day	93
	Ormskirk Railway	Mr Mackenzie	Mr Meek	Mr Greene	30
	Shrewsbury and Chester Railway	Mr Mackenzie, Mr Stephenson	Mr Robertson	Mr Meakin	25
	Mineral Line (Wales)	Mr Mackenzie, Mr Stephenson	Mr Robertson	Mr Meakin	6½
1847	Buckinghamshire Railway		Mr Dockray	Mr S. Horn	47½
	Birkenhead and Chester Junction Railway		Mr Rendel, F.R.S.	Mr Goodfellow, Mr Day	17½

Year	Contract	Partner	Engineer	Agent	Mileage
	Haughley and Norwich Railway	Mr Ogilvie	Mr Locke, M.P., F.R.S.	Mr P. Ogilvie	33
	Great Northern Railway		Sir W. Cubitt, F.R.S.	Mr Bartlett, Mr Milroy, Mr Ballard	75½
	North Staffordshire Railway		Mr R. Stephenson, M.P., F.R.S., Mr Bidder	Mr J. Jones	48
	Shrewsbury Extension Railway	Mr Mackenzie, Mr Stephenson	Mr Robertson	Mr Meakin	3
	Trent Valley Stations	Mr Mackenzie, Mr Stephenson	Mr Bidder and others	Mr Holme	—
	Blackwall Extension Railway	Mr Ogilvie	Mr Locke, M.P., F.R.S., Mr Stanton	Mr Burt	1¾
	Richmond and Windsor Railway	Mr Ogilvie	Mr Locke, M.P., F.R.S.	Mr Evans	16½
	Rouen and Dieppe Railway	Mr Mackenzie	Mr Neuman, Mr Murton	Mr Benyon, Mr C. Smith	31
1848	Chester Station			Mr S. Holme	—
	Oswestry Branch Railway	Mr Mackenzie, Mr Stephenson	Mr Robertson	Mr Meakin	2
	Loop Line (L. & S.W.R.)	Mr Ogilvie	Mr Locke, M.P., F.R.S.	Mr Evans	7
	Caledonian Railway (2nd Contract) (Stations, Maintenance, etc.)	Mr Mackenzie,	Mr Locke, M.P., F.R.S.		—
	Glasgow and Barhead Railway		Mr Locke, M.P., F.R.S.	Mr Strapp	11
	Barcelona and Mataro Railway	Mr Mackenzie	Mr Locke, M., F.R.S. Mr W. Locke	Mr Robson	18
1849	Royston and Hitchin Railway		Mr Locke, M.P., F.R.S.	Mr H. Harrison	13
1850	Shepwreth Extension Railway		Mr Locke, M.P., F.R.S.	Mr H. Harrison	5
	Birkenhead Docks		Mr Rendel, F.R.S., Mr Abernethy	Mr Dent	—
	North and South-Western Junction Railway	Mr Ogilvie	Mr G. Berkeley	Mr Evans	4
	Prato and Pistoja Railway		Italian Government	Mr T. Woodhouse	10
1851	Shrewsbury and Hereford Railway, and Maintenance		Mr Robertson	Mr W. Field	51
	Norwegian Railway	Sir M. Peto, M.P., Mr Betts	Mr Bidder	Mr Merrit, Mr Earle	56
1852	Hereford, Ross, and Gloucester Railway	Sir M. Peto, M.P., Mr Betts	Mr Brunel, F.R.S.	Mr Watson	30
	London, Tilbury, and Southend Railway	Sir M. Peto, M.P., Mr Betts	Mr Bidder	Mr White	50
	Victoria Docks and Warehouses	Sir M. Peto, M.P., Mr Betts	Mr Bidder	Mr Holland	—
	Warrington and Stockport Railway		Mr Lister	Mr Goodfellow	12
	North Devon Railway	Mr Ogilvie	Mr W. R. Neale	Mr P. Ogilvie, Mr Evans	47
	Mantes and Caen Railway		Mr Locke, M.P., F.R.S., Mr Neuman, Mr W. Locke	Mr J. Jones, Mr C. Jones, Mr J. Milroy	113
	Le Mans and Mezidon Railway		Mr Locke, M.P., F.R.S., M. Bergeron	Mr Woodhouse	84
	Lyons and Avignon Railway	Sir M. Peto, M.P., Mr Betts	M. Talabot, M. Thirion, M. Molard	Mr G. Giles, Mr Murton	67
	Dutch Rhenish Railway		Mr Locke, M.P., F.R.S.	Mr Ballard	43
	Grand Trunk Railway	Sir M. Peto, M.P., Mr Betts, Sir W. Jackson	Mr Ross	Mr Reckie, Mr Hodges, Mr Rowan, Mr Tait, Mr P. Ogilvie	539
1853	Crystal Palace and West-End Railway	Sir M. Peto, M.P., Mr Betts	Mr Bidder	Mr Watson	5
	Sambre and Meuse Railway		M. Declerq	Mr H. Harrison	28
	Turin and Novara Railway		Italian Government	Mr T. Woodhouse, Mr Hancox	60
	Hauenstein Tunnel		M. Etzel	M. Benyon	1½
	Royal Danish Railway	Sir M. Peto, M.P., Mr Betts	Mr Bidder, Mr G. R. Stephenson	Mr McKeon	75
1854	Arpley Branch Railway		Mr Lister	Mr Goodfellow	1½
	Woodford and Loughton Railway		Mr Bidder	Mr H. Harrison	7½
	Central Italian Railway	Sir W. Jackson, Messrs. Fell and Jopling	Italian Government	Mr Fell, Mr Jopling	52
	Turin and Susa Railway	Mr C. Henfrey	Italian Government	Mr C. Henfrey	34
	Bellegarde Tunnel	Messrs. Parent and Buddicom	M Talabot	Mr Goodfellow	2½
1855	East Suffolk Railway	Sir M. Peto, M.P., Mr Betts	Mr G. Berkley	Mr Watson	63

Year	Contract	Partner	Engineer	Agent	Mileage
	Inverness and Nairn Railway	Mr Falshaw	Mr Mitchell	Mr Falshaw	16
	Portsmouth Direct Railway	Mr Ogilvie	Mr Locke, M.P., F.R.S.	Mr Evans	33
	Caen and Cherbourg Railway		Mr Locke, M.P., F.R.S., Mr W. Locke	Mr Milroy, Mr C. Jones	94
	Coghines Bridge		Italian Government	Mr Dent	—
1856	Woodbridge Extension Railway	Mr Ogilvie	Mr Bruff	Mr Boys	10
	Elizabeth-Linz Railway	Sir M. Peto, M.P., Mr Betts	M. C. Keissler	Mr G. Giles	49
1857	Leicester and Hitchin Railway		Messrs. Liddell and Gordon	Mr Horn, Mr Harrison	62½
	Leominster and Kington Railway	Mr Field	Mr Wylie	Mr Field	14
	Minories Warehouses	Sir M. Peto, M.P., Mr Betts	Mr Tite, M.P.	Mr Holland	—
1858	Leatherhead, Epsom, and Wimbledon Railway	Mr Ogilvie	Mr Locke, M.P., F.R.S., Mr A. C. Crosse	Mr Ogilvie	10
	Worcester and Hereford Railway	Mr Ballard	Messrs. Liddell and Gordon	Mr Ballard	26
	Inverness and Aberdeen Junction Railway	Mr Falshaw	Mr Mitchell	Mr Falshaw	22
	Bilbao and Miranda Railway	Messrs. Wythes, Paxton and Bartlett	Mr Vignoles, F.R.S.	Mr Bartlett	66
	Eastern Bengal Railway	Messrs. Wythes, Paxton and Henfrey	Mr Hawkshaw, F.R.S.	Mr C. Henfrey	112
1859	Cannock Mineral Railway	Mr Field	Mr Addison	Mr J. Stephenson	10
	Crewe and Shrewsbury Railway		Mr Locke, M.P., F.R.S.	Mr Day	32
	Salisbury Station	Mr Ogilvie	Mr Errington, Mr Tolme	Mr Caswell	2
	Denny Branches		Mr Locke, M.P., F.R.S., Mr Errington	Mr Falshaw	3
	Victor Emmanuel Railway	Sir W. Jackson, Mr Henfrey	Mr Neuman, Mr Ranco	Mr Bartlett, Mr W. Strapp, Mr Blake, Mr Edwards	73
	Ivrea Railway	Mr C. Henfrey	Italian Government	Mr Dent, Mr Dixon	19
	Great Northern, Great Eastern, Great Southern Railways (New South Wales)	Sir M. Peto, M.P., Mr Betts	Mr Whitton	Mr Wilcox, Mr Rhodes	54
1860	Salsbury and Yeovil Railway	Mr H. Harrison, Mr Ogilvie	Mr Locke, M.P., F.R.S.	Mr H. Harrison	40
	Woofferton and Tenbury Railway	Mr Field	Mr Wylie	Mr Mackay	5
	Wenlock Railway	Mr Field	Mr Fowler	Mr Seacome	4
	Port Partick Railway	Mr Falshaw	Mr Blyth	Mr Falshaw	17
	Stokes Bay Pier and Branch Railway	Mr Ogilvie	Mr Fulton	Mr Evans	2
	Harleston and Beccles	Mr Ogilvie	Mr Bruff	Mr Boys	13
	Dieppe Railway (laying second road)	Mr Buddicom	M. Julien	Mr R. Goodfellow	—
	The Maremma, Leghorn, etc., Railway		M. Pini	Mr Jopling, Mr C. Jones	138
	Jutland Railway	Sir M. Peto, M.P., Mr Betts	Danish Government	Mr Rowan	270
1861	Disley and Hayfield Railway	Mr H. Harrison	Mr Errington	Mr Harrison	3½
	Knighton Railway	Mr Field	Mr Robertson	Mr Field	12
	Nuneaton and Hinckley Railway	Mr Field	Mr Addison	Mr J. Stephenson	5
	Shrewsbury and Hereford Railway (widening)	Mr Field	Mr Wylie, Mr Clark	Mr J. Mackay	51
	West London Railway (extension)	Mr Ogilvie	Mr W. Baker	Mr Evans	9
	Ludlow Drainage	Mr Field	Mr Curley	Mr Mackay	7
	Severn Valley Railway		Mr Fowler	Mr Field, Mr Day, Mr Dent, Mr Dowell	42
	South Staffordshire Railway	Mr Field	Mr McClean, M.P., F.R.S.	Mr Day	4
	Metropolitan Mid Level Sewer	Mr Ogilvie, Mr Harrison	Mr Bazalgette, C.B.	Mr Harrison	12
1862	Ringwood and Christchurch Railway	Mr Ogilvie	Captain Moorsom	Mr Evans	8
	Kingston Extension Railway	Mr Ogilvie	Mr Galbraith	Mr Evans	4
	Cannock Chase Railway	Mr Field	Mr Addison	Mr Cooper	3
	Coalbrookdale Railway	Mr Field	Mr Fowler	Mr Dent	5
	Ashchurch and Evesham Railway	Mr Ballard	Messrs. Liddell and Gordon	Mr Ballard	11
	Nantwich and Market Drayton Railway	Mr Field	Mr Gardiner	Mr Gallaher, Mr Mackay	11
	South Leicester Railway	Mr Field	Mr Addison	Mr J. Stephenson	10
	Tenbury and Bewdley Railway	Mr Field	Mr Wylie, Mr Clarke	Mr Mackay	12

Year	Contract	Partner	Engineer	Agent	Mileage
	Wenlock and Craven Arms Railway	Mr Field	Mr Fowler	Mr Dent, Mr N. Mackay	14
	Ludlow and Clee Hill Railway	Mr Field	Mr Wylie, Mr Clarke,	Mr Mackay	6
	Llangollen Railway		Mr Robertson, M.P.	Mr Gallagher	6
	Rio Janeiro Drainage	Mr Ogilvie	M. Gotto	Mr Honcox	—
	Mauritius Railway	Mr Wythes and others	Mr Hawkshaw, F.R.S.	Mr Longridge	64
1863	Epping and Ongar	Mr Ogilvie, Mr Harrison	Mr Sinclair	Mr Harrison	13
	Barrow Docks	Mr Field	Mr McLean, M.P., F.R.S.	Mr Dent	—
	Runcorn Branch Railway	Mr Ogilvie	Mr W. Baker	Mr Evans	9
	Tendring Hundred Railway	Mr Ogilvie	Mr Bruff	Mr Boys	3
	Worm Drainage	Mr Field	Mr Curley	Mr Mackay	
	Sudbury, Bury St Edmunds, and Cambridge Railway	Mr Ogilvie	Mr Sinclair	Mr Bell, Mr Boys, Mr Smalls	48
	Meridionale Railway	M. Parent, Mr Budicom	M. Grattoni and others	Mr C. Jones, Mr Charles	160
	Queensland Railway	Sir M. Peto, M.P., Mr Betts	Mr Fitzgibbon	Mr Wilcox	78¼
	North Schleswig Railway	Sir M. Peto, M.P., Mr Betts	Mr Rowan	Mr Louth	70
1864	Epping Railway	Mr H. Harrison, Mr Ogilvie	Mr Sinclair	Mr Butler	12
	Letton Drainage	Mr Field	Mr Curley	Mr Mackay	3
	Dunmow Railway	Mr Ogilvie, Mr H. Harrison	Mr Sinclair	Mr Butler	18
	Corwen and Bala Railway		Mr Robertson, M.P.	Mr Field, Mr Reid	14
	Wellington and Market Drayton Railway	Mr Field	Mr Wilson	Mr Mackay	16
	Enniskillen and Bundoran Railway	Mr Field	Mr Hemens	Mr Day, Mr Drennan	36
	Central Argentine Railway	Mr Wythes, Mr Wheelwright, Mr Ogilvie	Mr E. Woods	Mr Wheelwright	247
	Lemberg Czernowitz Railway		Mr McClean, Mr Stileman, M. Ziffer, M. de Herz	Mr Strapp	165
	Viersen-Venlo Railway	Mr Murton	M. Lange, Mr Bidder	Mr Murton	11
	Delhi Railway	Mr Wythes, Mr Henfrey	Mr J. Harrison, Mr Bidder	Mr C. Henfrey, Mr Mareiller	304
1865	Chertsey Extension Railway	Mr Harrison	Mr Galbraith	Mr Harrison	3½
	Dee Reclamation Works	Mr Field Mr Meakin	Mr Bateman, F.R.S.	Mr Meaken	—
	Evesham and Redditch Railway	Mr Ballard	Mr Richards	Mr Ballard	18
	East London Railway	Mr Wythes, Messrs. Lucas, Brothers	Mr Hawkshaw, F.R.S.	Mr H. Harrison	2½
	Hull and Doncaster Railway	Mr Field	Mr Harrison	Mr Stephenson	16
	Hereford Loop Railway	Mr Field	Mr Clarke	Mr Mackay	2½
	Hooton and Parkgate Railway	Mr Field	Mr Johnson	Mr Mackay	5
	London and Bedford Railway	Mr Ballard	Mr Liddell	Mr Ballard	36
	Llangollen and Corwen Railway	Mr Field			10
	Nantwich and Market Drayton (Widening)	Mr Field	Mr Gardiner	Mr Reid, Mr Mackay	11
	Boca and Barracas Railway	Mr Wythes, Mr Wheelwright	Mr Coghlan	Mr Simpson	3
	Warsaw and Terespol Railway	Mr Vignoles, F.R.S.	Russian Government	Mr H. Vignoles	128
	Chord Line (India)	Mr Wythes, Mr Perry,	Mr Rendel	Mr Perry	147
	Calcutta Waterworks	Mr Wythes, Mr Aird	Mr Purdon, Mr Lewis	Mr Paton	—
	Runcorn Bridge (Masonry only)				
1866	Ebbw Vale Railway	Mr Field	Mr Gardiner	Mr Mackay	2
	Thames Embankment	Mr Ogilvie, Mr Harrison	Mr Bazalgette, C.B.	Mr Harrison	¾
	Kensington and Richmond Railway (and Spurs)	Mr Ogilvie. Mr Harrison	Mr Galbraith, Mr Tolmé	Mr Evans	7
	Christchurch and Bournemouth Railway	Mr Ogilvie	Mr Strapp	Mr Ogilvie	4
	Moreton Hampstead Railway	Mr Ogilvie	Mr Margrafy	Mr Crossley	12
	Bala and Dolgelly Railway		Mr Wilson	Mr Field, Mr Day, Mr Drennan	18
1867	Sirhowy Railway	Mr Field	Mr Sayer	Mr Mackay	2
	Wolverhampton and Walsall Railway	Mr Harrison, Mr Ogilvie	Mr Addison	Mr Harrison	7½
	Czernowitz Suczawa Railway		M. Ziffer, M. de Herz	Mr Strapp	60
	Kronprinz Rudolfsbahn	M. Klein, M. Schwarz	M. F. Kagda	M. Fölsch	272

77

Year	Contract	Partner	Engineer	Agent	Mileage
1868	Silverdale Railway		Mr Forsyth	Mr Field, Mr Mackay	$13\frac{1}{2}$
1869	Nepean Bridge	Sir M. Peto, M.P., Mr Betts	Mr Fowler	Mr Willcox	—
1870	Callao Docks		M. Alléon	Mr Hodges	—
	Vorarlbergbahn	M. Klein, M. Schwarz	M. W. Paravicini	M. Fölsch	55
	Suczawa and Jassy Railway		M. Ziffer	Mr Strapp, Mr Edwards	135

CANADA WORKS AFTER THOMAS BRASSEY

Canada Works continued in business after Thomas Brassey's death, building locomotives, bridges, boilers and ships and in 1877 they built some of the floating pontoons of the Princes Landing Stage, Pierhead, Liverpool and one of the hinged walkways linking the landingstage to the river wall. The workmanship and ornateness of this walkway is superior to others of the same period.

In February 1886 "The Canada Works Engineering and Shipbuilding Company" was floated as a limited liability company and William Heap was one of the Directors of the new company. The prospectus quotes the bridges over the Jumna River on the East India Railway and the Victoria Bridge in Canada as examples of the class of work Canada Works had accomplished in the past.

The new venture was not a success and the new company finally closed down in 1889. William Heap and Co. were owed £900 but Canada Works paid out 15/- in the pound and later paid off most of the remainder.

A sad end to a great engineering works, but it did not die completely because when it went under we took over many of the old connections that had been forged by Thomas Brassey and to this day we still benefit.

Today there is little to be seen of Canada Works except the entrance gates and one or two of the smaller buildings that still stand. In 1972 part of the boulder road that ran

Bust of Thomas Brassey in Chester Cathedral.

through the works was relaid in the gardens in front of our Hoylake office and a few cobbles were set in the paving in the garden around our Eccles office as a memorial to a great engineering works. Today the site is derelict and overgrown; a dumping ground for rubbish.

When one stands on the site of Canada Works one can hear the first triumphant whistle of the "Lady Elgin" in 1854; the singing of the workmen and the chinking of their glasses as they enjoyed their party at the bottom of the coffer dam in the River St Lawrence; the cheers of the workmen as the "Wildfire" sailed for Balaclava; the creaking of the carts and the cries of the drovers as they carried the 100,000 tons of equipment through the dust and the heat of the Indian plains; the shriek of the locomotive as Victor Offenheim charged through the warring Prussian and Austrian armies, and a quiet voice saying "Mrs Brassey will be glad to possess all these crosses".

NOTE TO THE THIRD EDITION 1991

A strange coincidence occurred one Saturday afternoon in 1980 when the writer received a telephone call from an unknown reader in Derby, who had just returned from his daughter's school fete. On a jumble stall he had seen a box of Victorian drawing instruments that had belonged to a John Millar (no relation to the writer so far as is known), who had been a draughtsman at H.M. Dockyard, Pembroke Dock, for many years until he retired about 1910 and he asked if we were interested. The writer bought the drawing instruments and found under the top layer of instruments a visiting card belonging to Sir Thomas Brassey, Thomas Brassey's son, who later became Lord Brassey.

BIRKENHEAD'S MEMORIAL

In his lifetime Thomas Brassey was lionised as a hero, he was féted and decorated by kings and emperors and if he had wished he could have had honours heaped on him by his own country. His children restored St Erasmus' Chapel in Chester Cathedral and there is a bust of Thomas Brassey on the North Wall, but where is the reminder in Birkenhead of this great man and his superb works? A street is named after him and there is a seedy pub called "The Grand Trunk" but that is all.

The men who worked for Peto, Brassey and Betts were Victorian giants and they deserve to be remembered as does their leader. Birkenhead's past is not so illustrious that it can afford to ignore them and their deeds.

St. Erasmus Chapel, Chester Cathedral with Brassey's bust on the left. Thomas Brassey's children paid for the restoration of the Chapel as a memorial to their father.

CHAPTER 4

Heap and Arkle

HEAP AND ARKLE (1866–1892)

After making up his mind to start his own business, William Heap mentioned this to George Arkle a banker who was associated with Canada Works. Mr Arkle suggested that Mr Heap should take a twenty-five year old relative of his, Thomas Arkle, in Partnership and after some thought William Heap agreed.

T. W. Arkle was the son of William Arkle, an Accountant who lived at Thornwood, 7A Slatey Road, Claughton, Birkenhead and at the time he was unmarried and living at home.

THE ALBANY (1866–1870)

Late in 1866 Mr Heap took his farewell of Thomas Brassey and he and Thomas Arkle decided that their office should be in Liverpool because the port was booming and it had excellent communications with the rest of the world. They visited various offices that were to let and finally picked on the most splendid office block of them all. The Albany in Old Hall Street, and they proudly screwed their brass nameplate outside No. 6, Ground Floor, North Corridor on the Central Court side and stood back to admire the wording:

HEAP & ARKLE,
Engineers, Iron & Steel Merchants

We were in business.

The Albany had been built a few years earlier by Mr Naylor of Hooton Hall and his Architect was J. K. Colling and it is still an excellent example of a mid-nineteenth century office building. If one walks along the corridors of the Albany today one can savour the Victorian business atmosphere and one half expects top hatted, frock coated, bushy whiskered, gentlemen to walk out of the doors.

OUR FIRST AGENCIES

In 1866 the Industrial Revolution was an established fact in Britain, if not elsewhere, and it was about this time that modern business organisation as we know it was set up with proper sales departments etc. William Heap was well known in many countries because of his work with Brassey and it was his original intention to set up as an Iron Merchant and also to advise his customers on the design of structures and pumps, in other words to provide a consultancy service.

When some of the steel people heard that William Heap was setting up on his own account they suggested that if he would handle their products exclusively in a given area of North West England and not sell a competitor's, and if in addition he handled all their technical problems and provided a sales service, they in return would appoint him an exclusive Agent in that area and would pay him a small commission on all sales in that area. Outside the area he was free to sell what he liked and he could take on other Agencies provided that the products did not clash.

This was a new conception of business, but after some thought Mr Heap and Mr Arkle agreed and so a modern sales organisation was born with Heap and Arkle acting as the sales office for

The Albany, Old Hall Street, Liverpool, in 1866. The first office of Heap & Arkle.

The Albany in 1988.

The North Corridor in The Albany Building. William Heap's first office in 1866 was the last door in the left. (1988).

their Principals and advising customers on the technical and commercial questions that arose in exactly the same way as if the company had set up its own office in Liverpool.

The first Agencies that the company held were:

Eadie & Spencer
Clydesdale Tube Works
W. & J. Galloway & Sons, Rivet Works, Manchester

When William Heap first came to Wirral in 1853 the only bank in Birkenhead was the North & South Wales Bank at 62, Hamilton Square and so when Heap and Arkle was set up they opened an account at this branch. Mr W. H. Jones the bank manager reported that their capital was only a few hundred pounds, but he considered them prudent and highly honourable.

William Heap and Thomas Arkle worked very hard and they were given a flying start by orders that Mr Heap's old firm Peto, Brassey and Betts placed with them. Mr Heap's old contacts abroad also started placing orders with them and after a year or two the postman was delivering orders for iron and steel from India, Canada, Italy, Spain, the Middle East, North and South America and in all the other countries where Thomas Brassey had built railways.

Gradually they prospered and after four years in The Albany they decided to move office, for some reason or other, and again they chose another fine Victorian office building, Bank Chambers.

BANK CHAMBERS, LIVERPOOL (1870–1876)

In 1870 Heap and Arkle moved to Bank Chambers, 3 Cook Street. The Architect for the building was Charles Robert Cockerell who designed several notable Victorian buildings in Liverpool including the magnificent "Bank of England" in Castle Street and the offices of the "Liverpool & London & Globe Insurance Company" in Dale Street, next to the Town Hall.

Bank Chambers adjoined the Bank of England building and was a very impressive office block with large airy windows, which were by no means usual in Victorian offices.

Bank Chambers survived the savage attacks made on Liverpool in the last war by the Luftwaffe although the offices on the other side of Cook Street were destroyed, but unhappily some post-war vandal had it demolished and a most uninteresting annexe and yard for the Bank of England was built on the site and the dreary wall of the annexe has killed that part of Cook Street stone dead.

In this period Heap and Arkle added the following Agencies to those they already held:

Staffordshire Bolt, Nut & Fencing Co., Darlaston
Wm. Charles & Son, Steelmanufactures, Sheffield
John Varley & Co., Ironfounders, St Helens
Hopkinson & Clarke, Brassfounders, Birmingham

The business continued to prosper in a quiet way and William Heap was appointed to supervise the construction of a number of heavy contracts for India, including the wrought iron jetties for the Port of Calcutta and we supplied a number of bridges to America.

JESSOPS OF INDIA

In 1876 the trade with Jessops of Calcutta, the official Purchasing Agents for the Government of India had grown to the point that it could not be financed out of their own capital and they secured their first overdraft. In 1873 they had transferred their accounts from Hamilton Square to the North & South Wales Bank's branch at 62, Castle Street, because it was more convenient

Bank Chambers, Cook Street, Liverpool.

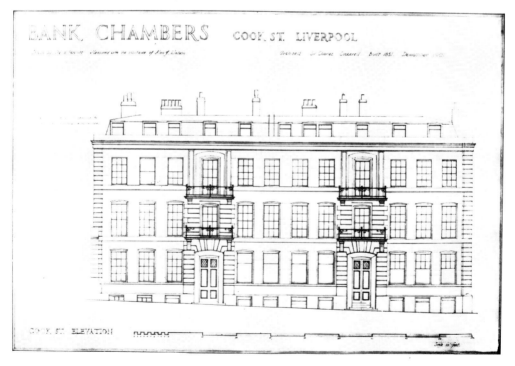

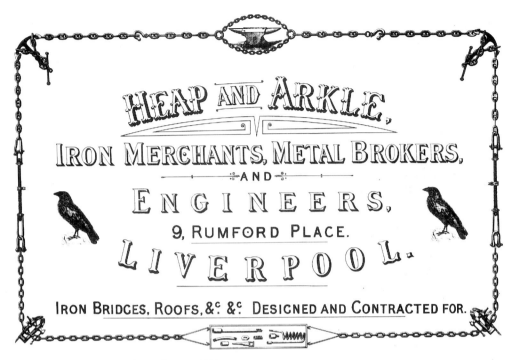

The cover of Heap & Arkle's catalogue c.1880.

than Birkenhead and although the North & South Wales Bank was absorbed into the Midland, our account remains there to this day.*

The men William Heap dealt with at Jessops in Calcutta were Mr Inverlock and Mr Rainford and they often consulted Mr Heap in his professional capacity and we sent out high grade Staffordshire irons, steel and pumping equipment to India.

The turnover was excellent, but Jessops were slow payers and so Heap and Arkle were forced to increase their overdraft, which in turn meant higher interest charges. They reluctantly concluded that they would have to reduce their overhead in other directions and so they decided that they would have to move to a smaller, and cheaper, office.

9, RUMFORD PLACE, LIVERPOOL (1876–1896)

Thomas Arkle mentioned their decision to move to his father who said that they could take over his office at No 9, Rumford Place because he was moving over the road to 8b and so Heap and Arkle made their third move in the ten years of their existence. This office block was pulled down about ten years ago to make room for Richmond House, where incidentally we supplied Dunham Bush heating equipment to the heating contractors, Messrs Crown House Engineering Co., Ltd of Liverpool.

In 1878 the British were engaged in a military action in Afghanistan on the North West Frontier of India; it was a difficult local war for the British because the tribesmen knew the mountains well and there were no roads or railways to enable supplies to be rushed to the troops and casualties were higher than they need to have been.

After the war was over it was decided to build a railway right up to the frontier and we were

*1991 Note. Sadly in 1984 the Midland Bank closed their branch at 62 Castle Street and after 111 years our account was transferred from this splendid Victorian building to the plastic bubble in Dale Street.

1873 Advertisement—Gores Liverpool Directory.

entrusted with the supply of the wrought iron bridge over the Bolan Pass on the North West Frontier. After the railway was finished, one train carried in sixteen hours what formerly two thousand five hundred camels had carried in a fortnight and a trading route that had existed for centuries was overtaken by the Industrial Revolution.

It was while Heap and Arkle were at 9 Rumford Place that they had our first telephone (Number 809) installed in 1883, which was only eight years after Bell spoke on his first telephone on 2nd June 1875.

THE DEPARTURE OF THOMAS ARKLE

During the 1880s relations between William Heap and Thomas Arkle became strained possibly because William Heap thought that his young partner was living rather extravagantly. During the first seven years of the partnership Thomas Arkle lived with his father in Slatey Road, but when he was thirty-two years of age he married and moved around the corner to a rather fine house at 19, Grosvernor Road, Claughton and then in 1881 he moved into an even larger, and grander house at 31, Grosvenor Road and here he lived the life of a prosperous gentleman with coach, horses and servants.

The houses are still standing and although they are decaying, the area is still very pleasant and a century ago it was one of the most fashionable areas for the merchants to live in.

In 1891 the firms capital was reduced to £4,900 because Mr Arkle suddenly had to withdraw all his capital and the following year he overdrew by a substantial amount and this was a complete write off. The same year the company suffered another loss of £700 in another direction and these losses caused problems because the Indian business was calling for more and more capital.

After many arguments, William Heap reluctantly had to terminate the partnership agreement and Thomas Arkle left the Company and the name of the firm became Wm. Heap & Co.

After leaving the firm Thomas Arkle set up on his own as an Iron Merchant and continued to trade in the City for another thirty-five years, but he did not appear to prosper too well because within three years he had moved from Grosvenor Road to a small terraced house in Albert Street, Tranmere and then moved to an even smaller house in The Woodlands, Tranmere.

The final years of the partnership were so unhappy and worrying for William Heap that when J. D. Crichton was writing some notes on the Company's history in 1935 he told Bessie, William Heap's daughter, that he did not propose to even mention Thomas Arkle because of the unhappy associations.

CHAPTER 5

William Heap & Co.

WM. HEAP & CO., 1892

The year 1892 was a very unhappy and troublesome one for William Heap because on top of the financial problem inside the office, there were external financial difficulties caused by the Great Fire of St John's, Newfoundland, which is dealt with later. Arrangements had to be made with the North & South Wales Bank for facilities and his brother-in-law, Charles, father of J. D. Crichton had to give a guarantee because the firm's capital was reduced from over £5,000 to a mere £839.

Although it was a very difficult time for William Heap his tough constitution enabled him to weather the storm and he even expanded the business, because just about that time we were appointed Agents for John Brown of Sheffield for the sale of armour plated steel, flanged plates for marine boilers, shafts, propeller bases, flues, heavy steel castings, railway tyres and axles.

The company's Agencies in 1892 were:

Clydesdale Iron & Steel Co., Mossend
John Brown & Co., Sheffield
The Staffordshire Bolt, Nut & Fencing Co., Darlaston
J. Wood Ashton & Co., Stourbridge

At this time William Heap's standing in India was so high that he was retained as a consultant by the Government of India where the inspection of bridges and cast iron structures were in question. At the same time the Government of India guaranteed every order placed with us by Jessops of Calcutta on their behalf.

Salthouse Dock, Liverpool, in the 1890's.

WILLIAM HEAP & CO.,
IRON & STEEL MERCHANTS & METAL BROKERS,
Office and Warehouse—1, RUMFORD PLACE, LIVERPOOL.

Telegraphic Address—"METAL, LIVERPOOL."   *Telephone—No. 809.*   *Private Cour supplied :: Customers.*

Plates, Angles, Channels, Tees and Rails, in Iron and Steel ; English and Belgian Rolled Girders. Section Books on application, Railway Tyres, Axles, Springs, Steel and Iron Forgings and Castings of every description. Boiler End and Furnace Plates, Serve Tube, flanged ready for use. Chains and Anchors, Vices and Anvils, Boiler and Gas Tubes, Rivets, Bolts, Spikes, Nails, and all descriptions of Fastenings ; Machinery, Bridges, Roofs, Piers, and all descriptions of Iron Structures.

RAVEN BRAND

Sole Agents for Liverpool and District for—John Brown & Co., Limited, Sheffield ; J. Wood &son & Co., Stourbridge ; Jas. Bown & Co., Birmingham ; W. & J. Galloway & Sons, Manchester ; Union Tube Co., Cambridge ; Staffordshire Bolt, Nut & Fencing Co., Darlaston ; Clydesdale Iron & Steel Co., Mossend.   (15)

Gore's Livepool Directory of 1894.

NO. 1 RUMFORD PLACE (1894–1896)

In 1894 William Heap moved from number 9 to an even smaller office at number 1 Rumford Place because of the continuing financial problems caused by the Great Fire of St John's and the Newfoundland bank crisis and it was in this office a year later that his seventeen-year-old nephew J. D. Crichton joined him.

The following year 1896, another young man joined as a bookkeeper, E. S. Piatt. The first task he was given to do was to write out the orders we had received that morning in the order book. In his best "copperplate" handwriting he entered the details of the orders for iron, steel and pumps from customers in the North West of England and abroad. One order was from Beirut in the Lebanon and young Piatt carefully wrote down the various items of steel plate, angle iron and bar, but the very last item on the order was for "One case of Woodward's Baby Gripe Water". Thinking this had been ordered in error, he went to see Mr Heap but he was told that frequently our customers abroad found it convenient to add this sort of thing on to an order and so we supplied the case of gripe water.

Although at this time we had typewriters all important letters had to be handwritten and young Piatt had to take copies in a hand press.

According to Mr Piatt, William Heap was a serious but kindly man with quite strict, self imposed, standards, and one of these was that he did not smoke in the office. One day Mr Piatt thought Mr Heap was out and went into his office to put some papers on his desk, only to find William Heap looking profoundly guilty, and uncomfortable, smoking a cigarette!

In the morning after he had attended to the mail and written his letters, William Heap used to go to the News Room and there would pick up the latest "intelligence" and exchange news with other merchants. In the evening he would leave the office at about 5-30 pm to go to his club and would return about three quarters of an hour later to sign the last letters and orders and then the office was usually closed about 6-30 pm.

It is rather surprising that our Hoylake office is open longer now than a hundred years ago, because whereas it used to open from 8-45 am to 6-30 pm, the mail is now opened at 7-30 am and the last person usually leaves about 6 pm, although our official hours are officially 9 am to 5 pm.

28 CHAPEL STREET (1896–1905)

After Mr Piatt had joined them the firm wanted more room and so they moved round the corner to a suite of offices at 28 Chapel St., Room 35 Chapel Chambers North where we had not only offices but a stores as well.

WILLIAM HEAP'S FAMILY LIFE

When William Heap first came to Wirral in 1853 he lived in lodgings, but in 1856 he was promoted from sub-manager to manager of the Bridge Department and had about five hundred men working under him. Thomas Brassey paid him well and so he decided to move into a house of his own and he chose to live at 14 Sommerville in Seacombe, which is about a mile and a half away from Canada Works across the other side of the Great Float.

Sommerville is a group of fourteen, large semi-detached houses, still standing, and although it is now in the middle of dull suburban development, in 1856 this pleasant group of houses looked out over rolling farm land down to the bustling River Mersey and the Liverpool shore beyond.

Most of the residents of Sommerville were merchants of one kind or another, who although they did not realise it were setting up one of the first dormitory towns in the country because most of them worked in Liverpool, but chose to live in the pleasant countryside of Poulton in Seacombe.

One of William Heap's neighbours was James Horsburgh who was a Partner in the firm of Horsburgh Halley & Co. who were Agents and Merchants with offices in Liverpool. James was very friendly with a flour merchant by the name of John Crichton and later they joined forces and the name of the firm was changed to Horsburgh Crichton & Co. at the same Liverpool address.

The next house to Sommerville was about a quarter of a mile away along the lane. This was Poulton Lodge, a large impressive house set in several acres of lovely landscaped, formal gardens, shrubberies and trees and in 1857 John Crichton and his family moved into this splendid house.

The Fawcett Preston beam pumps in Seabank Pumping Station, Wallasey, installed in 1894 at William Heap's insistence. Replaced in 1947 by K.S.B. Submersible pumps supplied by Heap & Partners Ltd. More water, less cost and beauty.

One evening James Horsburgh had a "social gathering"; one can hardly call those formal Victorian affairs "a party"; to which he invited several of his neighbours from Sommerville and Mr and Mrs John Crichton and their daughter Eliza. William Heap was introduced to Eliza and he was immediately impressed with the quiet, pleasant, but rather shy young lady of twenty-two summers and she found the well travelled, grave, courteous, bearded engineer of thirty-one years attractive.

Two years later on the 1st June 1859, William Heap married Eliza Mackenzie Burn Stuart Crichton at St Paul's Church, Seacombe, in the Parish of Wallasey, Wirral. The vicar, Edward Roberts, officiated and guests included William's mother, Eliza Mary Heap who travelled over from Isles House, Padiham for the wedding.

After their wedding William and Eliza lived at 14 Sommerville for eleven years and their first two children William Crichton Heap and Charles Edmund Heap were born in this house.

In 1870 they decided to move to a new house that had recently been completed at 2a, Falkland Road, Liscard which is almost opposite where Wallasey Town Hall now stands. Only a year after moving in, their eldest son William died; four years later another son Walter was born, but he only lived a year, and died in 1876 and five years later their only surviving son Charles died leaving only the two daughters Mary and Elizabeth Ann (Bessie).

William and Eliza were heartbroken at the deaths of their sons and the Falkland Road house was not a happy house for them and so in 1883 they moved to a substantial family house, Elm Mount in Penkett Road, Liscard, Wallasey where they lived for the remainder of their days.

Elm Mount is still standing and it is a solidly built, Victorian family house built on an elevated site and although the area is now built up when William and Eliza lived there it had glorious views over well cultivated fields running down to the river beyond.

WALLASEY COUNCIL

William Heap was a member of Wallasey Local Board, as the council was called in its early days, from 1879 until 1900, a period in which much of modern Wallasey was laid down, the Promenades, the Central park, the Water supply, sewage works and the other services we take for granted.

William Heap was a strong Conservative and rarely discussed politics with his wife's family because the Crichton's were equally strong Liberals. He founded the Primrose League in Poulton and Seacombe, but one blessing of those days was that, once the Councillors were elected, politics did not play much of a part in their work on the Council; there was of course always opposition of some kind, but it was not on party lines and the members, only numbering fifteen, had to work hard and harmoniously.

William Heap sat on a number of Committees but preferred to chair the Gas & Water Committee because rapid developments took place under his guidance, but not without opposition.

In March 1889 he clashed with other members of the Board when he advised that another borehole and pumping station should be constructed otherwise the district would run short of water in the foreseeable future. Some other members accused him of scaremongering and so he produced test figures showing that with No 2 beam pump working 24 hours a day and No 1 engine working 8 hours a day the total yield per 24 hours would be about 1,150,000 galls which was within 50,000 gallons on the peak demand on a summer day.

Two months later the "Birkenhead News" printed this piece: "Although the members of the Wallasey Local Board somewhat threw cold water on Mr Heap's statement that it would soon be necessary to provide for an increased water supply, it turns out that that gentleman was more sapient and far seeing than the rest of the Members of the Board. The Gas and Water Committee have already purchased a piece of land in Seabank Road for the purpose of erecting thereon a new pumping station. The price paid for the land is £2,400 so we expect that the total cost of the new pumping station will amount to a considerable sum."

The sequel to this story is that in 1947 we replaced the beautiful beam pumps in Seabank Road pumping station with submersible pumps, more efficient but beauty had departed.

In 1889 William Heap was elected Chairman of Wallasey Local Board and for some time he had been pressing for the Board to buy Liscard Hall Estate to convert it into a Public Park, but he was up against powerful opposition from the Finance Committee, amongst others, because the Board would have to borrow £25,000 which was a substantial sum, nevertheless, Mr Heap and his supporters felt that this was a bargain that future generations would appreciate.

On Tuesday 7th January 1890 there was a public enquiry held, the Inspector being Major General C. Phipps Carey and William proposed that the Board should borrow the money and purchase the estate and Mr Ball the Chairman of the Finance Committee opposed.

William Heap put forward figures showing that the purchase could go ahead without even increasing the rates and although the Finance Committee argued against him he won the day and Wallasey Local Board bought Liscard Hall estate for £25,000, and he had bought 37 acres of parkland for the astonishingly low sum of 1s-10d per square yard and then another 20 acres was bought later. This is why Wallasey now has its Central Park of 57 acres.

Time again proved our William right, because at the end of the very successful year they had not only carried out numerous improvements to the district, but actually dropped the rates. They were able to do this by the application of good business sense and staff numbers were kept down to an absolute minimum in the local Authority.

Another scheme which interested Mr Heap was the building of Wallasey Promenade; he was elected Chairman of a Committee to push a bill through Parliament and by visiting London he managed to do this with the minimum waste of time. The first length of Promenade was from Egremont to Holland Park and this was constructed in 1891; in 1897 it was extended as far as New Brighton; in 1901 Egremont to Seacombe and in 1906 New Brighton to the Marine Park.

At the same time the great sea defences were under construction and Mr Heap did much valuable work. These sea defences prevent much of Northern Wirral being swamped as they were since time began, until the Victorians took a hand.

In Council matters, William Heap's constant theme was the responsibility of the individual and he consistently told his audiences that it was a mistake to expect officialdom to do what they as individuals should be doing. In the 1890s there was a movement in New Brighton to set up a Council Committee to look into ways of improving New Brighton and this was Mr Heap's comments which sums up his approach that there were some things that were the council's responsibility and some the individuals.

"Mr Heap said that it was a very difficult question to deal with, in so much as the powers of the committee would be almost nil. Southport and Blackpool which had been mentioned had not been brought to their present state by the cold hand of officialdom, but by the public of the district forming a vigilance, or supervision, committee and preventing acts of vandalism or the putting up of buildings that would spoil the district.

If the ratepayers outside would get up such a committee as that and put on the Chairman of the Works and Health Committee they would formulate some scheme. But he said he could not quite see how a Committee of the Board could begin the work. To a great extent it was in the hands of private individuals rather than a Public Board. One complaint that he had heard was that anyone who wanted lodgings of a superior class—he meant men who were willing to pay three or four guineas a week—could not find them. How a Committee of the Board could take that up he could not see."

WALLASEY DISPENSARY AND OTHER WORKS

In the early days of Wallasey a "Dispensary" was set up which enabled poor people to receive medical treatment free of charge. For many years William Heap was the Treasurer of this scheme and was responsible for keeping its finances straight. Wallasey Dispensary was the oldest charity in the district and but for the medical services it provided, hundreds of poor people would have suffered or died.

William Heap was also on the Board of Management of the Central Hospital in Wallasey and the Cottage Hospital. For his services, he was presented with a magnificent silver tray when he retired, which he left to A. H. Atkins.

Another task William Heap carried out in his spare time was to act as Treasurer for Egremont Prestbyterian Church and the building of the present superb church in 1912 owed much to his careful husbanding of funds ready for the new building.

WILLIAM HEAP J.P.

In 1886 when he was sixty years old, William Heap was appointed a Magistrate and it is worth recording how this came about. A Mr J. M. Hawkins, who was prominent in local affairs in Wallasey, felt that in view of the public services rendered by William Heap he should be honoured, and so he organised a public petition which was signed by many hundreds of people. This petition was presented to the High Sheriff of the County of Cheshire urging that William Heap be placed on the Commission for the Peace. Shortly afterwards William Heap was made a Magistrate and according to his obituary, "he exercised a wise discretion to bear that common sense that had distinguished his successful commercial career and tempered his judgement with a large meed of mercy."

Life was much more violent and rough in Birkenhead and Wallasey than it is today, not only were the times harsher, but the inhabitants of North-Wirral in particular had only recently been forced to comply with reasonable standards of civilized behaviour. Until the middle of the last century the roads in the northern part of Wirral were either non existent, or very poor indeed and Bidston Moss was a dangerous swamp which only the locals could cross. This meant that the tide of history swept across the bottom of Wirral and left the inhabitants of Northern Wirral quite isolated. Shipwrecking was a favourite local pastime until the eighteen thirties, long after it had been stamped out in Devon and Cornwall and other parts of the country.

In the eighteen thirties even the Wallasey Magistrates were corrupt and often in league with the criminals. Wreckers had a safe haven in Bidston village and other outlying communities. Many of the old cottages in these villages must have seen on stormy nights, carts loaded with Brandy or Hollander Gin being quietly stowed away by muffled figures.

In 1839 there was a most violent hurricane which gave the wreckers great opportunities; they blacked out the lighthouses in Hoylake and Leasowe and put out false lights that lured two packages bound for New York on to the Hoyle Bank, and others were delivered up to them on the shore by the storm. Many a poor sailor was cast up on the shore by the storm, half drowned, only to meet his death by some fiercely wielded clubs held by murderers from Wallasey, Leasowe, Bidston and West Kirby. Fingers were cut off to obtain rings and there was one case of a woman biting off the ear of a female passenger to get her earings.

This was the final straw for the Liverpool Shipowners and they agitated so much that Superintendent Quick from Liverpool with a force of twenty policemen was sent to raid the homes of the wreckers.

The raid was highly successful and Superintendent Quick obtained clear evidence of the guilt of a number of the wreckers; but when the cases came before the Wallasey Magistrates they were most reluctant to commit the men for trial. They found every reason imaginable for not taking action, "The Liverpool Police had no right to act in Wallasey", "Superintendent Quick had not been given Authority to act by Cheshire Police" and so on. In spite of the Magistrates protests the case was pressed, the men stood trial and were sent to Botany Bay.

This was really the end of wrecking in Wirral, because not only were the corrupt Magistrates replaced by men like William Heap, but the Crosby Channel was opened to shipping, which meant that the main shipping lanes to Liverpool were moved from the treacherous banks off Hoylake to the much safer Crosby Channel. Then finally when Birkenhead Docks were constructed in 1850, the swampy moss at Bidston was drained by the river Fender through Wallasey Pool and it was then possible to build roads through the penninsula to Wallasey and the northern shore.

"SAVAGE BIRKENHEAD"

It was not only the wreckers whom law abiding citizens had to fear. The "Birkenhead

Advertiser" of Saturday 19th January 1889, printed the following editorial on "Savage Birkenhead": "The other night a policeman found two women on the ground in Claughton Road, worrying each other like dogs. What report would an Englishman bring home if he saw such a degrading and disgusting spectacle in a foreign land? But these revolting exhibitions are by no means uncommon in our 'Savage Birkenhead'."

The following week appeared a report headed—"Cannibalism in Lancashire"—a good arresting headline if ever we saw one.

"A disgraceful case of cannibalism was heard at Rochdale on Saturday. During a quarrel an old woman named Digman seized another female named Riley and bit a large piece of flesh out of her arm, leaving a wound one and a half inches deep. Digman was seen by byestanders to eat and swallow the flesh. The Magistrates sent her to prison for a month with hard labour."

They were fascinating times in Wirral, Middle Class gentility alongside tough, rough and knockabout working class. The "Birkenhead Advertiser" of 29th June 1889, gives this account of Sunday evening on New Brighton sands which illustrate the juxtaposition of the two life streams.

"*A Sunday Scene in New Brighton*

"A visitor to New Brighton gives the following experience:

"The scenes which occur every Sunday evening on the 'yellow sands' in New Brighton would afford much food for reflection for the moralist. They are certainly not of an edifying character. Bands of rough sporting characters infest the quiet shore at one end of the promenade and in full view of respectable visitors, play such pranks as would not for a moment be tolerated in the lowest quarter of Liverpool. They indulge in the questionable practice of throwing paper sandbags both at their companions and at innocent spectators and to vary the horseplay they frequently improvise sham prize fights.

For instance, shortly after eight o'clock on Sunday evening, while hundreds of people were promenading, two of the betting fraternity, got up as rustics, commenced to knock each other about, much to the alarm of the ladies, who thought that the pair of young blackguards were really pummelling one another. In a few minutes a large crowd assembled, a ring was formed and there were shouts of 'Fairplay' and 'Give them air', Several persons became very much frightened and there were loud calls for the police, but of course the ubiquitous man in blue was nowhere to be found.

"On going to the verge of the circle made by the mob the real nature of the affair was revealed. The two farceurs were simply showing off their prowess as acrobats and amateur boxers and a couple of individuals with big watch chains and chimney pot hats who were passing around the hat, were good enough to announce that the unseemly exhibition was in aid of 'an 'ospital'—they named an institution in Liverpool which I forebear from mentioning here. They further informed the admiring throng that they would accept nothing but silver, and curiously enough there were many greenhorns amongst the crowd who actually contributed sixpences and shillings!

"After the 'performance' the whole party proceeded at a rush along the shore to a neighbouring 'pub' where they spent the product of the collection.

"It is hardly possible to describe the disorder and hubbub occasioned by this rowdyism which it may be stated was perpetrated within a dozen yards of an open air prayer meeting. Hard by was a young man, described as 'a decayed artist', trying to turn a precarious penny by eleemosynary recitations; and in his immediate neighbourhood I noticed a youthful vocalist and his female partner, whose selection of comic and sacred music obtained a fair share of the patronage of the sand loungers.

"Further on promanders were crushing to get near a phenominal exposition of the 'delirium of drunkeness' and the delights of the 'Wild West Show' on 'Tea Pot Row' formed no mean attractions in the general satunalia of sport, escapades and hurly-burly.

"On the whole there are quieter places for the contemplative tourist than New Brighton sands, especially on a Saturday evening."

Is the writer alone in thinking that it sounds infinitely more interesting and enjoyable than television?

William Heap sat on the Bench twice a week and in general the cases that came before him are typified by the following list of the hearing on 1st February 1899.

Man summoned for kicking a horse.
Damage to glass in Wallasey.
Disputed Paternity of a child.
Maintenance orders.
Chimney on fire.
No muzzle on a dangerous dog.
Straying horses.
Unlighted carts.
Cruelty to a horse.
Case of bad language.
Four months for insulting ladies.

There was however one sensational case of a double murder that came before William Heap in May 1890, when a man by the name of Spicer was charged with the murder of his two sons aged 13 years and 3 years and the attempted murder of his wife.

It caused a sensation because although, as we have recorded elsewhere, North Wirral was quite lawless in the first third of the century the lawbreakers went undetected until Superintendant Quick, supported by honest Magistrates, came along, and the case of Spicer was only the second time that a man was committed for murder in the whole of the Hundred of Wirral.

William Heap was a good J.P. showing leniency when needed, but firmness with the evil doer and considering the heavy drinking of strong ale by many of the populace from early morning to late at night, which is not conducive to a quiet life, kept the peace well.

J. D. CRICHTON

J. D. Crichton
(1894–1935 Director 1915–1935).

In 1894 two years after the partnership with Thomas Arkle had been dissolved, William Heap had a conversation with his brother-in-law Charles Crichton about the possibility of Charles's son John Douglas, then a young man of seventeen years, joining the firm which was just starting to get on its feet again. After the talk John expressed an interest and joined William Heap in the small office at the top of Rumford Place.

In spite of the problems of the previous two years William Heap & Co. was one of the leading firms in Liverpool in the iron and steel trade and we had a very healthy export business as well as steady business from companies in the North West of England.

Not long after J. D. Crichton joined the firm, we received an order from Spain for steel for a steam ship which was to be built in a Spanish yard and so J.D. was sent up to Motherwell to see David Colville and Sons Ltd., and after negotiations he placed the order with them. Later, we placed more business with them and in February 1902 Mr Archie Colville offered us their Agency for the North West of England and certain countries abroad.

We accepted the Agency and this was the beginning of a very close relationship with Colvilles and we sold Colville steel in the North West of England, Canada and Newfoundland for over thirty years to our mutual satisfaction.

J. D. Crichton worked hard and the company continued to make good progress in this country and abroad and in particular in Newfoundland.

It was largely as a result of J. D. Crichton that the company started to develop our engineering side as well as the traditional iron and steel trade. At the time we were founded most engineers were Civil Engineers but they automatically handled pumps, steam engines and other machinery. For thirty years we had supplied pumps and other machines but we had not specialised.

In 1902 however we were doing so much pump business that we were offered and accepted, the Agency for the leading pump manufacturer in the U.K. at that time, Gwynne's Pumps. By now the business had expanded and so a new engineer by the name of Dr Rawlings was taken on to handle the "engineering" side. He stayed with us for three years and then left us to join the Sperry Gyroscope Co. where he made progress and eventually became their Managing Director.

Export orders cabled to William Heap from the Angel Eng. Company of St John's Newfoundland in 1881. Note the Victorian brevity of the instructions. The system worked well because we were trusted to carry out customer's requirements.

The instructions read:

Metal. Liverpool.

Send next boat—horizontal engine complete 10" cylinder pump attached. Two steady boiler makers. Eight shillings commence day. Passage paid. One year's work.

One plate Staff. iron 9'–0" × 4'–6" × 1/2"
     (Peculiar)   Backsight
60 boiler tubes 3" O.D.   12 foot long
pluralize. Ebullience. Nourished.
(Note—these are coded messages.)

Metal. Liverpool.   December 29th 1881.

Make best terms you can boilers makers, want general hands, one suitable as foreman.
Cable price twelve inch also date you could ship 10 inch.
                                        Angel.

94

CHAPTER 6

Canada and Newfoundland

NEWFOUNDLAND

By the time J. D. Crichton joined the company our trade with Newfoundland was substantial, because from the very beginning William Heap had been doing business with our oldest Colony.

In the early days there were no roads in Newfoundland outside the main towns, nor railways and the only way of reaching the small settlements scattered along the 6,000 miles of coastline was by sea. This applied to the whole of the Southern Coast, the North, North East and South West and in winter thousands were cut off completely from the outside world for months at a time.

Apart from the concentration of population in St John's and the Avalon Peninsular, the bulk of the people were in hundreds of small communities and even as late as 1920 there were only three settlements outside St John's with a population of more than 4,000 people and this in a country with a total population of about half a million.

Scene on Water Street, St. John's, Newfoundland in the 1880's.

It was strange that in a country with such difficult internal communications, that in 1866 it was easier to deal with Liverpool than with the next township, because that year Brunel's "Great Eastern" succeeded in laying the Atlantic cable from Liverpool to St John's and then on to New York.

Even stranger is that Newfoundland witnessed three great events which improved communications and shrank the world. As mentioned above, the first being that the Western Terminal for the Atlantic cable was Hearts Content in Newfoundland, the Eastern end being Liverpool; the second was when Marconi made the first successful radio transmission from Signal Hill, Newfoundland to Cornwall in England; and the third was that in June 1919, Alcock and Brown made their triumphant Atlantic flight from Pleasantville, St John's, to Connemara, Ireland.

The laying of the Atlantic cable helped us build up our business with Newfoundland by the enormous speed up in communications. Its laying was a great event because it had first been laid the year before but there were problems and it had to be recovered, but in 1866 "The Great Eastern" accomplished one of the most successful feats of her chequered career.

On the 1st August 1866, William Heap walked into the Exchange Newsroom on the Flags in Liverpool and saw the very first message to be transmitted over the Atlantic cable written on the slate; it read:

"Palmyra, screw steamer, hence at New York yesterday".

A new era of close communication with the New World had dawned.

On the 1st October 1866 a great banquet was given by the Liverpool Merchants and Shipowners at which the chief guest was the President of the Board of Trade, Sir Stafford Northcote Bart, M.P. The banquet was given in the Law Association Room in Cook Street and at 9-05 pm the wires were brought into the banquetting room and Sir Stafford sent a cable to the President of the United States of America. Receipt of the message was acknowledged back from Newfoundland at 11 o'clock and no "after dinner" speaker ever received such a thunderous ovation as was hammered out by those bewhiskered Victorian Merchants and Shipowners; they had witnessed a technological breakthrough and they knew it.

Recently, at the works of Dunham Bush in Portsmouth, we saw an operator type out on a computor terminal the dimensions of numerous holes that had to be punched in a sheet of steel by a multi-head press with a moving table. The punched tape for feeding into the press consul was coming out of the machine almost instantaneously. Nothing very remarkable about that, except that the signal had left the works by land line, had been bounced over the Atlantic via the communications satellite hovering over mid-Atlantic, travelled along another land line into a computor memory bank in Cincinnatti, Ohio, the computor had selected the programme and the answering signal was bounced back to the works in Portsmouth the same way in no time at all.

A staggering technological achievement and yet the press is a direct descendant of the Roberts Jacquard press first used in 1847 under a tarpaulin on the banks of the Conway, and the communications were direct developments of the communications experiments first witnessed so long ago in Newfoundland and Liverpool.

THE NEWFOUNDLAND RAILWAY

In 1880 Newfoundland decided to embark on a very ambitious and costly scheme for such a small colony—to build a railway right across the country. Work started in 1881 and we supplied much of the material for the original railway and later to R. G. Reid who ran the railway for many years.

The Newfoundland Railway made a great improvement to the life of people in the hitherto isolated communities and it was the only way of crossing Newfoundland until the highway was built after the last war.

Unhappily however the enormous capital cost of the building of the railway, added to enormous overspending in other directions, put a terrific strain on the finances of the Colony and almost brought it to the point of ruin. This unhappy situation was triggered off by a series of disasters which in turn almost ruined William Heap & Co., a couple of thousand miles away in Rumford Place, Liverpool.

THE GREAT FIRE OF ST JOHN'S 1892

Fire was no stranger to St John's, indeed as in the London Town of 1666 it was an ever present danger because of the streets of crowded timber buildings. In 1846 there occurred the first great fire of St John's which virtually destroyed the city, it started in Hamlin's workshop when a glue-pot which was being used for cabinet making overboiled and set fire. The flames rapidly spread through the crowded streets until by the next day St John's was in ruins.

After the fire, various proposals were made to reduce the risk of fire; Water Street was to be made 70' wide, there were to be at least ten streets constructed as fire breaks and it was proposed that the buildings on both sides of Water Street, and on the south side of Duckworth Street, should be constructed of stone, brick or some fireproof material. Regrettably there were arguments about the plans and the scheme was watered down, so that the rebuilt St John's remained a fire hazard.

The afternoon of 8th July 1892 was blistering with a wind from the North West, it had not rained for a month and the shingled roofs of the houses and office buildings were as dry as tinder. The previous day the firemen had been practicing with their hoses and they had emptied a water storage tank and it had not been refilled because the water mains had been turned off while a new connection was made.

About three o'clock in the afternoon, a fire started in a house near Fresh Water Road and it rapidly spread to the adjoining timber houses and in just over an hour all three were ablaze. Soon the white-hot sparks and, furnace-hot air set three more houses alight and soon there were twenty roaring away. By then the air was full of flying sparks and the high wind carried these some distance from the original outbreak and new fires started.

The firemen tried to stem the flames but there was insufficient water and soon their hoses were burnt and the spread of the flames was remorseless, eating its way down the hill into the heart of the city.

One building stoutly constructed of stone was the new Cathedral of the Church of England, which had been designed by Gilbert Scott and which was the pride of St John's. Terrified people rushed with their possessions to put them in the Cathedral out of reach of the devouring flames. Bishop Jones thought that the Cathedral was the safest place and he had his household goods removed into the great church, but the flames set siege to the great building and the outside temperature became so high that first of all the lead holding the windows melted and then the glass melted. Once the high temperature burning gasses gained entry into the cathedral it was not long before that too was ablaze from one end to the other.

All night long the fire raged and spread from building to building and by six o'clock next morning three quarters of the city lay in ruins. Two thousand houses, stores, four hotels, numerous printing presses, solicitors offices and all the great public buildings were razed to the ground and St John's had suffered the sort of total devastation that some European cities experienced in wartime.

When the cost of the fire came to be reckoned up it was found that the cost amounted to $20,000,000 but many of the buildings were either not insured or under-insured, and the total insurance carried by all the buildings only ammounted to $4,800,000.

Considering the extent of the devastation it was a miracle that there were very few casualties and it was a mercy that the fire occurred in mid summer because if it had occurred in winter thousands would have died in the sub-zero temperatures.

Tents were put up for the homeless and cash and supplies poured in from overseas, but the strain on the already overstretched economy was almost unbearable.

Even without natural disasters and ambitious railways, the Newfoundland economy was always under pressure because of the scattered population and the only logical answer to the underlying economic problem would have been to try to concentrate the population into larger towns, but in a free society this was not possible.

In addition to the difficulties already outlined, there were political problems and accusations of corruption were rife. Some idea of the overspending can be gained by the following figures showing the Public Debt: these figures excluded the enormous capital cost of the railway.

Newfoundland Public Debt in 1883. $1,549,313.
Newfoundland Public Debt in 1884. $4,133,202.
Newfoundland Public Debt in 1892. $6,439,367.

St. John's after the great fire of 1892.

The Anglican Cathedral, St. John's, after great fire 1892.

THE GREAT NEWFOUNDLAND BANK CRISIS

In addition to the internal problem in Newfoundland, there were external factors which added to the problems. World trade was in one of its periodic slump conditions, the fishing had failed two years in succession; in the United States, Canada and Newfoundland business slackened and commodity prices fell. As a result many businesses, large and small, started to fail. As money grew tighter, even the banks and brokerage houses started to go under and the Canadian stock exchange was suspended for ten days to try to stop panic.

The Colonial Governor was seriously concerned about the rapidly deteriorating situation and he sent a Memorandum back to the Colonial Office in London asking for a warship to be sent to prevent possible disturbances and possible attacks on people and property. In response to this request the Admiralty immediately despatched a Man o'War from the West Indies station.

Within two years of the Great Fire the Commercial Bank failed and the Governor reported that the Union Bank could not keep going much longer. Enormous borrowings had been made in London to finance some of the reckless extravagances and the Colony could not even pay the interest instalments that were due. On the 17th December 1894 a report sent by the Governor said that there could be no doubt that the Colony was, at the present moment, hopelessly insolvent; twenty per cent of the taxes were being distributed in poor relief, the Civil Service was badly underpaid and both political parties were hopelessly corrupt. Most of the Directors of the Commercial Bank, he wrote, would soon face criminal charges and he ended by calling for a Royal Commission to enquire into the running of the affairs of the Colony and in particular felt that the Civil Service should be modelled on the English, and that the elections should be organised in a fair, decent, and honourable way.

At this time we were doing a substantial business with Newfoundland and suddenly many of our customers found that, through no fault of their own, they could not pay our bills because they had either lost everything in the Fire or their bank had failed. They cabled William Heap, who himself was beset with problems caused by the termination of the partnership, but he immediately despatched the following cable:

"We will trust you, pay when you can."

One admires the lack of fuss and histrionics, bearing in mind that the Newfoundland Crisis put a great financial strain on William Heap, we like the acceptance that a man's word was enough, this was the style of Victorian business and rarely did it fail.

The British Government however acted in a very cautious and unimaginative way; nothing changes; and it was left to a Canadian Bank to sort out the mess and just as William Heap by his gesture forged links that still exist today, so the Bank of Montreal by a very shrewd and

99

courageous move stepped in with help and by so doing tied Newfoundland into the Canadian, rather than the British, finance system. They opened a branch of the Bank in St John's and lent the Government $400,000 and in return they became the Colony's Official Agents.

The loan was enough to prime the pump and within two years confidence had returned, the Colonial Government had received a sharp lesson and every penny that was owed to us by the Newfoundlanders was repaid with 5 per cent interest.

William Heap's shrewdness and judgement had proved sound and our Bank Manager started talking to us again.

THE ANGEL FAMILY OF ST JOHN'S

In 1882 the Government of Newfoundland had a six-hundred foot dry dock built in St John's by J. E. Simpson of New York and for ten years Simpson operated the dry dock on lease from the Government, but in 1892 Simpson went into liquidation and so the Government itself operated the dry dock for two years until in 1894 the dock was leased to Angel & Harvey.

Our connection with the Angel family started before this time and we did considerable business with the Hon. James Angel and his partner Alexander Brown while they were running James Angel & Co. and later Angel Engineering Supply.

As told elsewhere James's son, Fred, was instrumental in setting up our Newfoundland office and his son, Dr Jack Angel, was Chairman of Heap & Partner (N'F'Lnd) Co. Ltd., and his son Roger at one time worked in our Newfoundland office and both are still Directors (1988).

AN EDWARDIAN VISIT TO NEWFOUNDLAND

In 1954 the writer asked J. D. Crichton if he would write a few notes on his first visit to St John's and he gave the following account:

A Visit to Newfoundland 1904
by J. D. Crichton (written in 1954)

I have often wondered why my firm came to have a connection—a connection now nearly a century old—with Newfoundland.

I do know that my old senior had played a part in the building of the Grand Trunk Railway of Canada, and, maybe, the firm's link with the Oldest Colony, which was to be the youngest Dominion, followed on friendships made when he was superintending the building of the Victorian Tubular Bridge spanning the St Lawrence at Montreal.

My old partner could have solved the mystery for me, but I never asked him to do so, and he is long since dead.

I joined my firm in 1894, and one of my memories of those early days is of the great fire which swept St John's in the year 1892. The firm had then several accounts with people in St John's, chiefly small accounts, but one ran into quite a considerable figure. Following on the fire came a cable from the customer which told us that, because of the disaster, he could not meet his obligations at due date . . . so what? Back went the message "we will trust you". The debt was repaid in two years and a life long personal friendship had been added to a commercial friendship.

There followed, before the end of century, the building in Scotland of a number of steamers for the old Newfoundland Company, and visits by engineers from St John's who had to be on the spot when the ships, and perhaps particularly the ships' engines were being constructed. So more and more personal friendships were made—and in due course came the decision that I in turn should travel.

One afternoon early in February 1904, and that is just on fifty years ago, I boarded at Liverpool the crack ship of the Allen Line, R.M.S. "Parisian", with a first-class ticket to Halifax in my pocket for which my firm had paid £12.10.0.

The "Parisian" with her two smoke-stacks painted red and black with a white stripe between, and with her four pole masts, was one of the then Atlantic greyhounds, quite a monster in fact.

Lord Street, Liverpool about 1900. Note the offices on the left of our photographers Stewart Bale.

A monster of these days, though with her 5,395 gross tons register only one-sixteenth the size of "Queen Elizabeth". And old ways of arranging her set-up were still in evidence, skylights above her saloon, skylights with fitted seats around them. Nor had she promenade decks as we know them. But she was a fine vessel and a good sea boat, though her virtue in this last respect had, on that voyage, no great strain put on it. Just as decent weather came her way, as could be expected in the North Atlantic during February. There was no sun of course, and always that great sweep of water with Mother Cary's chickens skimming over it. Still, 48 hours out from Halifax the weather did deteriorate. The wind rose, the temperature fell, and the spray froze as it landed on the forecastle, and on the shrouds of the fore-mast. And when we made port the good ship was well down by the head, and the crew were clearing the ice away with axes.

And so to shore with, if I remember aright, no Immigration officials to trouble us. I certainly

The Allan Line "RMS Parisian" in the River Mersey. She carried J. D. Crichton on his first visit to Newfoundland.

had no passport. What happened to the emigrants on the Russian ship which followed us in, and came to lie alongside of us, I do not know. What I do know is that I walked ashore without hindrance, and crossed the quay to what was then known, and perhaps is still known as a "rig". I told its driver that I wanted to go to Newfoundland, and what was I to do about it.

He said that he guessed that I wanted the Ice Yard, and told me to jump in, the which I did. Wondering, all the same, that with so much ice about me, why a special yard to keep it in was needed.

Off we went through streets with snow piled high on either side, so that even from the rig I could only see the tops of the heads of the people using the sidewalks.

And on to the Depot of the I.C.R.—the Intercolonial Railway—and I knew then what the driver meant when I thought he spoke of the Ice Yard.

At the Depot I learnt that there was no immediate prospect of going to St. John's by way of Sydney and the Island Railway. The last train from Porte-aux-Basques had left over a fortnight ago, had reached the Topsails, and had then been snowed up. So the rig took me to a nearby hotel—I think it was the Halifax. There I was planted down in a lounge with a hardwood floor, and a surround of spitoons, and left to think things over.

It was the hotel people who came to my rescue. It seemed that there was a ship in port sailing for St. John's that very night, and I could probably get a passage by her. She was the "Ulanda" and by her I went.

How tiny she looked as she steamed past "Parisian", and how near the water I seemed to be. My most vivid memories of her short voyage were a sight through mist of the shores of Sable Island, and of being taught to play fan-tan by one Walter Munro, who afterwards was to be a Prime Minister of the Oldest Colony.

And so to a sight of the Cabot Tower, to the Narrows, and then up the hill to the Cochrane House, where I learnt and with a thrill that one of my fellow lodgers was indeed a Prime Minister, the Prime Minister – it was Robert Bond.

I had arrived.

Having announced my arrival, I was soon whisked off to the other end of the town, to meet people whose ideas about hospitality had surely reached perfection. Among them was a real live 'Honourable', and as I had never before met a member of an Upper House, I felt, and indeed came to know that I was in distinguished company.

Business and commercial matters were of course discussed, but I soon realised that the real concerns for my visit were sleigh rides, shooting over the flats of the South Shore, and teas at Donovans with young people spooning. It was that spooning business which now means that two young chaps that I know have a grandmother in St. John's. I am their grandfather, but not the husband of the very nice grandmother.

I went twice to St. John's in those far-away days, and it is not easy to sort out one's memories of fifty years ago. But I believe that it was when I went there on this first visit that one evening my host said to me "when the meal is over take a good snooze, for at ten o'clock we are going to a Duck Supper".

And at ten o'clock we climbed on to the rig, and set off for Paddy Strangs. The supper was "a bird a man" affair with whisky for all—for all except me for I had not graduated in whisky, and my tipple was Milwaukee Blue Ribbon Ale. Poker followed.

Well on into the morning the Jack Pot lay in a great heap, and when the fortunate one collected it he whispered to me in good Scots—"Man, this is what makes life in the Colonies worth living".

All good things must end, and one day I heard that the Railway ship "Bruce" would shortly be sailing for Sydney. The Railway was still closed, and there being no immediate prospect of any other way of leaving I bought a Saloon passage by her. She also carried Deck passengers, over a hundred of them.

The voyage to Sydney is a short one, but we never reached Sydney. For quite soon "Bruce" was in the ice and indulging in that cork screw motion which can produce sea-sickness in even experienced sea-farers. And it did.

It was of the highest wisdom to keep in the Saloon.

The decks were slippery with . . ., no, I leave you to supply the missing word.

Sydney was afar off, not because of mileage but because of ice. So the ship chugged her way into Louisburg. I had left the Oldest Colony, and had landed in the Oldest Dominion.

On now by an empty coal train, thence homewards by way of the Wentworth Valley, the Chateau Frontenac, the Heights of Abram, scaled two hundred years ago by the men of the 22nd Foot, whose Colonel and General was Wolff, and then once more to Halifax where on the Easter Sunday, I heard the men of the Leinster Regiment (the Royal Canadians) sing their Hallelujahs in the Chapel of its Citadel.

The Leinsters are no more, differences between Ireland and England have seen to that.

But the 22nd of the Line, now the Cheshire Regiment, boasts a special link with a famous Canadian Regiment "Les Vingt-Doux". Curious the changes which the years bring. Two hundred years ago the first settlers in Canada battling with invaders. And now descendants of both actually linked together in a special and proud military association.

I must end my story—for at Halifax a ship was waiting, and so then for me it was "Eastward Ho".

17 WATER STREET (1905–1911)

Meantime back in Liverpool.

By 1905 the Company had recovered from the earlier problems and was expanding in a modest way due to the increase in the rotating machines side and so once again a move of office became necessary—this time to Seaton Buildings at 17 Water Street where we occupied rooms number 2 and 12. and here we stayed until William Heap retired in 1910.

A. H. ATKINS

After Dr Rawlings had left us, J. D. Crichton advertised in "The Engineer" for a Sales Engineer and they interviewed several applicants including H. D. Platten and A. H. Atkins. William Heap and J.D. could not make up their mind and so they offered the position to Mr Platten who

Liverpool Advertisements (1910).

Arthur Henry Atkins in 1909, three years after joining William Heap & Co.

A. H. Atkins M.C., M.I.Mech.E.,
A.M.I.E.E.—Director 1915–1968.

accepted and almost immediately afterwards Mr Crichton left for a visit to Newfoundland keeping A. H. Atkins still on the hook.

On his return from Newfoundland, J. D. Crichton conferred with Uncle William and they decided that in view of their increasing business for rotating machinery that they would take on A.H.A. as well and so on Monday 9th July 1906, Arthur Henry Atkins joined Wm. Heap & Co.

H. D. Platten was a splendid man, but not in the same class as A.H. which may have been one of the reasons for the delay in offering him an appointment.

Within three years of joining the company A.H.A. was a partner and eventually worked for the firm for sixty-two years.

Arthur Henry Atkins was born near Dorchester in Dorset in 1883, the youngest child of Charles Atkins and his second wife Ellen. Charles had five children by his first wife and four by his second. A.H.'s parents were comfortably off and his childhood was spent in a very pleasant country manor house, constructed of cream stone and set in several acres of rolling Dorsetshire countryside.

After finishing at day school, A. H. Atkins studied engineering at Imperial College in London and then went to Weymouth to serve an apprenticeship with Cosens Co. Ltd., who are still shipbuilders and shiprepairers.

From Cosens, A.H. went to H.M. Dockyard at Chatham and there saw how not to do things. Tiring of the enforced idleness and holdups he joined W. H. Allen of Bedford and worked in their pump design office.

After Arthur Henry had joined Wm. Heap & Co. in 1906 he spent the first three years developing the firms business in the North West of England. The train service was excellent and A.H.A. used to board the train in Liverpool with his bicycle and would then travel to Manchester, Bolton, Bury, Accrington, Oldham, Preston and other Lancashire towns. On arrival he would then use his bicycle to go to see his customers. History does not record how long he used his bicycle, but it was certainly long enough for him to remind us in the 1960's that motor cars were an extravagance and that a bicycle was a wonderful machine for developing business.

In Manchester, A. H. Atkins developed a friendship with the Managing Director of Lancashire Dynamo in Trafford Park and he made a practice of calling to see him quite regularly. He was invariably entertained with a glass of sherry and at the same time was told about the various cotton mills that were being built or modernised, because Lancashire Dynamo had a very strong grip in the market. A.H.A. would then set about getting the orders from the mills for the boiler feed pumps and ancilliary equipment.

A. H. ATKINS FIRST VISIT TO NEWFOUNDLAND, 1909

In 1909 it was decided that Mr Atkins would supplement the work that J. D. Crichton had been doing in Newfoundland and so he set sail for St John's. As we have mentioned, we had old trading links with the Angel family in St John's and so he was invited to stay with Mr and Mrs James Angel at their home in Hamilton Street and he was looked after royally.

A fishing expedition was organised and he was rather startled to find that each man was issued with a bottle of whisky and after the fishing they built a fire, cooked their fish, yarned and drank their whisky.

Picnics and other outings were organised and he was taken to Topsail, Brigus and other places of interest by horse and rig and was entertained in the most delightful fashion.

The days passed pleasantly but Arthur Henry was getting quite worried because although everybody appeared to be interested in him, there was no mention of business. However he was meeting some very interesting people and he hoped that sooner or later they would get down to brass tacks, but the Newfoundlanders seemed to be quite loathe to discuss business with him.

It was a very disappointed young man who finally boarded the ship to sail back to England, because he had enjoyed himself enormously but he had nothing at all to show for the visit. He was leaning on the ship's rail, chin in hand, looking at the dockyard scene when he saw a procession of young boys making their way up the gangplank and after enquiring from one of the sailors, they made their way towards him. To his huge delight and astonishment each gave him an envelope containing some substantial orders for British equipment they wanted us to supply. His kindly hosts and people he had met wanted him to enjoy himself and to see something of Newfoundland and they did not want to spoil it by discussing business!

RETIREMENT AND DEATH OF WILLIAM HEAP

In 1910 William Heap decided that it was time for him to retire; the business was in the safe hands of his nephew John Crichton and Arthur Atkins and his health was beginning to fail. He had been working continuously for sixty-eight years, ever since he had left school and he felt he had earned a rest.

Regretably he did not have a happy retirement, because his health deteriorated still further, his wife Eliza had died three years earlier on 2nd July 1907 at the age of 72 years, but William was faithfully nursed by his two daughters and Nurse Dalzell and after a long illness William Heap died on Sunday 10th March 1912.

William Heap was buried in the family grave in Wallasey Parish Churchyard with his boys and his wife and after the funeral it was announced that his estate totalled £7,937-3-3 which although a substantial sum for the day, was not a fortune considering that he had been in continuous employment for almost seventy years, that income tax was very low indeed and that he was head of one of the leading firms in iron, steel and engineering in Liverpool.

Without doubt William Heap would have made more money if he had stayed in the family grocery merchanting business, but he would not have enjoyed such an interesting life, nor would he have met some of the giants of the Industrial Revolution, men whose genius changed the face of society.

William Heap's eldest daughter, Mary, died only three months after her father on 5th June 1912 and left Bessie alone. Elm Mount was too large for one person and so Bessie moved to 6 Hescote Park, West Kirby, Wirral and here she lived a bustling active life until she died on 23rd September 1939—her father's birthday—just after the last war broke out, the last surviving member of the Heap family.

ROYAL LIVER BUILDINGS (1911 to 1928)

After William Heap retired in 1910, A. H. Atkins and J. D. Crichton set out on a programme of expansion, particularly in Canada; they took on more staff and by 1911 the company's fortunes had improved to the point where they could afford to move into brand new offices in the newly built Royal Liver Building and they took over rooms 33, 35, 37 and 39 at a rental of £130 p.a. and we occupied this suite of offices until 1922 when we moved up to the second floor and rented rooms 231, 233 and 235.

The Liver Building is one of the trio of waterfront buildings that symbolises Liverpool—it was started in 1908 and finished in 1911. It was the first large multistorey reinforced concrete buildings in this country and its clocks faces are larger than Big Ben's. On the top of the two domed clock towers are the mythical Liver Birds, which local legend claims flap their wings when a virtuous woman passes by.

As in our earlier offices we had a room in Royal Liver where we kept our stock of Dunham traps, hand pumps and later Securex fittings.

The Heap Family grave set in a Sandstone bluff looking out towards Hoylake.

The Royal Liver Buildings,
Liverpool 1920.

CANADA

When William Heap set up in business in the Albany in 1866 he knew Canada well and in those days vast areas of Canada were owned and ruled by a private company "The Hudson Bay Company" in the same way as India was developed in the early days by "The East India Company". The Hudson Bay Company was originally chartered in 1670 by King Charles II and it did not give up its rights to the Canadian Government until 1868. It set up trapping and trading posts and forts all across Northern Canada and it is still thriving to this day as a great trading company.

HEAP AND PARTNERS (CANADA) LTD.

The development of our business with Canada started with the visits William Heap made to the Dominion in connection with the Victoria Bridge, but we first started to concentrate on the Canadian market when A. H. Atkins visited the country in 1910. Within four years they were so successful that they had opened up offices in Montreal, Toronto and Vancouver under the name Heap & Partners (Canada) Ltd. A.H. travelled all over Canada in search of business and in those days places that are now large cities such as Winnipeg and Medicine Hat were quite primitive, with dusty streets and bars fitted with swing doors as in the Wild West films.

In 1912 we had relinquished the Agency for Gwynnes Pumps in favour of The Rees Roturbo Pump Company of Wolverhampton and in the early winter of that year we received an enquiry for circulating pumps from a small company called the Charlotte town Light, Heat & Power Co. Ltd., in Charlottetown, Prince Edward Island. A.H. decided to follow up the enquiry and left Montreal for Prince Edward Island, but winter had set in with a vengeance and part of the journey was by rail, but because of deep snowdrifts the last part was made by sleigh. It was

107

an appalling journey in sub zero temperatures and to make matters worse, when he arrived he found that there were no hotel rooms available in what was then a comparatively small community.

After he had been to the power company the Manager and Chief Engineer invited A.H.A. to stay the night at his home. In the early days this was by no means uncommon and most people were delighted to offer hospitality to the handsome, cultured, amusing young Englishman and to hear the latest news from the Old Country.

During the course of the evening the whisky bottle was produced and Mr Atkins learned that the Charlottetown Power Company was going to build a complete new power station and distribution network to accommodate the expected growth in the community and they had sent out piecemeal enquiries for the various parts of the plant. After talking matters over with his new found friend, A.H. was able to offer a number of suggestions to improve their scheme and he suggested that they should use diesel driven generators, generate at a higher voltage than they had been considering to keep down transmission losses and then transform down locally to the required voltage. His hosts were so impressed with him that they asked him to submit a tender for the entire station, distribution network and transformer stations.

When Mr Atkins returned to England shortly afterwards, he travelled over to Manchester to see Crossley Brothers Ltd., Pottery Lane, Openshaw, Manchester and they gave him the cost of the necessary diesel generators. Enquiries were then sent out for the generators, fuel storage tanks, pipework, control gear, transformers, miles of distribution cable, cable towers and, of course, pumps.

After receiving our offer the Charlottetown Power Company placed the entire order with us and eventually it was installed to their entire satisfaction. A good example of how a bright sales engineer can develop business from unpromising beginnings.

In 1914 A. H. A. pulled off another notable contract by supplying two very large water pumps to the City of Ottawa Water Works. The city was running short of water, due to the rapid growth of the population and additional supplies were wanted urgently. There was no time to build a conventional pumping station and so we supplied two large diesel driven water pumps made by Rees Roturbopumps and these were mounted on two large rafts that were anchored in the river and the pumps drew water from the river and then pumped it ashore through a pipeline and so into the waterworks system.

By 1914 our Canadian business was being run from our head office at 726–730 Imperial Avenue, Montreal, under the direction of A. E. Myles, a dedicated, religious man and a member of the Plymouth Brethren. One cannot help noticing however that his strong religious conviction did not prevent him being a very astute business man.

One of the most important Agencies we held in Canada before the first war was that of Samuel Osborne Ltd. of Sheffield and we sold their range of high speed steels, milling cutters, twist drills and other tools all over Canada. In our Montreal warehouse we had a number of machine tools which we used for cutting and machining their steel.

When war broke out in 1914 we found to our surprise that Heap & Partners (Canada) Ltd. held almost the entire stock of high speed steel and cutting tools in Canada and although the U.S. manufacturers stepped up their supplies we were one of the major suppliers of these products, vital for the war effort, in Canada. More machinery was purchased at largely inflated prices to increase our output and the business worked flat out throughout the war. When peace was declared in November 1918, the plant and machinery was so worn out that the Auditors report for 1918 said that in his opinion the machinery and plant had been so overworked that it was almost worthless.

SAMUEL OSBORN (CANADA) LTD.

The Osborn business became so large that just after the war we decided to change the name of our Canadian company from Heap & Partners (Canada) Ltd. to Samuel Osborn (Canada) Ltd. The change took place in February 1919 but it was only a change in name and the company remained a wholly owned subsidiary of ours. Later we sold the Canadian business to Samuel

Osborn of Sheffield and it still thrives today. We rented the offices and warehouse to them until 1947, when we eventually sold the property to them as well.

DEVELOPMENT OF THE CANADIAN REFRACTORIES INDUSTRY

When war was declared in 1914 Britain's steel industry faced a very serious problem because until then we had imported dolomite from Austria which was used for making refractory brick for lining the steel furnaces, but with the outbreak of war we were cut off from these supplies, and without refractory brick a country cannot make steel and without steel it cannot wage war.

We represented Colvilles of Motherwell at that time, one of the best British steel makers and when they told A. H. Atkins of the formidable problem they were facing he offered to find out if we could obtain alternative supplies from Canada because he recalled someone telling him a few years earlier that there were dolomite deposits in parts of Canada.

Losing no time he cabled out Montreal office, told them of the problem and asked them to investigate if there were any substantial deposits of dolomite and magnesite suitable for making into refractory brick. The job was given to a junior Manager in one of our Canadian offices who made an excellent job of the investigation and he found that there were indeed enormous deposits of the refractory that were not being worked. Being a thorough sort of fellow he immediately resigned from our employ, borrowed some money and bought most of the land where the deposits lay. Next he bought an old tractor which he converted into a crude type of bulldozer and he was in business supplying refractory to British steelworks.

After the war, and this experience, we took more interest in refractories and we became the Agents for the whole of the U.K. for Canadian Refractories Ltd. and we continued to represent them until 1964, when Mr Atkins felt he was getting too long in the tooth to handle it.

Today Canada is one of the worlds leading producers of refractories and Canadian Refractories is a part of the Harbison Walker Group—the Worlds largest producers of refractories.

WORLD WAR I (1914–1918)

Just after war was declared in August 1914, A. H. Atkins volunteered for the Army, leaving J. D. Crichton behind to run the business, but towards the end of 1915 as the demand for men increased J.D. felt that he must volunteer as well.

The difficulty was to find somebody to handle the work normally being done by A.H.A. and himself. We had another partner, E. E. Baker but he was fully committed with running our business in Manchester. The problem was finally resolved when Mr Crichton's wife Hesther and his father Charles, offered to step into the breach.

WM. HEAP & CO. LTD. (1915)

In 1915 the company was converted from a Partnership to a limited liability company and Hesther Crichton, Charles Crichton and Eustace Baker were made Directors. Having settled his affairs J.D. then joined the Royal Artillery in January 1916. Shortly afterwards he was sent to France where he saw active service until 1918.

HESTHER WINGATE CRICHTON

Hesther Crichton was a remarkable woman, because she emerged as the strong figure in the company during the first World War and not only did she run the head office in Liverpool throughout the war but the business in Canada and England expanded considerably during this period.

It could not have been easy for a housewife and a mother to suddenly have to take charge of a small, but energetic, engineering company with substantial interests on both sides of the Atlantic.

A Social gathering at Colvilles about 1932.
John Crichton 2nd from left—standing. J. D. Crichton 4th from left—standing. Sir John Craig M.D. of Colvilles 5th from left—standing. Hesther Crichton—back row—7th from left—standing.

In 1917 some problem cropped up which could only be settled by a Directors' Meeting at which J. D. Crichton and A. H. Atkins were present, but they were both fighting in the trenches and could not return to England. Hesther decided that the only way to overcome the difficulty was to go to France herself and to hold the meeting there.

The war in France was at its bloodiest and the trains and the Channel boats were crowded with wounded and troops and it was a most difficult journey for a young unaccompanied woman making her own way to Paris, but at 4 pm on Wednesday 5th September 1917, Hesther called a Directors Meeting in the Hotel Grillon, Paris and the problems were duly resolved.

J. D. Crichton and A. H. Atkins had managed to obtain twenty-four hours leave to attend the meeting and after the mud and blood of the trenches it was bliss to have a hot bath, don clean clothes, attend to the business in hand and then to have afternoon tea.

After too brief a time with her husband, Hesther made her way back to Liverpool and A.H. (now called Tommy by all his friends) and J.D. returned to the front line where A.H.A. was to be awarded the Military Cross for gallantry in action.

A. H. ATKINS AND WAR SERVICE

Few men can, or could, say that they served in the armed forces in the Boer War, the Great War and World War II but A.H.A. was one of them.

In 1902 as a young man A.H. was serving with the Royal Artillery and when he rejoined the Army in 1914 he again joined the Gunners, but in 1915 he was seconded to the Royal Engineers to join a section working on Sound Ranging and he was promoted to the rank of Major.

Another officer working in the same section was Major W. L. Bragg, later Sir Lawrence Bragg, whose father Sir William Bragg had been awarded the Nobel Prize for Physics. One evening Arthur Atkins was with Lawrence Bragg when a telephone call came through from a very excited and proud Sir William to tell his son that he too had been awarded the Nobel Prize for Physics for his work in X-ray techniques in the investigation of crystals. Somebody found a couple bottles of wine and there was a great celebration. A week or two later Albert Einstein sent W. L. Bragg a post card congratulating him on the award.

W. L. Bragg was a Scientific Advisor on Sound Ranging and he gathered several bright young officers including A.H.A. into a team and they developed new methods of Sound Ranging. This is a method of pin pointing the position of enemy guns by using microphones strung out in an arc as close to the front as possible. The sound of the enemy gun was picked up by the microphones and the times measured on instruments and from this the position of the gun could be determined very quickly.

The leading members of Major Bragg's team were Tucker who developed a new microphone; Philpots who was an excellent instruments man and Atkins whose strength was organisation and the application of sound ranging to counter battery work. The British techniques became so good that in 1917 the Germans issued the following order:

"*Group Order.*

"In consequence of the excellent sound ranging of the English I forbid my battery to fire when the whole sector is quiet, especially in an East Wind. Should there be an occasion to fire, the adjoining battery must always be called on, either directly, or through the Group, to fire a few rounds."

After the war when this German Group Order was shown to Professor Bragg he wrote to A.H.A. "The joke was that the Tucker microphone at that time made it possible to disentangle the records of half dozen batteries firing at once, let alone two and to locate them all. One must give them full marks however for that bit about the East wind—they realised what was our worst adversary."

Major Atkins fought on the Somme front from March 1916 until June 1917 when the 4th Army went up to the coast. This period of trench warfare has been well recorded many times but through the mud, noise, and violence, more often than not lice infested A.H.A. retained his sense of humour.

After the war Major Atkins returned to the office in Liverpool, but he kept in touch with Professor Bragg and became a Member of the Field Survey Association which comprised the Sound Rangers and on one occasion after the war he gave a speech in honour of the chief guest, Sir John Davidson, who was a Cabinet Minister and in this speech he gave the following, not too serious account of how the Tucker microphone came to be invented:

"We have heard something about maps and about the very important part which they play under active service conditions, but most of us here represent that other branch of survey which was primarily associated with the location of enemy guns and other problems associated more closely with the artillery. Some of our guests have probably only a vague idea of the things that were done and the things that were possible with the wonderful apparatus which was devised under the direction and control of the Ordnance Survey. That it was possible to locate and report an active hostile gun in two to three minutes, and the position it was shelling, the muzzle velocity, the date it was made and the mark of the gun—that is quite normal and understandable. Under favourable conditions, however, we were able to look a little further into the future, and we were actually able on certain occasions to predict when a hostile gun was about to fire, and the target it was about to engage. Whilst we had the most wonderful mechanisms, none of them was sufficiently wonderful to turn fools into wise men, but at any rate we were able to go a long way along the road towards rendering various processes of war safer and more foolproof to our own people, and, in the opposite direction, more dangerous and effective from the point of view of the enemy.

We have heard a great deal in recent years about mechanisation, but very little has been said until just recently about the mechanisation of the 5-gallon oil drum. This simple and humble instrument is the basis of what was known as the Tucker microphone, and in a recent publication Bragg has given us some of the historical facts which resulted in the birth of this wonderful instrument. In 1916 it very soon became apparent that the type of microphone which we were then employing was unsuited for battle conditions. Tucker and Bragg retired to a farm in France in order to consider the whole problem and to try to develop something which would be more effective. This farm was well equipped and the sanitary arrangements attached to it were adjacent and in contact with the building. The exhaust went to atmosphere, and one morning shortly after breakfast Tucker went there to perform his usual functions, or at least one of them, and whilst he was so engaged a 6-inch mark 7 gun in our own lines commenced firing, and Tucker then noticed a peculiar tremor beneath him. Shortly after that had happened, the gun report came along, and was so violent that he actually oscillated on the seat. This gave Tucker a great idea, and he rushed away to get Bragg so that Bragg might confirm his impression. Before the gun ceased firing, Bragg had taken his place, and in due time Bragg was able to confirm that the violent disturbances which Tucker had experienced were entirely due to the gun. Bragg tells us that Tucker then followed this up by doing more delicate experiments with his nose on a mouse-hole, and eventually he produced the Tucker microphone, which was one of the most wonderful developments of the war and was the admiration of our allies as well as of ourselves, besides winning very great respect from our enemies."

WM. HEAP & CO., ST JOHN'S, NEWFOUNDLAND—1919

In 1919 Mr F. W. Angel visited Liverpool for talks with J. D. Crichton and A. H. Atkins about the possibility of opening up an office in St John's, and as a result Wm. Heap & Co. Ltd. of St John's, Newfoundland was opened with Mr F. W. Angel as President and Mr J. Boyd Baird and Mr J. W. Morris as Directors and the following year Mr Wm. C. Knight joined as Secretary and later became Treasurer and Director.

The first offices that we occupied in St John's were in the Board of Trade Building and here we appointed a young man recently serving in the army as our Sales Manager, one Hector Ross.

Extract from
The Telegram
of St John's
1919.

HECTOR ROSS

Captain H. H. A. Ross who was appointed Manager in 1919 had served with distinction with the Newfoundland Regiment in the 1914–18 War, and he was a hard working and hard playing man and under his energetic leadership the new company prospered until it was hit by the slump of the nineteen thirties. Even then we escaped relatively unscathed from the depression largely because the slump on the other side of the Atlantic was a year or two out of phase with the downturn in the U.K.

Hector Ross was fortunate in dealing with a number of interesting contracts including:

RE-RAILING OF THE NEWFOUNDLAND RAILWAY

As we have mentioned earlier we supplied most of the equipment used in the original Newfoundland Railway and when after many years service it was decided in 1925 to re-rail the line we again supplied the rails which were made by our old friends Colvilles of Motherwell.

We received the first order for part of the line in 1925 and then three more orders in 1926, 1928 and 1929. The 1928 order alone was for 114 track miles of thirty-three foot rails, tie plates, switch gear and points and this one order alone was worth £150,000. These orders were very welcome indeed in Liverpool and Scotland in the 1920's.

We chartered vessels to carry the steel from Scotland to Newfoundland and indeed we regularly chartered ships for Newfoundland until about 1966 when the type of business being done by our St John's office changed.

CORNER BROOK PAPER MILL

When this enormous paper mill was being planned we were associated with Sir W. G. Armstrong Whitworth & Co. of Openshaw, Manchester in the building of the mill and since then we have regularly supplied this important mill with engineering plant and machinery.

Newfoundland office staff outside 241 Water Street, St. John's in 1938. Hector Ross is the tall man in the centre.

Bowden Buildings, St. John's—our wartime offices.

BUCHAN'S PIPELINE

In 1927 we supplied the 6' bore Buchan's pipeline which was made by Mechans of Glasgow. The pipe was rivetted together from $\frac{5}{16}''$ and $\frac{3}{8}''$ plate and carried water from a dam almost one and a quarter miles across country to the power station.

An even longer pipeline we supplied was the eleven and a half mile long 20" pipeline from Bishop's Fall to Grand Falls.

Buchan's Pipeline 1927. 6' diameter—$1\frac{1}{4}$ miles long.

Buchan's Pipeline 1927.

114

DIFFICULTIES AND DANGERS

A recital of orders successfully carried out can sometimes make business appear to be too easy; it was at times, extremely difficult and much hard, patient work was put into these contracts. Even after we had secured the order there were, and are, considerable risks associated with export trade and to illustrate the unexpected difficulties that can be faced even when the goods were almost home and dry we relate a few of the problems we have encountered.

THE SHUNTING LOCO

We received an order from Newfoundland for a shunting locomotive and this was manufactured by a British firm and shipped out across the Atlantic. As it was being off-loaded in Newfoundland there was an accident and as a result the loco fell several feet on to the quay and it sustained severe damage.

Fortunately nobody was hurt and Hector Ross hurried to the scene of the accident and collected what was left of the loco and its shattered pieces. The situation was very serious because it would have taken months to get a new engine from England and so he put together the various broken castings and using them as patterns he had new parts cast in a local foundry. Then with the aid of the machine shop he rebuilt the engine completely to the satisfaction of our customer.

THE WHEEL LATHE

It may be thought that the normal way of off-loading in Newfoundland is to drop goods overboard if we relate the story of the Wheel Lathe, but we must take that risk.

The Anglo Newfoundland Development Corporation at Grand Falls carried out the maintenance of its own railway engines and wagons and they ordered from us a large wheel lathe for turning locomotive and wagon wheels and it was ordered "Delivered F.O.B. Wharf, Botwood", which was the shipping port for the paper mills: and it was the customer's responsibility to ship the lathe from the wharf to the mill.

As the lathe was being lifted and slung over the ship's side the sling broke, the headstock of the lathe landed on the wharf, but the long bed went plunging over the side into the deep.

This then posed a very tricky legal problem because the shipping company claimed that as the lathe was over the ship's side it was no longer their responsibility; the customer, very reasonably, complained that we had only delivered one third of the lathe "F.O.B. on the Wharf" and we were left with the problem that whilst we knew where the other two thirds of the lathe was we could not do much about it and we felt that the Shipping Company had not fulfilled its obligation.

Eventually after much arguing the customer agreed to pay for the one third we had delivered, the shipping company paid one third and we paid the remaining third. A new bed was ordered from England and eventually the customer had a complete wheel lathe.

THE ATLANTIC CABLE

As an example of the absolute necessity for good packing, there is the celebrated case of the bright steel bars which we ordered from a steel mill in the U.K. for delivery to our St John's Warehouse. The bars were to be packed in the steel mill suitable for export and delivered to us in St John's. In accordance with our instructions the rods were packed in very strong wooden cases and were adequately packed everywhere except, as we later discovered, at the ends of the rods.

The consignment of steel was loaded on board a vessel in Liverpool in the same hold as the new oil filled, Atlantic cable which had cost a small fortune to make and would cost another to lay on the bed of the Atlantic.

The voyage across the Atlantic was uneventful and the ship docked safely in St John's, but when one of the cases was being unloaded, the stevedores used only one sling fastened about the middle, instead of a two point lift which is usual. The sling was not quite at the centre of gravity of the case and as it was being lifted high into the air out of the hold, it suddenly tilted and the bright steel rods slid inside the box with such force that the end of the case burst open and to the dismay of the onlookers on deck the bright steel bars flashed through the air, singing into the hold below, like the English arrows shot from the Cheshire longbows at the Battle of Agincourt. There were no French knights in the hold of the ship that day but there was the giant, sleeping, serpentine coils of the trans-Atlantic cable and the rods embedded themselves deep in the coils of the slumbering monster and its life blood, or was it oil? seeped out and the multi-million pound serpent lay dying.

There were many sleepless nights in England and Newfoundland for some little time after that and the cable had to be returned to England for testing and then when all the punctures had been located new sections had to be made, joined in, and finally the whole cable had to be re-tested and shipped back across the Atlantic. In the meantime the cable laying ships and their crews were lying idle and the laying of the new cable was delayed for months at enormous cost.

Again the tricky question of responsibility arose; fortunately for us we were not involved because the accident happened in the ship's hold and the steel was still not our responsibility. The steel company felt that the accident was caused because the stevedore had not slung the load properly and the other party claimed that the damage had been due to the lack of packing at the ends of the bars.

A very costly court action took place and after a very long court hearing the judgement was given against the steel company and they awarded damages against them that were so heavy that the firm had to go into liquidation.

For the lack of a bit of packing costing a few pence in a small consignment of steel, the Atlantic Cable could not be laid for months, the cost of putting matters right had cost a fortune a company had been ruined and dozens of men lost their jobs.

Was it Mr MacMillan who said that exporting is fun?

EARLY MOTOR CARS

In the pre-first war period we received requests from some of our business friends in St John's about the newly popular vehicle, the motor car and we supplied the first car in St John's and what a car it was. One of the famous Rolls Royce Silver Ghosts that started being manufactured in Hulme, Manchester in 1906 and were produced until 1925. Later we supplied more Silver Ghosts, Rolls Royce Phantom I as well as Napier and Daimler motor cars.

We not only helped our friends by supplying motor cars, but we also engaged on their behalf chauffeurs and mechanics in Liverpool to go out to Newfoundland and some of them did very well. One of the chauffeurs, George Nightingale, later became Mayor of St John's.

HEAP & PARTNERS (N'F'LND) LTD. (1939–1978)

The original name of our Newfoundland Company was Wm. Heap Co., Ltd. of St John's, but to distinguish it from our Liverpool Company its name was changed in 1933 to William Heap & Partners (Newfoundland) Ltd. but this was a bit of a mouthful and so in 1939 it was simplified to Heap & Partners (N'F'Lnd) Ltd.

In 1935 Hector Ross was made a Director of our St John's company and remained so until in December 1938 he was taken into hospital for what was thought to be a minor operation to treat an old war wound, but sadly he suffered a relapse and died on the operating table. He was a splendid fellow who was missed in Newfoundland and England.

The company was now faced with an emergency with the sudden and unexpected loss of Hector Ross and so it was arranged that a young engineer named Tom Freeman would go out from our Liverpool office for six weeks until a permanent solution could be found: a formidable task for a young man who had only been with the firm less than a year.

116

T. S. A. FREEMAN

Tom Freeman—President (until 1978)—
Heap & Partners (Newfoundland).

Tom Freeman was educated at Oundle School in Northamptonshire and after leaving school served an apprenticeship at Cammell Laird's Shipyard in Birkenhead and when he came out of his time he worked for six months in the steam turbine department. Later Tom worked for Marconi in Birkenhead and B.I.C.C. in their Helsby Works.

A. H. Atkins was friendly with Tom's father, Sterry B. Freeman, who was the Superintendent Engineer for the famous shipping line Alfred Holt of Liverpool. Early in 1938 A.H. mentioned to Sterry Freeman that they were looking for a young sales engineer and he wondered if Tom would be interested. Tom was, and joined our Liverpool office on the 1st June 1938 and was employed as a sales engineer dealing with Saunders Valves, Powerflexible Tubing and other Agencies.

It was intended that eventually Tom would go out to Newfoundland for a further period of training but the death of Hector Ross accelerated these plans and Tom was told to go out to St John's to keep the flag flying until a permanent replacement was sent out, and a passage was booked for him on the S.S. "Nova Scotia" sailing for Newfoundland on 5th February 1939.

So Tom, armed with several pages of notes prepared by John Crichton about our customers in Newfoundland and the sound advice from A.H.A. that he should "learn to play bridge or you will be a social dud, because in winter there is nothing else to do there" set sail from the Mersey.

The North Atlantic in winter lived up to its worst reputation and for the entire voyage the "Nova Scotia" had to battle against ferocious, icy, gales and mountainous seas. At one time the Captain even resorted to pumping oil on to the sea, a practice that is not encouraged today.

Twelve days later at 4-30 pm on Friday 17th February the "Nova Scotia" finally made harbour in Newfoundland and disembarked her weary passengers. Recently "Concorde" made the same crossing in just over three hours.

After spending the weekend finding accommodation, Tom reported to our office 241 Water Street on Monday morning intending to spend a week or two in the office finding his way around, but instead he found that there were problems that had to be sorted out in the paper mills and mines on the island and he had to set out immediately.

It was a little different to working from our Liverpool office because outside St John's our nearest customer was 275 miles away at Grand Falls. At that time there were few roads and the railway was the means of transport and Tom found that instead of visiting a customer for a few hours one stayed for a few days.

So using the single track, narrow gauge, railway, which chugged across the frozen Newfoundland landscape at 20 m.p.h. T. S. A. Freeman visited Grand Falls, Corner Brook and Buchan's Mine and returned to St John's almost a month later. He then spent the days sorting out the office problems before leaving on another trip to Bell Island and the Wabana Mines and returned to the office to find another major crisis on his hands.

During the illness of Hector Ross another Agent in St John's, had contacted our largest Agency at that time, "Westinghouse International", and told them that in view of our problem it would be in their interest to switch the Agency to him. Westinghouse were considering this proposition and so Tom set sail for New York on 31st March to see Westinghouse at their office at 55 Broadway, New York.

We were first offered the Agency for this important Company in 1919 and we represented them for their whole range of products which varied from domestic refrigerators to large power station steam turbines. Although it may seem unusual to cover such a wide range, the difficulty with Newfoundland is that the total population is only about half a million and with such a small population our St John's office had always had to handle a much wider range than we have in England because the population is too small to afford the sort of specialisation we have in the U.K.

We were very successful for Westinghouse and we had secured a number of important contracts including the supply of a 32,000 KVA steam turbine generator and seven 2,250 KVA sets for the Anglo–Newfoundland Development Company at Grand Falls and the supply of all the original lighting at Gander Airport in addition to the control boards, runway markers, beacons and other electrical equipment, as well as the more run of the mill type of business.

After seeing Westinghouse in New York, Tom Freeman cabled A. H. Atkins telling him that he considered that A.H. should visit Westinghouse without delay and so Mr Atkins caught the next ship leaving Liverpool for New York, had more discussions with Westinghouse and as a result we were offered a long term agreement.

Ironically when we finally parted company with the grand organisation in 1969 it was at our request. We were always very proud to be associated with Westinghouse and we had enjoyed the interesting work, but although the business was very substantial it was not always very profitable, and our Newfoundland Board eventually took the view that we would be stronger if we parted company but it was sad after fifty years of close association.

To return to 1939, T. S. A. Freeman was made a Director in June 1939 at the request of our President at that time J. Boyd Baird, very rapid promotion for a young man who had only been in Newfoundland for a few months and who had only joined the company a year earlier, but in view of the responsibilities suddenly thrust on his shoulders and his success in tackling them, it was well deserved.

In this period just before the Second World War our business in Newfoundland apart from Westinghouse was in X-ray machines, machine tools, steel castings, Samuel Osborn cutting tools, Crossley Packings and Saunders valves.

War broke out in September 1939 and almost immediately it became difficult shipping material out from the U.K. because of the problems caused by the German submarines.

We have in our Hoylake office the 1939 Balance Sheet for Heap & Partners (N'f'lnd) Ltd. which was sent to us in 1940. The ship carrying the mail was torpedoed but later some of the mail, including our Balance Sheet, was salvaged from the Atlantic and although it is water stained and somewhat crumpled it is quite legible. What a story it could tell if only it could talk.

Later in the war all our correspondence was microfilmed and we exchanged correspondence this way with Newfoundland.

In 1944 A.H.A. had to visit Canada and he flew over the Atlantic in the hold of an R.A.F. bomber, a most uncomfortable and cold flight, but he was very grateful for the lift.

118

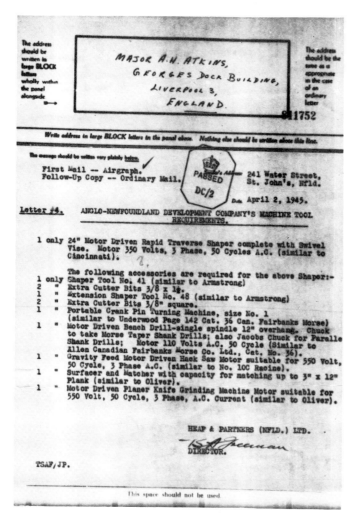

MAJOR A.H. ATKINS,
GEORGES DOCK BUILDING,
LIVERPOOL 3,
ENGLAND.

941752

Write address in large BLOCK letters in the panel above. Nothing else should be written above this line.

The message should be written very plainly below. ✓

First Mail -- Airgraph.
Follow-Up Copy -- Ordinary Mail.

PASSED DC/2

241 Water Street,
St. John's, Nfld.

Date April 2, 1945.

Letter #4.   ANGLO-NEWFOUNDLAND DEVELOPMENT COMPANY'S MACHINE TOOL
REQUIREMENTS.

1 only 24" Motor Driven Rapid Traverse Shaper complete with Swivel
Vise. Motor 350 Volts, 3 Phase, 50 Cycles A.C. (similar to
Cincinnati).

The following accessories are required for the above Shaper:-
1 only Shaper Tool No. 41 (similar to Armstrong)
2   "   Extra Cutter Bits 3/8 x 1½.
1   "   Extension Shaper Tool No. 48 (similar to Armstrong)
2   "   Extra Cutter Bits 3/8" square.
1   "   Portable Crank Pin Turning Machine, size No. 1
(similar to Underwood Page 142 Cat. 36 Can. Fairbanks Morse)
1   "   Motor Driven Bench Drill-single spindle 12" overhang. Chuck
to take Morse Taper Shank Drills; also Jacobs Chuck for Parallel
Shank Drills;   Motor 110 Volts A.C. 50 Cycle (Similar to
Allen Canadian Fairbanks Morse Co. Ltd., Cat. No. 36).
1   "   Gravity Feed Motor Driven Hack Saw Motor suitable for 550 Volt,
50 Cycle, 3 Phase A.C. (similar to No. 10C Racine).
1   "   Surfacer and Matcher with capacity for matching up to 3" x 12"
Plank (similar to Oliver).
1   "   Motor Driven Planer Knife Grinding Machine Motor suitable for
550 Volt, 50 Cycle, 3 Phase, A.C. Current (similar to Oliver).

HEAP & PARTNERS (NFLD.) LTD.

DIRECTOR.

TSAF/JP.

This space should not be used

*Microfilmed wartime
letter (actual size).*

CONFEDERATION AND AFTER

In 1949 Newfoundland became the tenth Province of Canada and this was to have a profound effect on our trade with our Canadian office.

We had represented many British companies for years in Newfoundland and had given them excellent service in what can be a difficult market, but when Newfoundland became part of Canada their Canadian Agents claimed Newfoundland as part of their territory and many companies had signed Agreements nominating one company to represent them in the whole country.

This practice of British Companies in employing one Agent in, say, Toronto or Montreal works well if the Agent is covering the whole country adequately; but the distances in Canada are so vast that frequently they do not give adequate cover on the mainland, never mind Newfoundland. Admittedly it is not quite as bad as British companies expecting one Agent to cover the whole of the U.S.A., as some do but it shows that some British companies do not understand the country properly.

Majestic Sales. Heap's showroom for Westinghouse Products in St. John's about 1966.

It reminds us of the enquiry we once received from our Newfoundland office for a very large boiler, and as most of the large boiler companies were short of work at that time we expected that they would be quite keen to quote; but they were less than enthusiastic. Later we spoke to the Director of a very well known boiler company and we asked him why they had turned the enquiry down; he told us that they thought it would be a waste of time because of the enormous advantages that the U.S. and Canadian boiler manufacturers had. We pressed him to name the advantages and he caused us to choke when he said "Well—they are right on the doorstep and we are not".

This man, now dead, was an excellent engineer and highly intelligent, was startled when we told him that St John's is nearer to Liverpool than it is to Montreal and without taking a check we were willing to gamble that his company in Manchester was just about the nearest large boiler maker to St John's!

In 1951 A. H. Atkins could see the enormous changes that were coming in Anglo–Newfoundland trade due to Confederation and so he sold out our interests in the Newfoundland office to friends and colleagues in St John's.

St. John's from the roof of Heap's office about 1966.

120

Heap & Partners (Newfoundland) Co., Ltd. St. John's 1976.

HEAP NOSEWORTHY LTD., ST JOHN'S (1978 TO DATE)

For many years we had a close association with William Noseworthy of Newfoundland and in January 1978, Peter and David Cook, sons of Eric Cook, formerly Director of Heap & Partners (Newfoundland) decided to amalgamate with Heap & Partners, St John's and a new company was formed known as Heap Noseworthy Ltd. The new company is now flourishing under the Presidency of David Cook and Peter Cook is a Director. Branches have been opened in Marystown, Grand Falls and Corner Brook.

Tom Freeman, who you will recall went out to St John's in 1939 fro six weeks, retired towards the end of 1979 and he died in Florida in 1987.

E. E. BAKER (1913–1928)

In 1913 the Canadian business was expanding so rapidly that it was decided to take on another senior engineer to handle our business in the Manchester area and eventually a thirty-six year old engineer Eustace Baker joined us.

E. . Baker — Director 1915–1928
Founder of Baker, Kelly &
Wallis.

E. E. Baker had worked for Brush Electrical Co. in Loughborough and moved north just before he joined us; he was an energetic and capable engineer and under his direction our business in the Manchester area expanded.

When J. D. Crichton joined the army in 1915, Eustace Baker was appointed a Director and on the 18th January 1917 he opened our first Manchester office in Room 44, 4th Floor, 30 Cross Street. This office was rented from the Star Insurance Company at a rent of £26 p.a. and we stayed in this office for four years until we moved to larger offices at 9 Albert Square in 1921.

Our business in Manchester in World War I, and after, was divided into two broad streams, the steel and refractory business and "engineering; the latter comprised Belliss and Morcom steam engines, steam turbines, diesel engines and air compressors, Rees Roturbo Pumps, Centrifugal Pumps, Greenwood and Batley Steam Turbines, Liptack furnace arches and Necker water treatment. C. A. Dunham business was handled from Liverpool. In 1928 Eustace Baker approached his fellow Directors and said that he would like to start up on his own and with the approval of his colleagues he bought the goodwill of the "engineering" Agencies in the Manchester area and on the 29th February 1928 E. E. Baker took over the office at 9 Albert Square and set up in business on his own account under the title E. E. Baker and the same day we moved our Manchester office to 1 Dickenson Street.

E. E. Baker was eventually joined by Dr Wallis and Mr Kelly and they changed the name of their partnership to Baker, Kelly and Wallis of Manchester.

Because of our common background we have long been associated with Baker, Kelly and Wallis; for example they handled the sale of Belliss and Morcom products in the Manchester area but we installed and maintained the plants. Similarly B.K.. represented the Saunders Valve Company in the Manchester area and we handled their products in the Liverpool area, until 1980 when we were allowed to sell Saunders valves anywhere in England.

E. E. Baker died on the 31st March 1960 and the business was then carried on by his son DeFoe Baker with the old partners.

In 1972 the Saunders Valve Company bought out Baker, Kelly and Wallis and after running the business for a couple of years put it into voluntary liquidation.

Like a Phoenix rising out of the ashes Foe Baker formed BKW (Manchester) operating from their old address in Eccles and we are sure that our long association with the Baker family will continue.

The menu card from the office Christmas Dinner held at the Exchange Hotel, Liverpool on 19 December 1928.

Captain Hector Ross took this back to Newfoundland with him and it rested in our St John's office until 1985 when it was given to the writer by Tom Freeman.

CHAPTER 7

Between the Wars

L. C. ASHCROFT (1923–1959)

In 1923 it was decided to take on another sales engineer to supplement the work being done on Dunham heating equipment and Belliss and Morcom engines and air compressors and in January 1923 we engaged Leonard Crossley Ashcroft who was then forty-two years of age and had formerly worked for Grayson Rollo Engraving Docks on ship conversion and repair work.

Len Ashcroft was a very active sales engineer who covered our area very well, although he could not drive a motor car. He planned his work in such a way that by using public transport in his hey-day, before and during the war, he made about the same number of visits as our present generation of sales engineers, who have the advantage of a motor car.

L. C. Ashcroft was largely responsible for developing the Dunham steam trap business in the early days and later as new products came along he sold vacuum pumps and condensate return

Mr. & Mrs. L. C. Ashcroft
on holiday in Llandudno.

pumps and in the Stoke on Trent area he probably sold more Dunham vacuum return line pumps per square mile than anyone in Europe. Practically every pottery had one installed and the potteries were a very happy hunting ground for him, as well as Liverpool, Manchester, Preston and North Wales.

The remarkable thing about L. C. Ashcroft was that his appearance hardly changed from the time he joined us until he retired at almost eighty years of age. Right up to his retirement most people thought he was in his fifties. Every year Mr and Mrs Ashcroft used to go to Llandudno for part of their holiday, and every year they had their photograph taken, Mrs Ashcroft with her Peter Pan of a husband never changing.

Len Ashcroft retired at Christmas 1958 at the age of 79 years. He died in 1966. Mrs Ashcroft died about 10 years later.

INDIA BUILDINGS (1928–1936)

Water Street, Liverpool about 1930.   *India Buildings about 1930.*

In 1928 the company moved office after a seventeen year stay in Liver Buildings and took up residence at 319 India Building where we occupied 135 sq. yards at a rental of £2-10s per sq. yard, and here we stayed for two years and then moved up to the 8th Floor to Room 847 where we had 120 sq. yards in a suite on the S.E. corner of Fenwick Street and Brunswick Sreet.

India Building has a most beautiful entrance hall with a highly decorated ceiling and it is a splendid office block. It was very badly damaged during the Second World War but happily the main structure survived and after the war it was restored to its former glory.

OSCAR SPEDDING (1915–1929)

After E. E. Baker had set up his own business in Manchester, our steel and refractories business continued to be run by Oscar Louis Spedding who had joined us just after the end of the First World War and who had been a Director since 1924.

Oscar Spedding was in some ways quite brilliant but he had one fault which at times almost drove his colleagues to distraction and that was he was not only extremely good at selling steel but he was an impulse buyer on a grand scale. It was this impulse buying that quite alarmed his fellow Directors.

In the slump years of the nineteen twenties all kinds of companies went to the wall and for an active man like O. L. Spedding, there were wonderful opportunities to indulge in his passion. One day he walked into our Liverpool office in Liver Buildings and announced with some excitement to a startled Major Atkins and J. D. Crichton that he had bought a cotton mill! After they had recovered their breath they asked him if he had taken leave of his senses. "No" he replied because the mill contained some hundreds of tons of scrap iron and he had taken out a lease on a scrap yard in Gorton, Manchester and he had arranged with somebody to dismantle the machinery and to transport the scrap to the yard. Not only had he done that but he had sold the scrap to a steel works and we had to feed the scrap to them at a certain rate.

A.H. and J.D. told Oscar in no uncertain terms that he must be mad because we were not scrap iron merchants and had no intention of becoming one. He replied that times were hard and he was sure he would make a profit.

Sure enough he did make a modest profit and A.H. and J.D. heaved a sigh of relief, but history reveals that it might have been better if Mr Spedding had made a loss, because he was now addicted. In a short space of time he bought another cotton mill and again made a small profit and then he bought a colliery that had gone into liquidation but this time he made a small loss.

Major Atkins and J. D. Crichton had a furious row with Mr Spedding and told him that this practice of buying derelict companies must stop because they were in grave danger of becoming nervous wrecks because they did not know from one day to the next what he was going to buy, and so a rather penitent Oscar promised to reform.

In 1928 Oscar Spedding secured an order for steel tube from John Thom the Wellsinkers of Patricroft, Manchester. There was some doubt about the financial stability of Thoms at that time and J.D. wrote to Oscar telling him to be careful. Oscar pressed on regardless and felt let down when John Thom announced that they were in financial trouble and called a meeting of creditors, but he quickly recovered his spirits and decided to attend the meeting himself on behalf of Heap & Partners.

It was announced at the meeting that the largest creditor was Heap & Partners and whilst this might have dismayed lesser men, Oscar Spedding saw it as a wonderful opportunity and he saved the day by announcing that instead of forcing the company into liquidation Heap & Partners would take over the wellsinking business and would run it as a going concern. He was almost chaired from the meeting because the other creditors knew we were financially sound, but his more conservative and cautious colleagues were speechless when they found out that they were the owners of one of the best known wellsinkers in the country.

Oscar Spedding was called to Liverpool by an outraged A. H. Atkins and J. D. Crichton and was asked how he could have done such a thing. We knew little about geology or the technique of sinking wells and the many problems were only too obvious and they felt that they had enough difficulties without being saddled with running such a specialised business.

After a somewhat heated, and one sided, discussion A.H. said that they had concluded that as long as Oscar stayed in our steel section he was open to temptation and with some reluctance, because he was a good steel salesman, they had decided to transfer him to our refractories section and he was to go to Montreal for a course of training with our Principals, Canadian Refractories.

Oscar Spedding said that he was sorry   that A.H. and J.D. were so concerned but he felt sure that the art of wellsinking was such a "hit and miss" affair that he could run it at least as well as the so called "experts", and given a chance he thought he could run it for a couple of years and not only recover our money but perhaps even make a profit. History shows that he was right, we did run the business for three years quite successfully and when trade eventually improved we sold the business and made a profit.

So far as J.D. and A.H. were concerned at that stage, this was entirely a matter for conjecture and they wouldn't listen to Oscar and so he was handed a return ticket to Montreal and details of his itinerary and hotel reservation. Oscar Spedding accepted the situation with good grace and within a week had sailed for Canada and Canadian Refractories.

It had been arranged that Oscar would report to Canadian Refractories on a certain day, but he did not appear that day, nor the next so Canadian Refractories cabled Liverpool and told A.H. that he had not appeared. We checked with the shipping company and found that the vessel had arrived on time and so they cabled Mr Spedding at his hotel. To their surprise they received a reply telling them not to worry, he was quite well, but he was engaged in a small business matter and would report to Canadian Refractories within a day or two. For the next few days the cable wires were hot as a now highly alarmed J.D. insisted that Oscar should report without further delay.

Eventually Oscar Spedding turned up at the Montreal offices of Canadian Refractories full of apologies, hoping that he had not inconvenienced them too much, but as it had been a fine morning the day he was supposed to report to them he had decided to walk to their offices. On the way he passed an auction yard and as he was a little early for his appointment he thought he would spend a little time taking in the local scene.

The auction was to dispose of the effects of a company that, in common with many others on both sides of the Atlantic, had been forced into liquidation by the World slump. Oscar noticed that one lot to be sold consisted of a couple of hundred barrels. He examined one of the barrels and found it to be in excellent condition and that it was partly full of some unknown liquid, he checked one or two others and found that some were empty and some contained liquid. Oscar reasoned that if a liquid were stored in a barrel then it must have some value and therefore one could buy the barrels only and there might be a bonus resulting from the unknown fluid. By now he had forgotten all about his appointment and was off in full cry, once again proving that a geographical change alters nothing in a man.

There was one small snag and that was that Oscar's financial resources in Canada were quite adequate for the original purpose of the trip, but were a bit thin for engaging in business enterprises but he felt that was a risk he had to take. He stayed, and eventually the barrels were knocked down to the Englishman with the beaming face.

Now came the most exciting part for Oscar, to find out what was in the barrels, he opened one and found that the liquid was lubricating oil — excellent, couldn't be better. Off came his coat and with the aid of a temporary assistant engaged on the spot he poured the partly filled barrels into others and by the end of the afternoon he had a number of full barrels of lube oil and the balance of empty barrels. Oscar felt it had been a good days work.

The next day he fully intended reporting to Canadian Refractories but he had a small problem and that was that he had spent all his, or rather the firm's, money, and he was a few thousand miles from base, so he decided it would be more prudent if he sold the barrels first, recovered his money and he hoped some profit as well, before going to see our Principals. Although Oscar Spedding had never been in Canada before he had a natural instinct to sort out customers and within a few days he had sold the oil and the barrels and had made a profit for the Company.

Unhappily, A.H. and J.D. did not appreciate his efforts and while he had been busy in the backstreets of Montreal his colleagues were so worried about what he might be up to that by mutual agreement with Canadian Refractories he was to be packed off back to Liverpool by the next boat.

The great difficulty facing A. H. Atkins and J. D. Crichton was that Oscar Spedding was extremely hardworking, very loyal, completely honest and a good salesman and they valued these qualities, but he was becoming a nightmare to them. They decided that in view of the refractories fiasco that they would give him one more chance and send him back to Manchester once again working in our steel section, but with the threat that if he strayed again they would have to part company.

All went well for a few months and their taut nerves were beginning to relax, but then early in October they tried to contact him in Manchester but found he was mysteriously busy on an "important contract" and he was out of town. On Thursday 18th October 1928 they were heartily relieved to discover that Mr Spedding was in Motherwell visiting our Principals, Colvilles Steel Works. A little surprised that he had not mentioned he was going to Scotland, but delighted that he was not off on one of his mad jaunts.

On Monday 22nd October an excited Oscar Spedding walked into India Buildings and after greeting A.H. and J.D. told them he was sorry he had been out of contact but he had great news for them. He must have seen their faces fall because he held up his hand and said "Before you say anything, I assure you we can't go wrong with this one." By now highly alarmed and coldly furious they demanded an explanation. Spedding told them that he had pulled off the biggest deal of his life and he was sure that they would be as delighted as he when they learned that they were now the proud owners of one of the Wonders of the World, no less than the "Big wheel" at Blackpool—the largest wheel in the World!

The iron nerve that had carried Major Atkins through the hell of the Battle of the Somme stood him in good stead now. Slowly he reached for his pipe, pulled his tobacco pouch out of his pocket, filled his pipe, lit it, took a long puff and then asked Mr Spedding if he would mind repeating what he had just said.

Oscar Spedding breathlessly told them that he had not mentioned anything to them before now because he did not want to raise false hopes, but now his negotiations were successfully concluded and all could be revealed.

In May 1928 he had read in the "Manchester Evening News" that Sir John Bickerstaffe, Chairman of the Blackpool Tower Co. had announced that reluctantly they had decided to pull the "Big Wheel" down so that they could build a new building to be called "Olympia" on the site. Spedding made enquiries and found that the "Big Wheel" would yield about 1,000 tons of scrap, so he had contacted a man known as Eli Ward of Eccles and they had agreed that Eli Ward's firm of dismantlers would take the wheel down and Heap & Partners had contracted to remove the scrap from the site and to sell it. On behalf of the Company Oscar Spedding had not only bought the wheel on Friday 12th October but he had then gone to Motherwell and signed a contract with Colvilles who had agreed to buy the scrap iron and steel and he had even arranged with the L.M.S. Railway Company to run a shuttle service of their lorries from the "Big Wheel" to special wagons that would take the scrap to Motherwell. Eli Ward's men would lower the scrap straight into the L.M.S. lorries below. It was true that there was a penalty clause regarding the dismantling time, but there should be no problems in this respect because the wheel had only taken six months to build.

A.H.A. and J.D. were worried and furious because the "Big Wheel" was a national institution like Blackpool Tower, it was so enormous that it carried nine hundred people, two hundred and twenty feet into the air. It was one thing to admire such an extravaganza but quite a different matter to own it because they could see that the problems ahead were immense, whereas Oscar Spedding's bubbling optimism blinded him to reality.

THE BLACKPOOL GIGANTIC WHEEL

Blackpool as a holiday resort was a Victorian development, as indeed were most other seaside resorts. In 1891 its population was only 25,000, but the working people of the north were getting more money, trains were making travelling cheaper and the working class were discovering the delights of the seaside. Men of enterprise saw this social change and started to cater for the visitors.

One such man was a Blackpool fisherman called Robert Bickerstaffe. He lived in a tiny cottage on the promenade and he could neither read, nor write, but he was intelligent and he became the first Manager of the Central Pier. Later, after he had saved some money, and borrowed more he built the first Wellington Hotel and then others such as the No. 3. Two of his sons followed him and took part in the development of Blackpool, one being Sir John Bickerstaffe, Chairman of the Tower Company and he was succeeded by his brother Alderman Tom Bickerstaffe, in turn his son Douglas Bickerstaffe became Chairman of the Tower Company.

Such men developed Blackpool particularly in the last twenty years of the nineteenth

The "Big Wheel" Blackpool about 1926.
The Largest Wheel in The World. In 1928
we found ourselves THE UNEXPECTED
OWNERS OF THIS WONDER which
could carry 900 people at one time.

century. Although Birkenhead ran the first trams in this country, Blackpool built the first electric tramway in Britain in 1885. It is appropriate that long after all the others that followed have gone, Blackpool's are the last trams still running in England, Scotland or Wales.

In 1889 the Opera House was built, South Pier in 1893, and the Tower in 1894. M. Eiffell had built his tower in Paris, and not to be outdone Blackpool too wanted a Tower to put the place on the map. In London a Mr. W. B. Bassett, R.N. had built a giant wheel at Earls Court and so a group of Northern business men decide to build a gigantic wheel on a site at the corner of Adelaide Street and Coronation Street which was then a bowling green and gardens.

A new company known as the "Blackpool Gigantic Wheel Co. Ltd." was floated with 50,000, £1 shares. The floatation was a great success and was oversubscribed, it was announced that as most of the visitors to Blackpool came from the north that preference would be given to subscribers from the north.

The first Directors were:

F. J. Astbury of Manchester.

James Pearson of Blackpool.

A. Bottomley of Halifax.

F. A. Badman of Birmingham.

And W. B. Bassett of London was the engineer in charge of building the wheel.

W. B. Bassett had built the wheel at Earl's Court and later built wheels in Vienna, Chicago and Paris. All have now gone except the wheel in Vienna, but more of that later.

A consulting engineer named Cecil Booth was appointed and he was also worth remembering as the man who invented the vacuum cleaner. In 1903 he demonstrated the first workable contraption for removing dirt by suction in Buckingham Palace to a marvelling King Edward and Queen Alexandra. The first of the thousands of salesmen who followed in homes all over the world, sprinkling dirt on to carpets and picking it up by the vacuum cleaner. Mr H. Cecil Booth was still alive in 1944 and at that time lived in Purley, Sussex.

W. B. Bassett was the driving force, the Blackpool Gazette described him in 1896 as "This bundle of nerves who conceived the idea, he is here, there and everywhere."

The first ground was turned in December 1895, the contract for the steel work was let to Arrol's Bridge, and Roof Co. Ltd., of Glasgow and the steam engines were to be supplied by Robey's of Lincoln.

By the end of January 1896, the ground was cleared and two 80' wooden platforms to carry two 3 ton cranes were built. The first of the four steel columns which were to tower 110' above the ground was started on the 4th February 1896, and the last was finished on 19th March 1896.

When the towers which were to carry the huge axle bearings were finished it was time to haul the axle into position before the wheel itself could be built. The axle was too large to be transported to Blackpool by rail and it had to be taken by road in a special trolley drawn by teams of horses. It was the largest solid axle ever made in Europe being 40' 8" long, 26" in diameter and weighed 30 tons. It was rolled up the slanting columns by a steam engine pulling cables fastened about the axle and it was placed in position in its giant bearing on the 9th April 1896.

Work started on the wheel itself in May and it was finished on the 8th August 1896. The thirty cars were built by Marshall Brown & Co. of Birmingham and they were conveyed to Blackpool by special horse drawn trolleys and arrived on Thursday 25th June 1896.

The wheel was driven by two 25-hp Robey steam engines and the power was transmitted to the axle by means of two steel cables each of which had been tested to 180 tons. These cables had a total length of 3,125' i.e. nearly $\frac{3}{4}$ mile and were joined by the longest splice ever made at that time.

The two hundred and fifty men employed on the wheel under the direction of W. B. Bassett built it in the space of 6 months and nobody was injured in building it, nor indeed on running it throughout its life.

If one wonders why this is mentioned remember that this structure stood 220' high and safety standards were very poor indeed. Men building such structures were frequently under the

The Tower and its Pal.

influence of alcohol and it is surprising that there were very few accidents. Kathleen Eyre in her book "Seven Golden Miles" published in 1961 tells a story of one gang of men who helped to build Blackpool Tower in 1891–1894 and some of whom later worked on the "Big Wheel".

"This gang walked into Blackpool from Weaton and called at the Eagle & Child every morning at 5 am for their first pint of the day, they then progressed via other hostelries until they reached the site in Blackpool. At night they would retrace their steps calling first at the Grosvenor, then the No. 3, the No. 4 at Langton, trudge across the fields to the Plough Inn at Staining and another stretch of the legs to the homely doorstep of the Eagle & Child once again."

The Tower is 518' high and in the 3 years it took to build only one man lost his life. It was opened on Whit Monday 14th May 1894 and K. Eyre again recounts during the opening ceremony it started to splash with rain. The gloom mongers shook their heads, but the wisemen said "Let it rain, it is worth a guinea a drop" and so it has proved ever since. When the weather is bad in Blackpool the Tower turnstiles click away merrily."

To return to the Big Wheel, the following facts may be of interest:

Height—220'
Weight—1000 tons
Number of cars—30
Weight of each car—3 tons 3 cwts
Length of axle 40' 8"
Diameter—26'
Weight of axle—30 tons
Number of spokes—250
Tensile test on spokes—50 tons
Drive—2–25-hp Robey steam engines
Speed of rotation—4 rev/hour
Number of passengers—30 per carriage (900 total)

When the wheel was finished it was then painted with two coats of paint and this took no less than $2\frac{1}{2}$ tons of paint.

At the bottom of the wheel a pavillion was built with a glass roof and here they built a replica of a Japanese street, with a Japanese Tea Garden. Remember that until only forty years before Japan had been completely isolated until Admiral Perry, U.S.N. had delivered his ultimatum that foreign shipping should be allowed into Japanese waters, so there was considerable interest in all things Japanese.

Finally on the 22nd August 1896, Mr James Pearson officially opened the Big Wheel and the public were admitted for the first time, adults 3d, children 1d, they could take a trip in the world's largest wheel! Great was the excitement, with Japanese lanterns, flags and bunting flying and bands playing. An enormous queue formed down Adelaide Street and in the first two and a quarter hours 4,000 people paid at the turnstiles.

The cars had padded seats running along their length and from the top on a clear day one could see, North Wales, Wirral, Isle of Man, Mull of Galloway, Scotland and five counties, some even said they could see Ireland, but the pubs were open all day in those times and the beer was stronger.

After they had travelled on the "Gigantic Wheel" the patrons could have tea or could complete their education by visiting, admission free:—

"Gordon's Exhibition of Tortures and Execution."

The official Souvenir and Guide to the Gigantic Wheel said:

"With the exception of the Forth Bridge, no feat of engineering has ever caused so much interest in that great home of the mechanic the North of Great Britain. The excitement of Londoners over the Great Wheel at Earl's Court was in a measure sentimental and it was looked upon simply and purely as a "show" and not one person in a thousand appreciated the difficulties or interested himself in the construction.

In Blackpool however, the chosen playground of the millions of sturdy craftsmen of Lancashire and Yorkshire, the steady growth of our massive structure was watched with an interest born of knowledge. Letters by the thousand were received enquiring as to the why of this, and the what of that, and many were the wagers that were referred to the decision of the Manager."

The wheel carried millions of people and a visit to Blackpool was incomplete without a trip on the Big Wheel, it was as much part of Blackpool as the Tower. It was remarked at the time that from a distance the Tower looked like a giant needle and at its side the Wheel resembled a giant cotton reel.

When the first war started however, in 1914, most of the men went off to France or Egypt and the women went on to war work. Nobody had time for the pleasures of Blackpool and on 18th January 1916 the "Blackpool Gigantic Wheel Co., Ltd." went into voluntary liquidation and the property and assets were bought by the Blackpool Winter Gardens and Pavilion Co. for £1,150 on the 30th June 1916. The Blackpool Gigantic Wheel Company was taken over by the Blackpool Tower Co. in 1928.

When the Tower Company took over they reviewed the viability of the Big Wheel and decided that tastes had changed and "The present generation demands something more exciting". The wheel also needed some maintenance work and so it was decided to pull it down.

Looking back, one wonders if Sir John Bickerstaffe and his Board were right, after all the Tower is still doing good business and the last of Walter B. Bassett's "Giant Wheels", that in Vienna is still pulling in the crowds to this day.

The Vienna Wheel was built at the same time as the Blackpool Wheel to commemorate the 50th Anniversary of the Emperor Franz Josef's accession to the Austro–Hungarian throne and in its first year carried a quarter of a million passengers. The Austrian wheel is smaller than its big sister in Blackpool being 209' high and although it originally had thirty carriages it now only has sixteen. Like our "Big Wheel" the Viennese wheel is in a famous pleasure garden called the "Prater" and the wheel itself is called the "Riesenrad". It was severely damaged in 1945 by an air raid and it was almost decided to pull it down, but there was such an outcry from the

Dismantling the Big Wheel 1929.

Lowering the 30 ton shaft 1929.

inhabitants of Vienna that the Authorities decided to rebuild it. Some of our readers may have seen the film "The Third Man" in which Orson Wells played the part of Harry Lime and which showed a meeting taking place on the "Riesenrad".

So here we were the unwilling owners of this marvel, which by now was beginning to haunt A.H. and J.D. like a giant monster overshadowing everything.

Eli Ward was convinced that he could have the wheel down for us in ten weeks with the aid of that wonderful new invention the oxy-acetylene cutter. Word spread around that men were being taken on and as the depression had thrown millions out of work there were hundreds of applicants. One man walked forty-two miles, only to find that there were no vacancies, so he had to turn around and walk back home. Sadly, although two hundred and fifty men were employed on building the "Gigantic Wheel", only twenty-three men were needed to dismantle it.

Work started on the dismantling on 5th November 1928 and the cars were taken off first and then auctioned on the spot. The first car was lifted off, not without some difficulty and sold to Mr J. Street for £13, it was put on a strong wagon pulled by three horses and removed to Layton. The wheel was then rotated and the diametrically opposite carriage was removed to preserve the balance. This was sold to Mr T. E. Peckett and others went to a Mr R. Hartley.

Mr Peckett bought most of them when he too was struck by the "Big Wheel Madness" or alternatively, Oscar Spedding had been talking to him, because on the 15th November 1928 the "Blackpool Gazette" reported an interview with Mr Peckett as follows:

'Mr T. E. Peckett of Riverlin, Sussex Road, Blackpool bought twenty-six of the cars and intends to form a "Garden City" with them at Poulton. He has acquired 3 acres of ground at Ray Lane close to Poulton Curve and there he will build "Big Wheel Garden City".

Mr Peckett said "There is a fine pond in the middle of the field which will make an ideal paddling pond for children and the people in my Garden City will have a fine view of the railway.

"I am going to open a banking account for the first child born in my Garden City and each carriage will have in front of it a fine stretch of garden. The carriages will be divided into three rooms, bedroom, sitting room, bathroom and lavatory—I have engaged a man to do the alterations. In the summer time I shall probably invite the Salvation Army band to give concerts in my 'Garden City'.

"Couples who have been living with their Mother-in-law and in other peoples houses will jump at the chance of having a nice 'Big Wheel' carriage all to themselves in my Garden City."

After this pronouncement we presume that the men in the white coats came for him because the Garden City was never built and the carriages were sold for weekend cottages, hen houses, summerhouses, garden sheds, sports pavillions and one was even used as a café. There may still be one or two of the carriages tucked away in the Fylde area. In 1958 one was being used as a summer house in Victoria Road Cleveleys, this was originally bought by Mr Archie Halliwell for seventeen pounds, but it cost him eighteen pounds to cart it away. In 1949 one was still being used as a caravan at Scorton near Garstang and even then one of the windows had the name of a young couple who had made the first trip in 1896 scratched on with a diamond.

So the carriages were sold and dispersed and work then started on dismantling the 1,000 tons of iron and steel, but before much progress had been made the weather intervened and deteriorated so much that work was not possible for weeks on end due to an almost unprecedented series of gales and high winds and the first piece was not removed from the wheel until 8th March 1929.

On the 14th March an oxy-acetylene cutter named Mr Ainsworth was at the top of the wheel waiting for a refill of gas and he looked over the side and immediately became dizzy. He crouched down and clung on to the wooden platforms between the rims of the wheel and could not move. Fortunately his plight was seen by three of his work-mates and they climbed towards him, but it took almost an hour before they could strap him to a stretcher and lower him to the ground. He later recovered and was the only casualty during the whole life of the "Big Wheel", apart from the occasion some years before when some people were accidentally forgotten and left suspended in one of the carriages all night.

Oscar Spedding organised his part of the work quite well and the L.M.S. lorries kept up a busy shuttle service between Adelaide Street and the Railway Goods Yard but time, and the penalty clause, was against them.

The shaft finally down 1929.

It may have been Oscar who hit on the idea of selling medals made out of the metal recovered from the "Big Wheel". They were sold for 6d and 1/- and on one side there was a picture of the wheel and the words "Blackpool Gigantic Wheel" and on the other side were the vital statistics of the wheel. Some of these medals are still in existence.

Most of the men doing the dismantling were ex-Royal Navy, and they worked steadily; at lunch time they retired to the "White Swan Hotel" in Back Hey Street, and there Mr and Mrs Jackson feasted them on a pint of beer, a plate of Lancashire Hot Pot, bread butter and pickles for 4d.

By the 18th May 1929 only the legs and the thirty ton axles were left and finally in June the "Big Wheel" had gone completely. As the "Blackpool Gazette" commented sadly "The Tower has lost its Pal".

The delays caused by the bad weather meant that we could not dismantle it by the specified time and although we were not much over the time it not only wiped out all the profit made by selling the scrap but involved us in a loss of £1,566 4s 2d.

A rather weary Arthur Atkins and J. D. Crichton invited Oscar to Liverpool once more and told him that he would have to give a written undertaking to the Company, pronouncing not to get involved in such ventures in the future, and if he would not agree then very reluctantly they would have to part company. After thinking the matter over for a little time Oscar Spedding told them that this sort of business was in his blood and on the 25th September 1929 he resigned from the Company. By mutual agreement he took over the Gorton scrap yard and set up in business on his own as "Iron Merchant" at 161 Oldham Road, Manchester. In 1935 he moved office to 34 London Road and was at that address until 1944 and from there we have lost track of him.

A. H. Atkins had a real affection for Oscar Spedding and loved telling tales of his adventures.

The running of our Manchester office was then taken over by Mr H. A. Scott Barrett who mainly concentrated on the steel side and refractories.

"Note to Third Edition 1991" –

After reading the above a Mr Unsworth of Bowden contacted us and told us that he was the Auctioneer who sold the Big Wheel in 1928 and he told us that Oscar left his London Road Office at the time of the Manchester Blitz, Christmas 1940, when he moved to Eagle Works, Staley Bridge.

Oscar Spedding died in 1958; he did not make a fortune, but the World is a poorer place without him and in Mr Unsworth's words, "he was a great character".

Ironically in April 1990 a new 180' diameter Ferris wheel was opened in Blackpool close to the Tower.

JOHN CRICHTON JUNIOR AND THE CRICHTON FAMILY

J.D. and Hesther Crichton had six children, Mary (b. 1905), John (b. 1906), Helen (b. 1908), Charles (b. 1909), Margaret (b. 1911) and Patrick (B. 1921). In 1981, the writer visited Mary Potts (née Crichton) then 76 years old; she told the writer how she remembered being sent to stay with William Heap at Elm Mount and she still had the peg doll dressed in it's original clothes, that she used to take to Elm Mount on her visits. Mary said that Elm Mount was rather gloomy for a child, but its saving grace was the garden and William Heap's two servants, Martha and Ivy who were very kind to Mary Crichton and when the elders were upstairs having a nap, Martha, who was Welsh, took Mary into the Drawing Room and taught her to play "chopsticks" on the piano. From this beginning came a love of keyboard playing and Mary eventually studied at the Royal College of Music and became an authority on the harpsichord and for many years taught the harpsichord and gave Bach recitals. Mary Potts died early on Christmas morning 1982 and in Cambridge her friends gave a Bach Memorial concert in her honour.

John Crichton went to Oundle School in 1921, and his brother Charles followed the next year. Charles wanted to be a film producer and so, one day he walked in Alexander Korda's office and announced that he wanted to be a Film Director! He was given a job in the cutting room and eventually, he did became a famous film director and made a number of postwar comedy films including "The Lavender Hill Mob", "Hue & Cry", "The Titchfield Thunderbolt", "He Who Rides The Tiger" and "Divided Heart".

Although now over 80 years of age, Charles Crichton is still producing films for cinema and television and he is a close friend and associate of John Cleese, in spite of an age difference of over 30 years, and they have worked well together for over 10 years' because they have similar tastes in comedy. Their last film, "A Fish Called Wanda" launched at the Edinburgh Festival, in 1988 has been widely praised and is a major success in the U.K. and U.S.A. and was acclaimed as one of the 10 best films made in the 1980's.

John really wanted to be a motor mechanic but his father, J.D. would not hear of this, because he felt that he would not be able to earn enough money as a motor mechanic to support a wife. Eventually John joined Heap & Partners as an engineer, and after a period of training, was sent out to our Newfoundland office to assist Hector Ross and there he met Emma Angel, daughter of our old business friend, Mr Fred Angel, and subsequently they married.

After three years in St John's, John Crichton and his bride, returned to Liverpool and after training with some of our Principals went to run our Manchester office, there he remained until 1935, when J. D. Crichton retired and John was then made a Director and moved back to our Liverpool office once again.

RETIREMENT OF J. D. CRICHTON (1935)

In 1935, J. D. Crichton decided he wanted to retire as he was approaching 60 years of age and had worked for Heaps for over 40 years, mainly on the iron and steel side of our business. J. D. Crichton and A. H. Atkins worked well together for 30 years, and in all that time, they never used their Christian names but always either their surnames or more usually, their initial J.D. and A.H.

In politics, J.D. was a Liberal whereas Uncle William was a staunch Tory. In those days a good Tory considered a Liberal a dangerous Radical, and at times a Tory would cross the street rather than have to greet a Liberal, and vice versa, and there was an unwritten rule that Politics were not discussed in the office. After retiring, J.D. and Hesther Crichton went on a tour round the World and then J.D., at the age of 60 years, became a student and went to Sorbonne in Paris and eventually gained a degree in the French language.

John Douglas Crichton returned to the office in 1941 so that his son John could join the Navy, and during the war he did a great deal of work for the Free French Forces in the U.K. and after the war he called in to see A.H. at regular intervals until he died in his 80's.

GEORGE'S DOCK BUILDING (1936–1941) (1941–1945 part)

After J. D. Crichton had retired at the end of 1935 A.H. decided that we would have to look for cheaper accommodation because although India Buildings were splendid offices we had suffered through the world slump and had to cut our cloth accordingly.

The first Mersey Tunnel had recently been completed and one of the ventilation shafts had a small office block included in its structure and although the Mersey Tunnel Joint Committee occupied most of the offices they were not using a suite of offices in the basement and so they were advertised as being to let and offers were invited.

A. H. and L. C. Ashcroft walked over to see George's Dock Building as it is called, and thought that the offices were ideal. They were in the basement and at the foot of the stairs there were two further small rooms that we could use as stores.

On returning to India Buildings they submitted a sealed tender offering £1 per square yard for the 127 square yards of offices and £5 p.a. for the 8 square yards of stores. Our offer was the highest submitted and we moved into Georges Dock Building on the 6th January 1936 and saved over two hundred pounds a year in rent.

Compare the architecture of the ventilation shafts for the first Mersey Tunnel built over

*George's Dock Building 1935.
Our office was through the
door on the extreme left.*

forty years ago with that of the shafts for the second tunnel opened in June 1971. The latest shafts are concrete monstrosities more fitting for a steelworks, whereas Georges Dock Building and the other ventilation shafts of the old tunnel have style and grace.

A newcomer to our staff at this time was Mrs E. M. Roughton who joined as a temporary secretary to J. D. Crichton in 1935, and stayed until she retired in 1965, she joined Miss M. L. Ellis. who came as Secretary to Mr Atkins in 1933 and who eventually became our Company Secretary and played an important part in our history, Miss Ellis retired in 1969. We were lucky to have the services of these two outstanding women at the same time.

*George's Dock Building from the
Dock Road. The overhead
railway in the background, like
the horse, now gone, alas.*

CHAPTER 8

World War II

THE 1939–45 WAR

After returning to Liverpool early in 1919, A. H. Atkins and Sir Lawrence Bragg corresponded regularly and they saw each other periodically, indeed they and their families became close friends.

A.H.A. retained his interest in Sound Ranging and in 1929 put forward some new ideas for wind and temperature correction which were considered by Professor Bragg and the War Office, but a new type of career Army officer with a petrified mind had taken over the development of Sound Ranging.

In 1939 when it was obvious that a Second World War was coming Professor Bragg visited Larkhill to have a look at the latest methods of Sound Ranging and he was horrified with what he found. It had become far too complicated and was, in his opinion, far inferior to the equipment that was being used in 1918. Professor Bragg then wrote to the War Office telling them of his fears and suggesting that the War Office should write to the two most successful Sound Rangers of the First War, Philpots and Atkins, inviting them to give an independent report on the new "improved" equipment. This was done and the letter to A. H. Atkins was sent a couple of days before war was declared and A.H. agreed immediately.

On the 19th September 1939 Arthur Atkins travelled down to Cambridge University and met Professor Bragg, Mr Philpot and a Captain Hodgkinson in the Cavendish Laboratories and subsequently they saw a demonstration of the latest Sound Ranging Equipment at Larkhill and later that month at Foulness.

On the 2nd October 1939 A.H.A. wrote to the War Office telling them that the new equipment was far too "gadgety" and recommended that a fresh start should be made by going back to the 1918 instrument and developing from that simple, but effective, device. That being done he then returned to his desk and his business.

It was obvious to Professor Bragg that the pre-war Army Officers responsible for the changes were not capable of straightening out the mess and so he wrote to the War Office saying that in his opinion it would be an enormous help if they could persuade A. H. Atkins to take it over because he thought Atkins "so eminently sound on practical details".

Lt. Col. Sir Henry Imber-Terry replied "I hope very much we shall be able to get Atkins because he is just the fellow I want to run a show which has every sign of becoming quite big."

Accordingly the War Office wrote to A.H.A. and asked him if he would rejoin the Army to sort out the Sound Ranging mess. After making arrangements regarding the running of our office A.H.A. put on his uniform again in February 1940 and at the age of sixty joined the Royal Engineers at Larkhill.

It was one thing asking A.H. to straighten things out but quite another thing achieving it, because he was put under the Command of the very officers who had caused the mess, and they did everything they could to stop Major Atkins taking action. Their first step was to keep him well away from the Sound Ranging instruments themselves and they tried to side-track him by putting him in charge of training men in Sound Ranging, but with their inefficient and complicated instruments.

A.H. had however been invited by the War Office to improve Sound Ranging instruments and technique and he was a match for the "Establishment" dinosaurs, because in secret, he and Sir Lawrence Bragg set to work on new instruments which were developed from the 1918 models and because they were denied facilities at Larkhill they had some of these instruments made by students working for Sir Lawrence at Cambridge University.

Several times A.H. almost despaired of getting anything done and the Army "red tape" infuriated him. On the 23rd April 1940 he wrote to Professor Bragg and told him that he had to give a one and a half hour lecture to a number of officers on how to send in reports to the C.B.O. "In the last war we just rang up and told him that certain hostile guns were active and left it at that, but there are now about one hundred and twenty forms to fill in."

While our officers were learning how to fill in forms the German Panzers unleashed their power and might and the British and French Armies reeled back, France fell and the British Army escaped by the miracle of Dunkirk.

The trauma of Dunkirk and the coming to power of Winston Churchill galvanised new thought and action, and although the fossilised officers still continued to resist, they were slowly pushed to one side because Professor Bragg saw to it that A.H.A. was supported by the War Office wherever possible.

By July 1940 the Germans had brought up long range guns on to the French coast and they started shelling the South Coast of England. The R.A.F. had the power to attack but it was essential to first locate the gun emplacements, but as the English Channel was in between it was necessary to develop new methods of long distance Sound Ranging.

On Wednesday 4th July 1940 a meeting was held in Room 94, Shell Mex House, London, which was then occupied by the Ministry of Supply to see what could be done about the long range German guns. Those present were:

Chairman: Lt. Col. H. M. Paterson, A5., M. of S.
Dr C. T. Paris, D.D.S.R., M. of S.
Col. P. J. K. Warren, O.B.
Major G. H. Hinds, O.B.
Professor W. L. Bragg, Cavendish Laboratory, Cambridge University
Capt. T. G. Hodgkinson, A.D.E.E.
Lt. Col. J. A. Leigh, R.A.S.S.
Major K. F. Mackey Lewis, R.A.S.S.
Major A. H. Atkins, R.A.S.S.
Major R. B. Eastwood, 1st S.R. Bty. R.A.
Lt. P. de K. Dykes, 1st S.R. Bty. R.A.
Col. G. Rutledge, D.N.O. Admiralty
Major C. T. D. Lindsay (Secretary), A5., M. of S.

The meeting was given all the information known at that time about the large German coastal guns which was:

Calibre—11"
Muzzle velocity—5,900 ft/sec.
Max. range—120 miles
Elevation—52°
Vertical height—225,000 ft.
Minimum velocity or trajectory—3,000 ft/sec.
Angle of descent—56½°
Time of flight—237 sec.

It was decided that urgent work should take place at Larkhill to develop new instruments and techniques but as one or two of the officers present were the "gadgety minded" men, this posed a problem for Bragg and Atkins, and although things were slowly improving they decided to continue the good work by having modified instruments made by the students at the Cavendish and A.H.A. quietly arranged for testing to be done at Larkhill.

Even at that stage of our country's peril A. H. Atkins was still not given a completely free hand and in August he wrote to Professor Bragg "The work being done in Cambridge will be a great help as we are not supposed to do any experimental work, but rather to use our equipment for training men on practical work."

The work continued throughout 1940, in spite of every obstacle, and slowly new instruments and methods were developed and these were to have a most important bearing on the future conduct of the war.

Early in World War II many scientists and Army officers thought that Sound Ranging was finished and would be superceded by Radiolocation, as Radar was known then, but Bragg whilst acknowledging the importance of Radar felt that S.R. had an important contribution to make. The critics argued that whereas in the First War battles were largely fought from static positions, the Second War would be a battle of movement and therefore S.R. would be useless.

The war in the desert between the 8th Army and Rommel's Afrika Corps proved that Bragg and his colleagues were right and the critics wrong. The desert war was indeed very mobile at times, as first the British, and then the German and Italian armour pushed across vast distances of the desert; but in between the pushes there were quite long periods of static warfare when the artillery came into action and that was when Sound Ranging came into its own. According to one witness who wrote to Bragg, 'Our men in the desert handled the Sound Ranging with skill, determination and incredible bravery."

At this time Major Atkins's only son Jim was in the desert as a young Captain with the 2nd Gurkhas who formed part of the 8th Army and in June during a particularly swift dash across the desert they nearly captured one of Rommel's senior commanders, General von Arnim. He just escaped but they captured the considerable stock of champagne which he carried with him and that evening the 2nd Gurka's mess had a very merry time.

Sad to relate that Jim Atkins was killed later when the Gurkhas were battling for Mount Casino in Italy.

The work on the development of improved, simple, Sound Ranging instruments continued in England and other scientists joined in, such as Professor, later Sir John, Cockcroft—he and Professor E. N. de C. Andrade made important contributions. Even the ploy of pushing Major Atkins into training was used to advantage because quietly he trained the young men in the simpler techniques and later they put this to good use.

In January 1942, John Crichton, one of our Directors, was killed in the Mediterranean and his father J. D. Crichton who had returned to temporarily run the office felt that he could not carry on and so Major Atkins was released from the Army and returned to Liverpool but he was retained to act in an advisory capacity afterwards. He had been at Larkhill for two and a half years and much of that time had been a struggle but his work was accomplished and Britain once again led the world in Sound Ranging.

After the desert war was won, Sound Ranging was used throughout the battle for Italy and later in the struggle for Europe and the work done at Larkhill and Cambridge bore fruit.

In 1944 in a last desperate gamble, Hitler launched his secret weapons against England, first the V1 flying bomb and then the V2 rockets. The British knew that new weapons existed but not their precise form, but when the first V1 was launched it was detected immediately, not by Radar, but by Sound Ranging.

On the 8th September 1944 the first V2 rocket fell on Chiswick at 6-43 pm and sixteen seconds later the second fell on Epping: a new type of warfare had started. Within minutes of the launch a report was ready for Churchill giving the time of the launch and the trajectory—again all plotted by the improved Sound Ranging instruments.

The Germans kept quiet about the new weapon until 6th November and Churchill in his book "Triumph and Tragedy" said, "I did not feel the need for a public statement until November 10th. The news media had put it about that the Chiswick explosion was caused by a gas main exploding and so after the official announcement on the 10th November this rocket went down in Cockney history as 'The Flying gas main'."

In April 1945 Sir Lawrence Bragg was invited by the War Office to visit Belgium to see Sound Rangers detecting V1 and V2 weapons and on the 24th April he wrote to A.H. "What impressed me was the short time in which it had all been done. The apparatus on the line system is standard telephone type worked directly with Standard Telephone and Cables". All the gimmicks and "gadgetry" had gone and Sound Ranging was once again a superb method of detection, simple and effective.

Altogether Germany launched 1,300 rockets against Southern England and every single one of them was plotted by sound ranging equipment.

The following letter written by Sir Lawrence Bragg to Arthur Atkins after the war sums up A.H.'s contribution. The "Ellis" referred to in the letter was Professor Ellis, Scientific Advisor the War Office.

Cavendish Laboratory,
Cambridge
18th December 1945

"Dear Atkins

Your heart would have warmed if you had heard what Ellis, who is scientific advisor to the War Office, had to say about Sound Ranging. He was one of our guests at an annual Cavendish dinner, which we have started again after the war. He has been analysing records of all the battles. He made a very nice reference to it in his speech, saying how it had saved the day both in the cross Channel battle and in locating the V2 trajectories, and afterwards he said to me that he could not sufficiently praise the people who had studied it and developed it in the first years of the war, when it might so easily have been discarded altogether with all the new radar methods—and that it had turned out in the end to be a real war winner. I'm sure you would have felt that all the work you put in at Larkhill was well worth while because you were the key man who saw it all through. I think that its value, which was fairly obvious in the first reports which came through, has shown up even more clearly in the analyses which have now been made. I wish you could meet Ellis, I'd like you to hear it all first hand. He had been going into the figures for all the big attacks, assessing the results of counter battery work and so forth.

A very merry Xmas to you all. Do come to Cambridge again and drink port with the dons. I see a bit of Philpot, we work together as advisers to the anti-submarine establishment, and we were talking about you when we were travelling together to Scotland last week."

So Arthur Henry Atkins' Army career which started in the Boer War with Cavalry, finished with a weapon that will dominate man for the forseeable future—the rocket.

"THE BLITZ"

The main weight of Hitler's aerial attack against the civilian population of this country was suffered by London and the South of England, but although the German air attacks against Merseyside were of comparatively short duration, in concentrated ferocity they matched any onslaught launched against the British Isles, and the people of Merseyside showed that they could behave with the same courage and determination as the Londoner.

The importance of Liverpool to the British war effort was obvious and for this reason she was given special consideration by the German Luftwaffe.

In his memoirs Churchill wrote that the dominating factor throughout the war was the Battle of the Atlantic. Half our food and almost all our raw materials needed to wage war had to be shipped over the seas to this country. London our largest port was largely immobilised because it was too dangerous to take ships through to the East Coast and so the main load was taken by our second largest port, Liverpool, and those ports of the Clyde.

A second reason for Liverpool's importance was that the Battle of the Atlantic was directed from there. At the beginning of the war the Head Quarters for Western Approaches was in Plymouth, but with characteristic shrewdness Churchill could see that Britain's main artery would lie in the North and so on the 4th August 1940 he wrote to the Admiralty suggesting that the H.Q. should be moved North. There was some opposition to Churchill's view but in September the Admiralty agreed, started to plan the move and in February 1941 the H.Q. of Western Approaches under the command of Sir Percy Noble, was moved to Derby House, Chapel Street, Liverpool.

The Battle of Britain began on 8th August 1940 when the German Air Force sent wave after wave of bombers carrying high explosive bombs and incendiaries and dive bombers against London. The next day 9th August a small raid was made on Liverpool and the first bomb to fall on Liverpool fell on the L.M.S. Goods Station in Carlyle Street. The following night the sirens wailed just before midnight and at half past twelve a string of bombs fell on Prenton in the Wirral. Again the following evening there was some bombing of the Wirral and seven high explosive bombs fell on Wallasey resulting in 32 casualties.

So throughout August, September, October and November there were light raids on Merseyside averaging one every other night and bombs fell on Liverpool, Wallasey, Birkenhead, Meols and Port Sunlight. Although these raids were modest they were tiring because people did not get a proper nights sleep. They would go down to their shelter if they had an Anderson shelter in the garden, or if they didn't have a garden they used a street shelter or tried to sleep under the stairs or under the steel "table shelters" that some houses were equipped with.

Unlike German cities we did not have many deep purpose-made air raid shelters which was typical of our unpreparedness for war. It was always surprising that the Germans were able to live through the sustained bombing by the Allies in the later stages of the war, until we discovered the existence of the deep, purpose made, reinforced concrete shelters that could accommodate whole populations. The Anderson shelter was made of corrugated steel and was really a small steel shed sunk into the earth three feet and with a couple of feet of soil or sandbags on the top and back and a blast wall of sandbags or an earth bank in front. They were somewhat damp and in some areas tended to flood but they were extremely effective and the writer, who was a child in the London area at the time, saw one huge crater with an Anderson shelter right on the edge of the hole so that one side formed part of the wall of the crater and yet the family inside although badly shaken, were alive and unharmed.

On the night of 28th November the first full scale attack was made on Merseyside; the sirens sounded just before 7-30 in the evening and for the next two and a half hours there was heavy bombing and two hundred people were killed.

The next heavy raids were the "Christmas raids" on 20th December the sirens sounded at 6-30 pm and from that time until 4 am there was continuous and intensive bombing of Merseyside by high explosive and incendiary bombs. There were many fires started, one of them being a gasometer we had supplied to Linacre Road Gasworks in the nineteen twenties. A number of small fires were started around our office and the neighbouring Cunard Building and Dock Board Office sustained some damage, but luckily this time we escaped. The worst incident that

The blitz. May 1941. Queen Victoria looks out over the devastated centre of Liverpool and is not amused by the half finished street air raid shelter in the bottom right hand corner of the photograph.

141

Watching bodies that had been taken from the wreckage being photographed for identification. Liverpool May 1941.

night was when a series of five railway arches that were being used as air raid shelters were hit and later forty-two bodies were recovered.

The following evening there was another heavy raid from 7 pm until 10-30 pm and again from midnight to 3-30 am and this was even more intense than the previous night's raid.

The next night the main attack was switched to Manchester, and Liverpool had a comparatively quiet night and then there was a lull with only three raids in January 1941 and two in February and all remained quiet until March. Then the German Air Force made what Churchill called "The Luftwaffe's Tour of the Ports", starting on the 8th, 9th, 10th and 11th by saturation bombing of Portsmouth, on the 11th they attacked Manchester, on the 12th Merseyside and the 13th and 14th the Clyde where 2,000 people were killed.

The Merseyside attack on the 12th March started at 9 pm when the first German aircraft dropped parachute flares over the Merseyside area and bombing started almost immediately. The main weight fell on Birkenhead and Wallasey, 250 people were killed in Birkenhead and 160 in Wallasey. Much of the old property in Borough Road, Birkenhead was flattened and Birkenhead General Hospital had to be evacuated. This time Liverpool escaped comparatively lightly and there were only 101 killed in March.

April was very quiet but on Thursday 1st May 1941 the Germans started a ferocious attack on Merseyside. It began with a comparatively light raid between 11 pm and 1-30 am and there were about one hundred incidents in Liverpool and nine in Bootle, but the next night was a brilliantly moonlit May night and this time the Germans did not need flares.

The attack started at 10-45 pm and went on continuously for four hours with wave after wave of German bombers; the air was filled with the whistle of high explosive bombs dropping and of the bark of anti-aircraft guns, the crashing of shrapnel from our own anti aircraft shells on roof tops and the crump of bombs falling a little way off and the enormous explosion of sound as bombs fell nearby. Interspersed in this cacophony of sound was the tinkling crashes of thousands of incendiary bombs falling on roofs tops or roads, the thermite they contained catching fire immediately on impact. Rather attractive to look at, some 3″ in diameter and just over a foot long, the magnesium alloy case was painted silver and the fins at the top were olive green.

If the firewatchers could catch them in time they could be extinguished with sand bags or the use of a stirrup pump might be able to contain the fire, but the great problem was that so many were dropped at one time that it was impossible to tackle all the fires.

Our old offices, India Buildings after the blitz. Badly damaged but the flag still flies.

The badly damaged Goree Piazza in front of Cunard Buildings.

Saturday 3rd May 1941. Georges Dock Building, centre, still standing proud after Friday night's air attack during which our fire fighters spent all night on the roof and saved the building. When our men tried to leave the building in the morning the doors were blocked and so Mr Piatt and Mr Kirkland had to wind their way down the stairs and escaped through the Mersey Tunnel back into Liverpool. Their first task was to buy hats for themselves because they were going back into the office at the base of Georges Dock Building, and war or no war, standards had to be maintained!

That evening Mr Piatt our Company Secretary and Mr Kirkland our refractories salesman were on the roof of Georges Dock Building on Firewatching duty. By midnight the whole area near to the Pierhead was ablaze and they were in the centre of a huge conflagration and they were kept busy attending to the incendiary bombs. Mr Piatt had been issued with a steel helmet, as had all firewatchers, but he disdained to wear it and instead wore his customary bowler hat that was green with age. The air was full of the shriek of falling bombs and the terrific crash as they exploded, all around the buildings were blazing furiously, the Mersey Docks and Harbour Board still standing but with smoke pouring out of its windows, the Cunard Building and worst of all the Corn Exchange Building which was like a furnace with flames leaping high into the sky. Suddenly a bomb dropped quite close on the Goree Piazza and the blast blew Mr Piatts bowler hat clean off and away into the swirling smoke blackened air. He stopped and then danced with rage and shook his fist at the bombers overhead and then resumed his firefighting.

The bomb that had fallen on the Goree Piazza had hit a pub at the end and as sometimes happened in dockside pubs in wartime the customers had lingered over their drinks longer than they should have, they received a direct hit and there were many casualties. An ambulance driven by a young girl picked its way through the burning streets and just as it reached the Goree it too was hit and the girl was killed outright.

All Friday night the fires raged, many of them out of control, smoke and dust were everywhere and the firemen, the A.R.P. wardens, the ambulance drivers, the policemen and the firewatchers fought through the blazing shambles to rescue the wounded and to bring out the dead and they did their duty with dirt streaked clothes, black faces and red rimmed eyes.

When morning eventually came a very grimy Mr Piatt and Mr Kirkland looked out on a smoking scene of almost total devastation. Miraculously the noble group of buildings at the

Cook Street, Liverpool, May 1941. Bank Chambers are on the left. Our offices from 1870 to 1876.

*Looking towards George's Dock
building May 1941.*

Liverpool May 1941.

145

Pier Head. The Liver, Cunard and Mersey Dock buildings were still standing and Georges Dock Building where our own office was, had been badly damaged by high explosive blast, fire and water but had survived. As they made their way down from the roof the inside was a wreck and the doors leading to the street outside were blocked by wreckage and rubble, but Mr Piatt and Mr Kirkland were not defeated, nor trapped, because they climbed over the debris down to the stairway leading to the Mersey Tunnel below which our staff were supposed to use as an air raid shelter during daylight raids. Down the stairs they went and came out of the door set in the side of the main tunnel near to the large ventilation grilles; then they walked out of the main entrance to the Mersey Tunnel and back into burning Liverpool.

After a clean-up Mr Piatt and Mr Kirkland decided that the first thing to do was to buy new hats because Mr Kirkland's was a casualty in Georges Dock Building; they found a shop that was open early and although Mr Piatt was lucky and found a hat to fit him, Mr Kirkland had trouble.

In these days our staff worked every other Saturday and it was Miss Ellis's turn to work, she arrived at Georges Dock Building and was surveying the wreckage and the little groups of people standing before a smouldering ruin that was their office yesterday, when Mr Piatt and the tall Mr Kirkland walked around the corner with very grave expressions on their faces, both wearing hats but Mr Kirkland's was sitting like a pimple on the top of his head.

After the firemen and demolition men had cleared most of the wreckage away our office was found to be in a very sorry state, but it had not been fully destroyed because it was in the basement. Our staff had then to clear up the rubbish and broken glass, the smashed partitions, the wet smouldering rubbish and to salvage what they could of our filing cabinets, furniture and the safe which we still have; but for months afterwards there was glass in our files.

The Heinkels and Dornier bombers came back the next night and every night for a full week and one of Britains main arteries was badly cut and bleeding profoundly. In spite of all however moral was as good as anywhere in Britain and that war time joker "Lord Haw Haw" was greeted with derision when he announced over the German radio that "they are flying the white flag in Scotland Road". In those days there was probably the greatest concentration of pubs in the land in Scotland Road and, as any Magistrate presiding over the early morning courts in any of the world's seaports would confirm, the residents of this celebrated

Huskisson Dock, Liverpool, after the ammunition ship S.S. "Malakand" had exploded, May 1941.

146

thoroughfare were not noted for diffidence when it came to a fight. It took more than the might of Goering's Luftwaffe to knock the spirit out of Scotland Road — it took the post war planners of Liverpool who amongst many other crimes against humanity destroyed a community and left a wilderness devoted to the motor car in its place.

Early one morning at 1-55 am a land mine gently floated to earth supported by its light green silken cords and parachute and exploded on the Junior Technical School in Dunning Road. The three storey building collapsed on top of the basement air raid shelter where 300 women and children were sheltering. The coal fired boilers in the basement exploded and added to the agony. After days of toil the rescuers eventually pulled out 164 dead and 96 badly injured people making this one of the worst single incidents in the war.

Homes, churches of all denominations, schools, factories and ships were destroyed or badly damaged, the docks were full of ships containing food, steel, oil and ammunition and the story of one of these vessels the S.S. Malakand commanded by Captain Howard Cooke Kinley, should go down in history.

The S.S. "Malakand" sailed into the Mersey from U.S.A. loaded with 1,000 tons of high explosive and docked in Huskisson Dock at the beginning of May. At 11-15 pm on Saturday 3rd May one of the German planes shot down a barrage balloon and the gigantic blazing, partially inflated, elephantine monster fell on the foredeck over No. 1 hold and started a great blaze. All around them the dock sheds were ablaze but the crew started the pumps and in 15 minutes heroically put this fire out. Whilst they were fighting this fire, seven high explosive bombs fell on the neighbouring sheds and the air was full of showering incendiary bombs, a number fell on the deck where they again started fires and once again the crew dealt with them.

The sheds on the East side were now utterly demolished and the ruins were blazing fiercely, the shed on the south side was like an inferno, and the flames enveloped the S.S. "Malakand" so that the heat blistered the paint near the men and the heat and smoke made breathing difficult. Under Captain Kinley's directions the hoses were turned on to the sheds but they were quite useless.

Captain Kinley then went to get help from the Auxiliary Fire Service, but found their station deserted because they were out fighting fires in other sheds, but eventually he found them and spoke to their chief, Fire Officer John Lappin, and told him of the "Malakand's" cargo in hatches 1, 3 and 6. Officer Lappin immediately telephoned the A.F.S. H.Q. and told them of the situation and although he had not enough men and equipment they moved to the vicinity of the ship. The whole time the area was under ceaseless bombardment from the Heinkel's and dive bombers.

It was apparent that the fires were too great for the available men and equipment and Captain Kinley warned John Lappin of the danger, but they continued to fight the blazing buildings as long as possible.

Around 3 am when it was obvious that the fires could not be controlled, John Lappin and Captain Kinley went to the A.F.S. Head Quarters for more equipment and they were loaned some oxy-acetylene cutting equipment, because they had decided to try to cut a hole in the port side of the ship to try and scuttle her. The firemen were still fighting the fires enveloping the "Malakand" when they returned but as they were approaching the vessel, she exploded with a fantastic flash and roar. Looking at the scene of devastation it seems impossible that anybody could live; there were a number of casualties, the driver of the fire engine that had arrived from Speke was killed as were several of the ship's crew, and most of the other crewmen and firemen were injured including Captain Kinley. They had fought all night against impossible odds with a complete disregard to their own safety and welfare. After reading of the men's exploits and looking at a photograph of the devastation, which residents of these Isles would not be proud to be British?

In another part of the City at Clubmoor, a train loaded with ammunition was hit and set on fire, a number of railwaymen and police realising the danger to the immediate community, started to uncouple those wagons that were on fire, when first one wagon exploded and then another and the air was filled with the noise of explosions and the shriek and whine of lethal flying shrapnel. In spite of the enormous danger they carried on with their task and were about to shunt part of the train away when the blast from one explosion blew Signalman Peter Stringer out of his box to the floor below, although badly shaken he climbed back into the signal box and set the signals so that George Roberts and another thirty-four year old, John Guinan and the other heroes could shunt most of the ammunition out of danger.

At 5 am on Thursday 7th May the last of the Dorniers and Heinkels left the smoking ruins of Merseyside and although people did not realise it, they would not return because Goring had switched the attack elsewhere and Churchill felt "thankful that the Germans did not persevere on this tormented target".

From the mouth of the estuary to Garston, ships, warehouses and dockside sheds were ablaze, ships carrying not only ammunition but wheat, sugar, meat, bacon and other foods for the defenders' of these islands. Out of one hundred and fourteen berths, sixty-nine were out of action and the tonnage landed was cut to a quarter because there was 40,000 tons of shipping sunk in the port.

The devastation was tremendous and the casualties appalling; in the comparatively few days of blitzkreig Merseyside suffered one per cent of all British casualties, including Army, Navy, Air Force, Merchant Navy and civilians in all theatres of war during the six year duration of World War II. There were 3,995 killed outright and 3,489 seriously injured; in one week, 2,315 high explosive bombs fell on the area, 119 landmines and millions of incendiary bombs. In Bootle, 80 per cent of all the houses in the Borough were damaged by bomb blast or fire; Liverpool and Litherland had 40 per cent of its dwellings totalling 90,000 houses destroyed or damaged and in Birkenhead no less than 25,000 out of its 34,000 houses had suffered some damage or had been destroyed and in the whole area there were 70,000 homeless people.

The blitz on Merseyside was a major engagement of the war and as Winston Churchill wrote after the war was over, "Had the enemy persisted, the Battle of the Atlantic would have been more closely run than it was, but as usual he turned away".

After our staff had salvaged as much as possible of the office furniture, filing cabinets and stocks of Dunham traps, Securex fittings and Saunders Valves, we were in business again immediately but although we argued with the Mersey Tunnel Joint Committee we had to leave the building as they did not consider it was safe. So Mr Piatt and John Crichton started the almost impossible task of finding new office accommodation in Liverpool, but hundreds of others were on the same trail and so the search was widened and widened until eventually Mr Piatt found two basement rooms in Grosvenor House at the bottom of Watergate in Chester.

So after seventy-five years in Liverpool we had to move to the lovely city of Chester, but we still retained our lease on the George's Dock offices and later A. H. Atkins prevailed on the Mersey Tunnel Committee to allow us to use part of the office after emergency repairs had been carried out and he used this office when he was on leave and later when he came out of the Army he used George's Dock which he preferred to the rather tatty Chester office.

Tatty though it might have been at that time, Grosvenor House is not without interest as it is on the site of the Roman bath house and one of the west walls contains a small Roman arch which was the arch leading into the first of a series of hypocausts. When Grosvenor House was being constructed in 1779 they discovered two rooms with hypocausts and one of these had blue, red and white mosaic flooring, but unhappily they were destroyed by the builders.

GROSVENOR HOUSE, CHESTER (1941–1945)

On the 23rd July we moved into Grosvenor House and occupied two small basement rooms which we used as offices and there was an adjoining wine cellar that was converted into a store for our stocks of Dunham traps, Saunders Valves and Securex fittings.

Not long after moving in, John Crichton left to join the Navy, and although his father J.D. came in for a few months he found it difficult to pick up the threads. The main inside work was done by E. S. Piatt, Miss Ellis and Mrs Roughton and the outside sales and technical work was handled by L. C. Ashcroft working on Dunham heating equipment, steam engines, turbines and air compressors for defence establishments. Mr Kirkland, who had the important job of making

Grosvenor House, Watergate, Chester. Our offices were the two basement rooms on the left and the wine cellar on the right was our stores. (1941–45.)

Right to left—Miss Ellis, Mrs. Roughton and The Author, Britannia House, December 1975.

sure that the steelworks were kept supplied with refractories, travelled all over the country advising steel companies on refractory matters.

Shortage of staff meant that all our people had to do jobs that were done by others in peacetime and to Miss Ellis and Mrs Roughton fell the unusual task of prepairing food for the staff on a "Baby Belling" electric cooker. One Saturday morning after everybody had left Mrs Roughton was just leaving on her way to the hairdresser when a load of Saunders Valves arrived. She unlocked the office and with the help of the driver off-loaded the valves and then carried them down to our basement stores. Similarly in the evening our two ladies would carry quite heavy parcels of Dunham traps or Saunders Valves to the Post Office if the men were unable to go.

At this time Mr Atkins was in the Army at Larkhill and sometimes Miss Ellis had to take papers down to Salisbury Plain for A.H. to attend to and to get various correspondence up to date. On one of these occasions she was staying with the Atkins, who were renting a house at that time, when Professor Bragg sent a message that he was going to visit them that day to discuss some Sound Ranging matter with A.H. Mrs Atkins was in a dilemma because being wartime there was not much food in the house and certainly nothing suitable for a Nobel Prize Winner however simple and human he might be.

A little while later Mrs Atkins was standing in the kitchen discussing the problem with Miss Ellis when A.H. entered the room holding a dead chicken by the neck. The sliding door on the chicken coop was faulty, he explained, and by the intervention of Divine Providence, the catch failed just as the unfortunate hen poked her head out and the heavy door killed her instantly.

Without a word Mrs Atkins took the dead bird and rushed off to the yard to pluck it, and that evening Sir Lawrence Bragg dined like a king off Coq-au-Vin, but if it had not been for the intervention of Providence he might have gone hungry!

Our Newfoundland office was very good at organising food parcels for our staff, particularly at Christmas, when each member of our staff received a food parcel.

It is an indication of the ridiculous way our Post War Government loved State control for its own sake and kept rationing in this country long after it had been dispensed with even by Germany and Italy, that when the writer joined the firm in 1952 it was still necessary for the food parcels to be sent and they only stopped when a new Government came in and scrapped all the unnecessary rationing. These post war years were most important because Europe was free to make progress at a time when we were held back by controls and permits for everything, and Britain has paid a very high price for the Socialist State. Still the writer must take his share of the blame—he voted for it at that time. We wanted, and still want, to build a new Jerusalem but it is now clear that Socialism almost ruined the United Kingdom.

LT. JOHN CRICHTON, R.N.V.R.

One of the conditions A.H. laid down when he agreed to rejoin the Army was that John Crichton, who was then in his thirties, should not be called up. The War Office agreed, because they were so anxious to get A.H.'s services. In 1941 however, John Crichton was most unhappy at having to stay behind looking after the firm and so he made arrangements for his father J.D. to come out of retirement, and for a monthly report of the activities of all our Agencies to be sent with him no matter where he was; and then satisfied that all would be well he joined the Navy with the rank of Engineering Lieutenant as he was already in the Royal Navy Volunteer Reserve.

After a period of training, John joined H.M.S. "Galatea" which had been part of the 2nd Cruiser Squadron based at Rosyth and had taken a gallant part in the Norwegian Campaign, but after John joined her she sailed for the Mediterranean to become part of Admiral Cunningham's 15th Cruiser Squadron based on Alexandria.

The war in North Africa was at its height and first Rommel and then the British 8th Army gained the upper hand in the desert war, but towards the end of 1941 the Royal Navy started to inflict devastating blows on the Axis supply convoys that sailed between Sicily and North Africa. In September 1941, 28 per cent of all cargoes shipped to Rommel's forces in Libya were sunk and after appeals by Mussolini, Hitler personally intervened and in September ordered Admiral Dönitz to transfer six "U" boats from the Atlantic into the Mediterranean, but in October the losses were 21 per cent, and then in November no less than 63 per cent, he again intervened personally and ordered four more "U" boats to be transferred from the Atlantic to the Mediterranean theatre of war. This personal intervention by Adolph Hitler had a profound influence on this company because one of the submarines transferred from the Atlantic was the U-557 with her young crew.

The new "U" boats quickly achieved success because U-81 sank that "much sunk" Cammell Laird built aircraft carrier "Ark Royal". The Germans had frequently claimed to have sunk it when they had not, but the U-81 was successful.

Twelve days later the 15th Cruiser Squadron, including H.M.S. "Galatea" were out looking for prey. Admiral Cunningham had taken his battle squadron, "Queen Elizabeth", "Barham" and "Valient" to sea, when they were intercepted by U-331 which penetrated a screen of destroyers and hit the "Barham" with three torpedoes and she sank taking 56 officers and 812 ratings down with her.

On the 15th December five supply ships for Rommel's Afrika Korps sailed from Taranto in three separate convoys. The situation in North Africa was so serious for the Axis forces that to protect these vessels there were no less than one battleship, a close escort of eight destroyers, two or three cruisers with three destroyers in support as well as the "Littorio" and "Vittorio Veneto" with four destroyers in close support. At the same time two light cruisers "Da Barbiano" and "Di Giussano" loaded cases of petrol at Palermo and escorted by a high speed motor torpedo boat made ready for the quick dash across the straits from Sicily to Libya.

British reconnaissance planes spotted the ships and four destroyers "Sikh", "Maori", "Legion" and H.M. Netherland Ship "Isaac Sweers" were despatched at high speed from Gibralta. Force "K" from Malta comprising the cruisers "Aurora" and "Penelope" and two destroyers "Lance" and "Lively" were ordered to leave Malta but this order had to be delayed because of Malta's shortage of fuel oil.

Commander G. H. Stokes in charge of the four destroyers from Gibralta brilliantly intercepted the enemy fleet and H.M.S. "Sikh" torpedoed "Da Barbiano" and then the "Di Giussano" and then the destroyers resumed their passage to Malta.

While this battle was going on, the heavily escorted Taranto convoy was getting underway and so Admiral Cunningham ordered the 15th Cruiser Squadron, "Naiad", "Galatea" and "Euryalus" and nine destroyers to sail from Alexandria to intercept the enemy. There were insufficient destroyers to allow the battleships to sail and as the cruisers only mounted 6″ guns they were well outgunned by the huge enemy force. To overcome this problem Admiral Cunningham resorted to a ruse by sending the fast minelayer "Abdiel" out to sea and while strict radio silence was enforced in Alexandria H.M.S. "Abdiel" created a radio diversion by pretending that the battle squadron was at sea.

The ruse was successful and on the 13th December the Italian convoys were recalled and in the confusion, two of the Italian supply ships collided violently and although they reached harbour they were out of action for many months. Two more supply vessels were torpedoed by H.M. Submarine "Upright" and finally the "Vittorio Veneto" was torpedoed and badly damaged by H.M. Submarine "Urge" and was out of action for months.

Off Alexandria however U-557 positioned herself in the swept channel waiting for the battle squadron to return and she lay there submerged with only her periscope showing above the waves. The battle squadron did not return, because it was safe in harbour but the 15th Cruiser Squadron did, and on the 15th December the "U" boat commander picked up H.M.S. "Galatea" in his sights, waited until the range was point blank and then sent a salvo of torpedoes crashing into her hull.

H.M.S. "Galatea" sank and only 13 officers and 141 ratings were rescued and 22 officers and 448 ratings went down with the ship including Lt. John Crichton, Director of Heap & Partners. A ship's engine room is not the safest place to be if she is torpedoed.

John Crichton left a son John and his widow Emma who was expecting another child later christened Andrew, but the British losses were not in vain because the transfer of the ten "U" boats from the Atlantic eased the enormous pressure on the shipping carrying supplies to Britain at a time when we were very hard pressed in the Atlantic and when on the 22nd November the entire fleet of operational "U" boats was transferred to the Mediterranean, Hitler had made a strategic mistake. In his memoirs, the German Admiral Dönitz stated, "The most important task of the German Navy and therefore the German 'U' boat arm, and the task which overshadowed everything else was the conduct of operations against shipping on Britain's vital lines of communication across the Atlantic.

The number of "U" boats transferred to the Mediterranean should have been kept down to a minimum and to have denuded the Atlantic as we did and put an end to all operations there for something like seven weeks was, in my opinion, completely unjustifiable."

Of the "U" boats transferred to the Mediterranean no less than seven were sunk by the British in the months of November and December and throughout the war out of 41,000 young Germans who went out to sea in "U" boats 26,000 never returned.

After the death of her husband Emma Crichton returned to her native Newfoundland where she still lives, her sons John and Andrew were educated at their father's old school Oundle and Andrew after serving an apprenticeship at Metropolitan Vickers in Trafford Park, Manchester, worked in our St John's office from 1965 until 1972 as Technical Director before he joined the staff of Memorial University, Newfoundland in the School of Business Administration and Commerce. In January 1976 Andrew Crichton was elected the 7th President of the St John's Board of Trade.

CHAPTER 9

Post War

EMPIRE BUILDINGS (1945–1971)

In August 1945, just after the Second War was over A. H. Atkins decided that it was time to consolidate the Chester and George's Dock offices again in Liverpool. As well as office accommodation we wanted more space for our growing stocks of Dunham steam traps, Securex fittings and Saunders Valves. After searching the Pier Head area we found that the Mersey Tunnel Joint Committee as well as owning Georges Dock Building also owned Empire Buildings, an office block in Spellow Place which runs between Fazakerley Street and Union Street in Liverpool. There was a small suite of offices to let on the first floor and in the basement there was an air raid shelter which we could convert to a stores. After the inspection A.H. signed a lease for the offices and basement air raid shelter.

Empire Buildings was built about the turn of the century with a view to attracting cotton brokers, because all the rooms had good light and beneath the windows and the north, west and east there were long, wide, benches where the cotton samples could be examined. The Mersey

Empire Buildings. The cobbled road in front is reputed to be the oldest stretch of cobbles in Liverpool.

Tunnel Committee had bought it before they started to bore the tunnel because the docks entrance ran beneath and they did not want any complaints from the owners. It was very solidly constructed and in 1945 when there were not many motor cars about it was very convenient.

A year after we had moved in the Mersey Tunnel Committee put the building on the market and after the building did not reach its reserve at the auction, Major Atkins put in a bid and bought it for £25,000. Empire Buildings was to become our home for the next twenty-five years, the longest we have ever stayed at one address and the reason is simple to explain. As we owned the building it was easy for us to take over an office or stores as they became vacant and we could choose, within reason, what we did, and so Empire Building was able to accommodate our post war expansion with ease.

At this time A.H. was sixty-five years of age and he decided we would have to take on new men to expand our home trade in the post war era. At that time our staff was quite small because of the war time man power difficulties and comprised Major Atkins, his secretary Miss Ellis, E. S. Piatt the company secretary who had been with us for almost fifty years, L. C. Ashcroft, Sales Engineer, J. G. Kirkland, Sales Engineer, Mrs Roughton, Secretary and H. H. Peers who shared his time between the stores and helping with the accounts. A. H. Atkins's only son Jim had been killed in the war as had our Director John Crichton, so a future generation of Management had been wiped out fighting for freedom.

After considering the matter for some time A.H.A. decided to offer one of Belliss & Morcom's outside supervisory engineers, H. H. Gwillam, a position with us as Manager, with a view to becoming a Director.

H. H. GWILLAM (1946–1951)

We had known Mr Gwillam for some years because he was in charge of outside erections for

Florence Colliery—Stoke-on-Trent. Four 4,000 CFM, 750-hp Belliss & Morcom Air Compressors. One of the hundreds of plants we installed and maintained.

Some of the men who powered the workshops of the world. A team of outside erectors posing beside a 600 kw Belliss & Morcom Steam Engine about the turn of the century.

Belliss & Morcom in the Potteries area and we handled the technical sales. We were successful in obtaining a number of contacts for combined power and heating schemes where we used a B & M steam engine, or steam turbine, and then used the exhaust, or passout, steam at say 1 p.s.i. for process and space heating by utilising a Dunham vacuum pump, unit heaters and convectors. On these jobs H. H. Gwillam co-operated with us in every way.

In 1946 Mr Gwillam joined us as Sales Manager and then Belliss & Morcom asked us if we would take over the responsibility for not only selling, but installing and maintaining, all their plant in the North West of England. We accepted and ran their team of about eight outside erectors for twenty years, maintaining their steam engines, steam turbines, air compressors and diesel engines.

In May 1947 H. H. Gwillam was made a Director and he then appointed new Sales Engineers to increase our sales—E. Jones was taken on and then A. J. R. Jones. Mr Gwillam was an energetic and capable Sales Engineer, he had drive and his Belliss & Morcom connections were invaluable and he was responsible for starting our post Second War expansion.

It was through Mr Gwillam's efforts that we became Agents for the K.S.B. Manufacturing Company, because he picked up a number of enquiries in 1946 and 1947 for submersible pumps and sent the enquiries to several firms including K.S.B. We were successful in obtaining the contracts and placed the orders for the pumps with K.S.B.

The K.S.B. Manufacturing Co., Ltd. were Agents for the whole of the U.K. for K.S.B. of Germany, one of the largest, and best, pump manufacturers in the world. The firm was run by Mr Bowen and during the 1939–45 war they could not obtain supplies of German pumps and so the enterprising Mr Bowen and his foreman Mr Barrow set about making submersible pumps in a garage in Gravesend using the German drawings and their production steadily increased throughout the war. When the war was over Mr Bowen went over to Germany and it was agreed that he could continue to make pumps in England as well as selling German-made pumps again.

We were offered the K.S.B. Agency in 1947 for German and British built pumps and Mr Gwillam secured contracts with a number of water authorities in the North West, where we supplied and installed British built pumps, rising mains and control gear.

One such contract was for Wallasey Water Board where we replaced the original beam pump that had been installed at the insistance of William Heap in 1889 when he was Chairman of the Water Committe. (See page 88).

The beam pumps were enormous, the beam being supported by superb Doric columns and the steam engine was lovingly tended by the fitters and kept in a gleaming condition with the brass work highly polished. After it was taken out and the submersible pump was installed all that could be seen was the rising main coming out of the ground, the engine minders had gone and scraps of paper and rubbish lay about the floor.

The new pumps were of course much more efficient than the old pumps and the cost of extracting each gallon of water was reduced appreciably, but some of the beauty had gone out of engineering; inevitable, but rather sad.

E. H. PIATT (1896–1948)

For half a century E. H. Piatt was our book-keeper and Company Secretary and he served the Company well. During the "blitz" on Liverpool his home in Wallasey had been damaged and when the office moved to Chester he moved home to the small village of Prees which is about six miles south of Whitchurch. Mr Piatt did not drive a motor car, but during the war the journey was not too difficult because he could get a bus into Whitchurch and then take a train to Chester.

After we had moved back to Liverpool however, after the war it meant that as well as the journey to Chester he then had to catch another train to Birkenhead and then catch the ferry to Liverpool.

After a while Mr Atkins suggested to Mr Piatt that he should consider moving back nearer the office to cut down the travelling, because although Mr Piatt was leaving home at the crack of dawn he did not arrive at the office until between 10-30 am and 11 o'clock and then he had to leave mid-afternoon to make the long return journey back arriving home every evening after 7 pm.

Mr Piatt had a rather excitable nature and although he was kindly, he could also be stubborn and he dug his heels in and according to A.H. would not even discuss the possibility of the move. This led to increasing bad feeling, until on the 12th February 1948, A.H.A. told Mr Piatt that the firm could not suffer the inconvenience any longer of Mr Piatt living so far away from the office and that he must insist that he should move nearer to Liverpool.

A short time after this exchange Mr Piatt walked in A. H. Atkins's office with his hat and coat on, banged the office keys on the desk and announced that he had resigned from the Company! After half a century's devoted work he just walked out!

It was highly regrettable that these two men should have parted company on such terms after working together so long and one is compelled to conclude that they were both at fault. Mr Piatt for being so stubborn and unreasonable and A.H. for allowing him to depart in this way.

After Mr Piatt had departed H. H. Peers took over as Company Secretary until he left in 1953 and was replaced by Miss Ellis who was Company Secretary for twelve years, until a young Accountant, R. P. Vine joined us in 1964 and became Company Secretary shortly afterwards.

As our post-war business developed. H. H. Gwillam found that the task of running the Belliss & Morcom outside erectors as well as the increasing sales work was becoming difficult and so he suggested that theyshould take on E. J. Howell, a young outside erector working for B. & M. to assist him. At this time Jim Howell was working in Granada in the Windward Islands and on his return to England he was interviewed and in August 1949 joined us.

For the first three years E. J. Howell lived in Manchester and combined sales work in the Manchester area with supervision of the Belliss & Morcom fitters.

A month before Mr Howell joined us, H. H. Gwillam took on another outside sales engineer, B. P. Hague who was formerly at the Automatic Telephone Company and he was engaged in the Merseyside area. Another newcomer was a very bright young lady who joined us at that time straight from Blackburn House School, Mary Seaton and a couple of years later Sam Durkin arrived—one of our most versatile men. (Sadly both Mary and Sam died a couple of years ago, both in their early fifties.)

THE UNSETTLED YEARS

Arthur Henry Atkins, over a period of more than sixty years, handled the company's affairs with great wisdom and ability but the hardest problem he found to solve, and one which caused him much difficulty, was the question of handing over to a successor; he was an outstanding man and they are not easily satisfied when they have to hand over the reins.

In 1951 when A.H. was approaching his seventieth year H. H. Gwillam decided it was time for him to take over, but A.H. did not want to hand over power; although Mr Gwillam felt he was in a strong position, the outcome of the power struggle was that he resigned from the Company on the 30th December 1951. The old lion was not finished yet!

Then there followed an unsettled period of three or four years in the life of the Company which was caused by Mr Atkins difficulty in finding a successor that he could be happy with and this problem was exaggerated by his habit of privately encouraging several people into thinking that they were the Crown Prince.

In April 1952 A.H. wrote to the University of Liverpool saying that he was looking for a young graduate engineer for sales engineering work and shortly afterwards he interviewed J. Millar, a twenty-five year old engineer who had served an apprenticeship at Metropolitan Vickers before going to study for an engineering degree. During the interview A.H. mentioned to Millar that he was an old man, that he did not have a son to take over and somebody would have to take over soon. Just an old man thinking aloud, but it could be misleading. At the end of the interview A.H. asked Millar when he graduated and on being told Saturday 6th July said "Good, start on the 8th". There had been no mention of salary, nor the precise details of the work but still—"somebody had to take over"!

Eight weeks after J. Millar joined the Company, a twenty-five year old ex-public schoolboy Mr Essenhighe, son of Mr Justice Essenhighe, joined the firm and not long afterwards told J. Millar in confidence that he had high hopes, because during the interview....

In May 1953 a Scots ex-Indian Civil Service Engineer joined the Company and was appointed Manager. He was a competant engineer but after a lifetime in India it was not easy for him to adjust to life in a very small firm. He introduced one innovation however and that was to put a large map on his office wall and when he went out making his visits he put a coloured pin on the town he was going to. Similarly he had different coloured pins for the other sales engineers. Like most of these visual organisational aids, they are pretty harmless but quite useless.

This map caused our Manager to get rather angry because some of the wags in the office used to alter his pins while he was out, so that if he had gone to Bolton he would press the pin into that town on the map, but when he came back at night he might find his pin stuck into the top of Snowdon, or in the middle of Lake Windermere.

This organisational chart was abandoned after A.H. had strolled into the Managers office one morning and puffing his pipe had studied the map. When the Manager arrived back later in the day A.H. asked him what on earth he had been doing on the Bar Lightship out in the Irish Sea!

Our next white hopeful, was a tall, very pleasant, Old Etonian and whilst nothing was actually promised distinctly gained the impression that...

One after the other our hopefuls became disillusioned and departed until a really serious contender came along, who was Managing Director of an Egyptian company. In September 1953 he had a talk with A.H. and he told Arthur Henry that as the Egyptians were making life uncomfortable for the British in Egypt he had decided to leave while the going was still comparatively easy. It was agreed that he would resign from his position in Egypt and would join the "House of Heap" as Manager—with a view to better things . . .

The new man had a good brain, but he was not an engineer and his strength lay in administration and organisation; talents which were ideal in a large organisation. He was very pleasant and affable and if he had a fault it was that at times he overstressed his high connections. For example before he joined the firm he gave as references, the British Ambassador to Egypt, the ex-Ambassador, the British Consul General and others. Included in the list were four Knights as well as a deprived Director of Barclays Bank who didn't have a title. A case of overkill considering that he was joining a firm employing a dozen people and this really didn't go down too well.

The new Manager joined us early in 1954 and his chief contribution was in analysing our sales and the areas of profit and loss and he soon showed his forté lay in inside administration and not in developing sales which was a bit awkward as this was also A.H.'s role.

Soon one could detect a smiling restlessness in A.H. as reams of figures were produced proving this or that, and A.H. was soon telling of the old couple who ran a shop for years and couldn't tell where the profit came from. Then their bright, University trained, son took over the business and he completely re-organised it and put in all kinds of wonderful systems and by the end of the year he could account for every penny he had lost.

In January 1955 J. Millar spent a couple of weeks in hospital for a minor operation and during this time received a note from A.H. hoping that he was feeling better, saying that the office was doing fine and mentioning that as from 1st January J. Millar was to be a Technical Director, as was E. J. Howell. He added a P.S. to the effect that our Manager had left.

This latest departure had more serious consequences because most of the comings and goings had affected the Saunders business and they, understandably, felt that things had gone too far and A.H. received a telephone call saying that if he let the Manager go, then we should lose the Saunders Valve Agency.

The Pierhead, Liverpool. For over a century our offices were within a few hundred yards of the waterfront but in 1971 we moved "over the water" to Hoylake.

This was a bitter blow to A.H. because more than once he had helped Mr Saunders when he was struggling in his early days, but although he had perhaps not been wise in all of his choices of potential successors, it had not been an easy time for him because he had the interests of the Company at heart. One could also admire his courage because he did not hesitate for one moment and agreed with the Saunders Valve Company to terminate the Agency but arranged that we should get normal merchants terms. Having done that he then said "Now we must improve our service and our sales".

This was done and eventually good relations were restored with the Saunders Valve Company and in due course we were again appointed their Agents.

There is nothing like an execution for concentrating the mind of a man and this was really the end of the uncertain years and A. H. Atkins and his family did everything they could to help the new Directors and to enable the transfer of power to take place smoothly and A. H. Atkins and his younger colleagues worked well together for the next thirteen years until he died in harness. At times he was brilliant and at others quite difficult but this was not because of an age gap of over forty years, but because regarding the particular matter in question he had always been difficult.

BRITANNIA HOUSE, HOYLAKE (1969 to date)

In 1967 one of our men saw a small notice stuck on a lamp-post near Empire Building stating that the whole area around our office was to be redeveloped to make way for the new buildings for the "Liverpool Daily Post & Echo" and the new headquarters for the "Royal Insurance Company", and further it was said that buildings were to be compulsorily purchased. If true this was serious news for us because we had sunk all our capital into building up stocks and we had not allowed for the possibility of having to buy new buildings.

The location of some of our Liverpool offices for over a century.

1 The Albany
2 Royal Liver Buildings
3 India Buildings
4 George's Dock Building
5 The site of Empire
  Buildings

159

Empire Buildings from Union Street. In the basement we built up the largest stocks of Diaphragm Valves in the world.

We sought a meeting with the Planning Officer and he confirmed that the notice was true, he mentioned that they were planning a small industrial estate for small displaced firms such as ours on a site off Scotland Road and asked if we wanted to move there. We did not, and do not, think that Liverpool's Planning Officers could successfully plan a Sunday School Outing and so we politely declined the offer, which is just as well because Empire Buildings had been demolished four years before their scruffy site was ready.

For over a century we had been within a couple of hundred yards of the Pier Head and the enforced move raised a number of problems which could seriously affect our business. The choice of location was extremely important, we had to be in an area which would suit our staff and our customers and we had to have enough room to expand. A wrong move could be disastrous and indeed this was later proved when a firm of heating engineers almost as old as we were chose the wrong area and the resulting problems forced it to close down within eighteen months of moving.

We wanted to stay in Liverpool because of our long associations with the city and we started an intensive search of Merseyside to find suitable premises but we had the same problem as when we were bombed out during the "blitz", but whereas during the war we had to contend with the mad Führer, our problems now were caused by the so-called "Planners" who were driving small firms such as ours out of the city centre without making adequate provision for them, because the planner's were too engrosed with their latest toy "the elevated pavement" that now disfigures Williamson Square, Byrom Street and other areas of the city and are almost completely unused. (The walkway schemes were officially abandoned, May 1979).

This very week, January 1976, the "Planning Department" has just announced that they are concerned at the number of small businesses that have left the centre of Liverpool over the last few years and they have now started an enquiry. This will of course enable them to justify their existence for a little while longer, but we can give them the answer right now.

Of the dozen or so small firms that occupied Empire Buildings in 1967 all but a couple have been forced to leave Liverpool or have closed down, because when they were all forced out on the streets they either could not find suitable premises or else they could not afford them. Each small firm provided employment, created exports, paid their rates, used the cafés and restaurants, patronised the small shops and contributed to the commercial life of the city. Indeed the small firms created Liverpool as a great commercial centre, not the Planners.

If the Planners want to know why the centre of Liverpool is dead or dying they should look in the mirror and then go to see the other guilty men—the City Council!

After months of searching it was obvious that we could not find anything to suit us at a price we could afford because too many others were also looking and so, very reluctantly, we decided that after over one hundred years we should have to leave Liverpool. We bought two maps of the North West of England and on one we marked the geographical location of our customers and on the other we marked the weight of material despatched from our stores. To our surprise we found that although most of our Merseyside customers were on the Lancashire side, when we considered our "tonnage" distribution more than two thirds of the weight sent out had to cross the Mersey. This altered our ideas of the location of our premises because the factory distribution side was a very important consideration and so we switched our attention to the Wirral.

Just about the first building we had noticed when we had started our search were the partially derelict buildings of the old Hoylake Steam Laundry, that had been laying empty for a few years. In view of our latest decisions we looked at them with fresh interest.

The buildings which were first built in 1900 were in a shocking state, in some places the roof had been torn off, in other areas the wooden floor had rotted and caved in, most of the windows were smashed, a colony of wild cats lived in the pipe tunnels under the floor and the general impression was of rot and decay.

Closer examination however, revealed that things were not quite as bad as at first appeared, the splendid wooden roof trusses in the main building although covered in peeling paint were in fact quite sound and the brick work was not too bad.

We called in a firm of Surveyors to give a report, but we might as well have saved our money, because to say the least they were not encouraging and they valued it at about half the asking price. After considering the report we decided to buy at a price that was more than the valuation but less than the asking price, because from our point of view the location was right; the premises adjoined Manor Road Station on the electrified railway line running into the centre of Liverpool, and so were convenient for our staff; the shape and size of this broken down building were ideal and lastly we could re-build it in stages as we could afford it.

In February 1968 after consultation with A. H. Atkins it was agreed that our sister company William Heap & Partners Co. Ltd., would buy the premises and we would be tenants as we had been in Empire Buildings, but before we could put this plan into effect A.H. died on the 1st March 1968 at the age of 85 years.

This altered our plans and so we decided to purchase the building ourselves and A.H.'s daughter Joan Turner and her husband Alan, kindly agreed to make us a loan to help us to buy the building and later when we came to rebuild the main building they assisted us again and we appreciated the help they gave us at a critical time.

After buying the premises early in 1969 the first thing we had to do was to clear away the tons of rubbish left by the previous owners. We had intended to sub-contract this work but we were unable to get one firm to tear down the old pipeworks, knock down useless partitions and clear away the accumulated rubbish of three quarters of a century, in the time we wanted and so we decided to do the work ourselves.

One day all our men, went over to Hoylake and set to work and by evening we had cleared away hundreds of tons and we are sure that even the Victorian navvies would not have been disdainful of our efforts.

We appointed Carl Thompson a Partner in the Birkenhead firm of Architects Furber & Thompson (now Carl Thompson Associates) to convert our plans into Architectural drawings, and he made an excellent job of the conversion.

We rebuilt over a period of two years and paid for the work by ploughing back all our profits plus help from our bankers the Midland Bank Co. Ltd. who helped us with financing some of our stock, as well as the loans from the Turners.

As it turned out fate was being kind to us because although it was inconvenient to move when we had to it was just as well that we did because the following year inflation started to increase and if we had left it only a little longer it would have been extremely difficult.

When we had digested the cost of the rebuilding we started to buy more machinery and equipment and we purchased a 3 ton mobile crane, a fork lift truck, a 4′ 6″ Radial Arm Drill, a centre lathe, milling machine, grinding equipment, paint spray and a number of specially designed test machines.

We had been working with the Onward Consortium of Local Authorities' in developing a new form of heating unit for schools of the future which eliminated the use of a boiler house. Our Principals Dunham-Bush built the prototype when the Consortium changed their ideas and so we bought it from Dunham-Bush at a reasonable price and then we designed a full air conditioning system for the offices and workshop utilising the direct fired air handling unit in conjunction with a 20-ton Dunham-Bush packaged water-chiller.

By good fortune the main building faces South and when we did our calculations we found that we would get an appreciable solar gain if we used the large windows proposed by the Architects and so we incorporated these, but had them made of tinted double glazing.

There are conflicting arguments about the pros and cons of large windows in buildings, the use of double glazing certainly increases costs, but not by all that much, and certainly if cooling is needed in summer then the initial capital cost is increased. On the other hand we wanted our people to look out over a garden and we hate "Fortress Architecture" which almost eliminates windows completely.

Installing the Dunham Bush Air Handling equipment in Britannia House. January 1971.

162

A good example of a "Fortress" is our old friend the new Royal Insurance Building, which is completely out of sympathy with the other buildings in the area and looks as if a sandy fort from the Sahara has been built at the Pier Head by mistake. Look closely at the arrow slits that have been provided instead of windows and you may see "Beau Geste" pointing his rifle at the attacking tribesmen rushing off the ferry. This building overlooks one of the most interesting commercial rivers in Europe and yet the staff might as well be working underground. The argument that staff would spend all their time looking out of the windows instead of working is fallacious.

Britannia House, Hoylake. Before and after—October 1970—March 1971.

We reasoned that we need heating most days of the year in England and so we wanted the advantage of solar gain especially as the "Onward" air handling unit is too small to handle our heating load on exceptionally cold days.

It has worked out very well and our fuel charges are extremely low for such a building and more important, our total energy costs the first year we were in were about the same as we paid the previous year in Empire Buildings yet we now occupied four or five times the area and had a machine shop as well.

The main block was ready for us to move into at the end of March 1971, and to prevent any interruption to the output of our stores the move was carefully planned, some new bins were built in Hoylake and others were to be knocked down in Liverpool and rebuilt in Hoylake. We calculated that we needed a 5 ton and a 10 ton articulated lorry leaving Liverpool alternatively every hour from 8 am until 7 pm every day for nine consecutive days.

We moved over a section at a time and then we transferred some of our stores staff over with each section together with the relevant orders and so output continued without a break throughout the whole of the move. All our men from the office and the stores took part in the moving of the stock.

At 5 pm on Friday 19th March our Liverpool office closed down for the weekend and we then started to move it over to Britannia House. Our girls turned in on Saturday and Sunday, packing and unpacking, sorting out files and at 9 am on Monday morning we were ready for business and for the first time in one hundred and five years Heap & Partners did not have a Liverpool office.

Thanks to the careful preparation and hard work by all our staff the move went without a hitch, we had moved the largest stocks of diaphragm valves in the world from an underground stores in Liverpool to Hoylake and during that month the stores, under Brian Aves, actually increased output.

The move to Hoylake enabled us to recruit some of the excellent local people on to our staff, Bill Smith and his daughter Fay, Mrs Halewood and Mrs Neil and the bright, hardworking, youngsters on our staff.

DEATH OF A. H. ATKINS, 1st MARCH 1968

About the middle of February 1968, A.H. went home from the office not feeling very well and two weeks later he died on the 1st March 1968. He had seen that the firm was continuing to make slow, but steady, progress and he was quite ready to go.

Although he was eighty-five when he died his brain was clear and active up to the end and his opinions were always worth listening to, even if one did not agree with him.

A. H. Atkins was like a diamond, brilliant, but turn it and the colours are quite different as a new facet catches the light, and several people could have as many opinions of him. He had a warm personality and the gift of almost always having a smile on his face, a superb vocabulary, great wisdom, particularly where his own interests were not involved. He was a good engineer, had great personal courage and loved his country and his company which he guided for sixty-two tumultuous years, through booms and slumps and two World Wars. Many people loved him and a few disliked him but nobody ignored him and one had a terrific admiration for him because he was such a splendid man.

In his life he suffered great personal sorrow, his only son Jim was killed with the 2nd Gurkha Rifles in Italy, and his daughter Elizabeth died at the age of twenty-one years.

Recently we met a lady who worked as a Secretary for Heap & Partners in the 1920's and she described A.H. as one of the "Gentlemen Engineers" and that just about sums him up. We miss him still.

THE DEVELOPMENT OF OFFICE EQUIPMENT

When William Heap first started this Company in 1866 communication with our customers at home and abroad was by letter and, to some part of the world, by cable.

Denise Pegler and our Phillips 353 Computer—Britannia House. (1976)

As recorded earlier, even after the invention of the typewriter right up to the turn of the century all important letters were handwritten and only more mundane matters were typewritten. Ironically, the arrival of fax is once again demanding good legible handwriting because most fax messages are handwritten and it is no good being able to send letters half way round the world at the speed of light if the scrawl is illegible.

Copies of letters were taken by pressing the original in a copying press where the pressure was exerted by turning a screw thread. It was the job of the office junior to carry out this slow task at the end of the day and we still have examples in our archives of this type of copy. We did not have a copying machine until the 1960's but that was primitive compared with our latest machines.

William Heap had been in business for seventeen years before we installed what is arguably, the most important piece of business equipment ever invented, namely the telephone. It was in 1883 when our first telephone, number 809, was installed and although it was primitive compared with our latest digital kilostream network with its facilities for group discussion and switching from office to office, it was still a tremendous leap forward in communication and today all our outside engineers have telephones fitted in their motor cars.

In 1924 the Company bought a "Dictograph" dictating and recording machine for £47.10s which had a cylindrical waxed drum which had to be skimmed up after use. This machine was not very good but it was the forerunner of the ubiquitous pocket tape recorders we all use.

Computers are dealt with later but we bought our first, a Phillips 353 visible record computer, in 1970 and again this was primitive compared with our present systems because today our customer's computers can talk directly to our machine which can translate "languages' and book orders direct.

ROYAL LONDON HOUSE, MANCHESTER (1960–1972)

We have already related how E. E. Baker opened our first Manchester office in Cross Street, in 1917 and how we finally transferred our Manchester office in Dickenson Street to Colvilles in

1935. We were then without an office in Manchester until well after the Second War.

In 1958 J. Mottershead joined us from Metropolitan-Vickers Electrical Co. Ltd. or rather A.E.I. as it had then become (the decline of that great company co-incided with its change of name to A.E.I. and the takeover by "the Group") and by 1959 our business in the area had progressed to the point when we felt it would be desirable to open an office in that great city again.

On the 27th January 1960, we opened our post-second war office on the second floor of Royal London House, Deansgate, Manchester. We had chosen this area because in those days car parking was easy in the streets at the back of the building. We stayed on the second floor for several years, but then when we wanted more room we moved to a large suite of offices on the 4th floor.

We had hardly recovered our breaths after the Hoylake move in 1971 when towards the end of that year we were told that the rent of our offices in Manchester was to be doubled and we could not have a long term lease. At the same time parking meters were introduced, some only allowing a thirty minute stay which made it extremely difficult for us to operate and so we decided that the time had come for us to move our Manchester office as well.

VICTORIA HOUSE, ECCLES (1972 to date)

When we started our search we decided to find accommodation near to the superb network of motorways that have been built in the North West over the last few years and although we had some difficulty we eventually found the ideal building for us, right in the centre of Eccles, close to an access point to the motorway and with an adjoining stores. The price was very reasonable because there was a snag: it was extremely difficult to get goods vehicles into the car park to gain access to the stores, which was of course essential.

After looking over the stores, the writer mentioned it to his wife Dorothy who immediately suggested that we should build a turntable and added that the Co-op store in West Kirby had such an aid. The next day we telexed John Mottershead in our Manchester office and told him that our "Traffic Consultants" had suggested a turntable.

Victoria House, Eccles, Manchester.

166

We then went ahead and bought the property with the help of a small loan from the Midland and sought a quotation for the turntable, but found we could not afford it.

This was a blessing in disguise because J. Motterhead designed a motor driven turntable, made some sketches and we had the table fabricated by a Manchester firm and we installed it ourselves.

It was designed to take a 10-ton vehicle which we thought would be the largest lorry that would use the turntable but we forgot one vehicle that uses the turntable and which can weigh up to 18 tons loaded—the very first vehicle to drive on to the turntable—the one that nearly gave us heart failure—the dust cart!

Fortunately we had made a very robust design and the safety factors more than adequately accommodated the additional weight, but the sequel is that several months after this we were talking to the Manager of the Co-op store in West Kirby and we mentioned that they did not appear to use their turntable and to our amusement he told us that it had never been used since the day it was installed because this "professionally built" turntable had buckled the first time a lorry drove on to it—and that was not the dust cart!

Our lease in Royal London House expired at the end of June and it had taken us three months to find the Eccles premises and we did not buy it until March 1972, so it only gave us three months to have drawings done of the conversion, go out to tender and have the building gutted, rebuilt, new toilets constructed and a new heating scheme installed. In situations like that when work has to be done quickly the safest way is to do it yourself—or at least as much as possible and to keep control yourself. A second problem was that the work had to be done at the absolute minimum cost and yet we wanted the same high standard we had achieved in Britannia House, Hoylake.

The writer started work on the Architectural drawings that Friday evening and work went on all night and all Saturday until evening when we went out to a party. On Sunday work started early and went on all day and by midnight there were half a dozen detailed Architectural drawings finished, the specification and bills of quantity were drawn up.

Two local builders gave us a price and within a week W. Britain & Son Ltd. of Eccles had started work. Peter Bolt, one of our inside engineers, designed the heating scheme and with the help of one or two of our boys installed the scheme as well.

CARR LANE STORES—HOYLAKE (1972 to date)

(This eventually grew and grew until now it is our largest site.)

By the 19th June a very poor building had been converted into a top class, heated office block and stores at a very reasonable cost and on the 22nd June we held a party to celebrate the opening of Victoria House a week ahead of time.

Since then the office has made considerable progress and the turnover has increased considerably, particularly the stock turnover from the stores. Once again we didn't want to move but fate was kind in making us do so.

In 1971 we rented from the old Hoylake U.D.C. a plot of land on their Carr Lane Industrial Estate, which is about a quarter of a mile from Britannia House. In 1972 we started the first phase by building 2,000 sq ft. of stores area, in 1977 we expanded this building to about 8,000 sq. ft. and in 1981 we built two additional factories on this site, giving us a further 10,000 sq. ft. of floor area plus a two storey office block named "Rallim House". This is now our largest site and will enable our expansion to continue.

 OUR LOGO

As long ago as 1875, we had a corporate symbol or "trade mark" which was a raven and early advertisements featured this bird, but the "Raven" trade mark was sold before the first war.

In 1970, after we had bought Britannia House, we found we were the proud owners of a magnificent flag pole and so we decided that we must have a house flag, this in turn meant that we needed a symbol designing.

We were advised that it is not an easy matter to design a logo for a company and indeed the writer had made several attempts, but the difficulty of incorporating the initials of Heap & Partners is that too often one ends up with something that resembles an advertisement for the elegant, and beloved, Harold Wilson's favourite bottle of sauce.

Accordingly we went to see a company that specialises in this type of graphic design and as artistic ability is now equated with scruffy, unkempt, appearance, it was obvious we were in the presence of genius. After making enquiries about our business and background, the "artist" retired to his equivalent of the ivory tower and a couple of weeks later produced a most dreadful design that looked like a mound of sand with the initials HP carved in one side. It might have been suitable for a third rate desert oil exploration company, but not for us.

We told the "artist" that we did not like the design and asked him if he would let us have an alternative; he did not seem to be very pleased and reminded us that we were engineers and not artists, and that they, the "experts" knew best. Nevertheless he agreed to submit further designs.

A week later he came back again and said that they felt we should accept the original design, because in the matter of artistic judgement we should not rely on ourselves but take the word of the artist. He must have thought we were as simple as the Directors of the Tate Gallery who will buy any old rubbish as long as they are told it is "art"; so we parted company.

A couple of days later we were talking to a couple of our chaps, Peter Bolt from the Sales Office and Malcolm Coram from the workshop and we showed them the proposed logo. After they had stopped laughing they said that they could do better themselves, so we told them to see what they could do.

Within a week they had produced half a dozen different designs, all infinitely superior to the "experts" efforts and we chose our logo from the selection. This symbol was also adopted by Heap & Partners (Newfoundland) Ltd. (see page 121).

It is only large organisations that have to rely on "experts" and small companies have splendid opportunities to rely on their own efforts and judgement.

THE ROBOTS OF WHITEHALL (Written in 1975 under a Labour Government)

In 1889 William Heap advised a meeting that "Central Government can teach us nothing" — times have not changed in this respect. Many of the problems besetting us today are directly due to bad Government decisions made since the war, mainly by Labour, but including some by the Conservatives. The "overkill" of the Welfare State; the expansion of Government spending which now accounts for no less than 60 per cent of the Nation's income, leaving only 40 per cent for private industry which alone has to create the Country's wealth; the situation now where the difference between the "take home" pay of a Manager and those working for him is less than in the U.S.S.R.; the bleeding of industry by penal taxation; the crippling Capital Transfer Tax and the proposed Wealth Tax which will largely eliminate family businesses in this country if nothing is done soon; the increase in murder and manslaughter that jumped so dramatically as soon as the death penalty was removed by Parliament.

If this is true our readers may ask why do not the politicians do something to put matters right, well we think we have the answer—we are not being run by human beings at all but by ingenious robots!

During the last Labour Party Conference in Blackpool one young lady, writing in a Sunday newspaper, came near to the mark when she reported that she had just seen the then Minister of Industry, Mr Anthony Wedgwood Benn, "Out on loan from Madame Tussard's Waxworks". This amused us because we had then been battling with the Department of Industry for over a year and we had already proved conclusively that the Department of Industry is controlled by the Robots. If our readers think we are joking we give our experiences.

In 1966 we received a visit from a member of the Board of Trade which was then responsible for industry, and we were told that because Merseyside was a Development Area the Government wanted to encourage investment and growth in the area, we were eligible for certain grants to help with our expansion. We dislike the grants system because it is extremely wasteful and we should be much happier to pay lower taxes and to make our own decisions. The Government, and the Civil Service, love this method of re-distributing our money of course, because it gives them the excuse to create another vast army of civil servants to administer the scheme and they think they know better than us—"Whitehall knows best". However we have to live with the system as it is and so we applied for, and received, certain grants for machine tools, test rigs, our computer, and some help was given with the new building. We appreciated the assistance given, but to keep it in perspective the total grants given for everything over a four year period came to less than the tax we pay in one year and was a "flea bite" compared with our plough back of profit over the last fifteen years.

In 1974 our business had expanded to the point where our computer was almost fully loaded and we knew that if we did not take action it would be overloaded within a year or so. In view of this we decided to order three peripherals: a "line printer" and two new memory banks and disc drives.

We made a routine telephone call to the Department of Industry and we were told somewhat casually by a young lady that as we had been given a grant for the computer we should no doubt be eligible for a grant for the new peripherals because they were definitely eligible. We were told the amount of the grant was less than £2,000, but still welcome because of the high tax on industry.

We submitted our claim to the local office of the Department of Industry on the 27th March 1974 and five weeks later on the 29th April we received a reply asking for a breakdown of our employees activities and for Architects drawings of our buildings, including an overall drawing of the whole site. We wondered why this was necessary since we were only applying for a grant for the computer peripherals, but we collected all the information together and sent it back by return.

Some time later we received a telephone call from one of the men dealing with our claim at the Department of Industry and he said that they had received the drawings showing the layout of our buildings at Hoylake but he could not understand them and he wondered if we could answer some questions over the telephone. After getting prints of the drawings out we told him to fire away. As usual when we are dealing with a telephone call we made notes of the queries as we went along, which was just as well because afterwards we had to pinch ourselves to make sure it really happened and if we had not had the notes we should have felt like "Alice in Wonderland". The conversation went as follows and referred to the simplest drawings of all, an outline drawing of Britannia House showing the various buildings and their use, and the other a plan of the buildings and grounds:

Man from Ministry—"Where is the boundary of your premises on the drawing?"

Answer —"The boundary is that line going around the perimeter."

Man from Ministry—"Where is the machine shop?"

Answer —"The machine shop is the rectangular building marked 'Machine Shop'."

Man from Ministry—"Where is the assembly area?"

Answer —"The assembly area is the rectangular building marked 'Assembly Area'."

Man from Ministry—"There is no mention on your application form of the machinery or plant situated on the land in front of your office?"

Answer —"Sorry it is our turn not to understand, there is nothing in front of our office but a garden."

Man from Ministry—"Your drawing clearly shows a structure and we must know its purpose before we can go further."

Answer —"Can you describe the shape of the machinery?"

Man from Ministry—"They look like overlapping circles with squiggly lines running out from the centre."

Answer —"Now we see what you are referring to—those 'overlapping circles' are an Architects symbol for a tree—they are the trees on our lawn!"

Man from Ministry—"How many trees are there in your garden?"

Answer —"We have no idea, sixty or seventy, but we cannot see what this has got to do with an application for a computer grant. If you think it is essential we shall go and count them!"

Man from Ministry—"No that will not be necessary but we shall have to visit your premises as we are still not clear about certain matters."

It was only then that we realised that we were not dealing with a human being at all, because a normal person would have shrieked with embarrassment at displaying such ignorance and would have babbled apologies, but our man was completely unaffected and indeed as we later discovered they only show any sign of emotion if their transistors overheat.

Later when we had studied him more we learned that he was only programmed to carry out certain functions and we really grew rather fond of him because he was quite harmless, but all the same this first discovery was a bit of a shock.

It was sometime later when we found out that our man could only operate from a range of about 25 miles from his radio beacon, whereas the man in charge of him had more sophisticated circuitry and at times one would swear that he could almost think and he received signals from London a couple of hundred miles away. But for real electronic wizardry some of those political models operating out of London are superb, some can receive signals from thousands of miles away—even as far as Moscow!

Later we received the promised visit from our fellow who brought along a companion: although our reader may think it rather extravagant to send out two men on such a small matter we later found that they are invariably sent out in pairs and it is not as silly as it sounds, because if one of their batteries runs down the other can tow it back to base.

Our little fellows mechanically moved about our premises and ran through their entire programme without once getting their tapes twisted.

"Show us your production areas."

"The production areas are the machine shops and assembly areas."

"This area where you store castings awaiting machining or assembly is 'non productive' and therefore 'not approved'."

"How much time does your cleaner spend cleaning up around the 'productive area' as opposed to the 'non productive area'?"

"How many of your men in your workshops are engaged on 'productive' as opposed to 'non productive work'?"

"A man who stacks castings in the 'non productive area' is 'non productive' and therefore 'not approved', but a man who stacks the same castings in the 'productive area' is 'productive' and 'approved'."

"The man who drives the fork lift truck in the 'productive area' is 'productive', but if the same man uses the same fork lift truck to load the finished valves on to your vehicles for despatch is . . ."

We interrupted and pleaded with them to let us try this fascinating new game, and so rather doubtfully they told us to try.

"He is non-productive!" we said.

"Absolutely correct" they said approvingly: and we like to think with a little admiration.

It was fascinating and we could have listened to them for hours.

At the end of the tour they spoke:

"Not approved:

1) The breakdown of your factory does not comply with the Ministry's ideas of 'productive' and 'non productive areas'.

2) The proportion of your 'productive' and 'non productive' workers is not in accordance with the dictate. There is an out of balance of two people." "Not approved" said one, "not approved" said the other and away they glided back to their control centre in Bootle.

Later we received written confirmation to this effect and so we timidly suggested that although we were not attempting to challenge the all embracing wisdom of Whitehall there were a couple of small points we should like to draw to their notice—they don't call us "Uriah" for nothing!

A) Although the Ministry undoubtedly knew what they were talking about we could not be quite as unproductive as indicated because with a very small staff we assembled, part machined and tested 2·5 per cent of the world's output of diaphragm valves—as well as doing many other things.

B) We hesitated to mention that at times even our office people, yes even Directors, had to do productive work and two of our non productive people had designed and made the control gear for the world's largest diaphragm valves.

C) We were in an area of high unemployment and although we were still quite small we had trebled our staff over the last three years and planned further expansion.

"Not approved" came the reply.

We could not rid ourselves of the small nagging doubt that perhaps Whitehall might just be a little bit wrong, particularly when the Chief Robot announced that he was granting millions of pounds to various workers' co-operatives and even overruled the Ministry's own advisors who pointed out that he could be losing millions. This has since proved true.

We felt that although the sum involved was small it was indicative of the problem being faced by small companies and so we wrote to the local office of D. of I. asking for an appointment to discuss the matter. A week later we recieved a letter from the D. of I. saying that the matter was receiving attention. Ten days later we received another letter saying that if we wanted an appointment would we telephone and speak to their staff.

Again the Systems Programmer was not being as foolish as might seem, by writing two letters without making any progress he had been able to justify the existence of their staff and as a bonus had employed another Government Department, the Post Office, in delivering useless letters, therebye helping them to transfer their loss elsewhere. Finally we were being told to use the state telephone system to do what we had asked for in the first place.

If we had been willing to join in the game we should have telephoned and then received a letter saying the matter was being attended to, copy to the Deputy Director, and so on. It could have snowballed until we brought our Manchester Office into the correspondence. The Ministry would need more men and so should we, and before long the unemployment problem would have been solved.

At that stage however we had not seen the ingenuity of the scheme and we have to confess that we thought they were just wasting more time and money and so we resolved to go to London to put our case, to Millbank Tower where the chief of all the Robots lived, because if any dialogue were possible it must surely be at the great control centre itself.

As we walked through the sunlit London streets to our appointment, we wondered why the Department of Industry needed such an enormous skyscraper and then the answer struck us 'So they can send out their signals all over the country, and incidentally so they can receive signals from afar".

We were whisked up, by a smooth silent lift, to the floor below the Chief Robot himself. We had asked to see him but he was engaged in delivering a programmed speech to the House of Commons, and we were ushered into two of the Chief's assistants. They were definitely equipped with more electronics than the D. of I. models in the North. One said that he was not one of those dreadful Civil Servants we apparently thought ruled the land; no, he had in fact been employed in industry doing a useful job, but had been tempted into the Ministry quite recently.

We told them of our concern about bad Government, at the apparent absurdities of some of the Department's decisions and the lack of any real concern for industry, apart from that controlled by the agitators. We even suggested that it might be worth while the Department's time seeing how we operated since by any standards we have a tremendous output for such a small firm and they might be able to apply the lesson's elsewhere. They were such sophisticated models that at this they produced an electronic chuckle that went on so long that we became quite worried, until it suddenly stopped and one pronounced:

"Your premises are not approved—there is no flexibility", and the other echoed:

"Not approved, you do not fit into a pigeonhole, not approved."

So we left.

We returned to Hoylake determined to fight on for Britain, and our grant; we could beat the Germans, the Japanese, the Americans and the Russians with one hand tied behind our back but that Department of Industry, that was really something! To be fair to ourselves, foreign competitors are human beings and so the odds are more or less even.

We decided to try writing to the Chief Robot again; there was an outside chance that we might be able to activate one of his circuits if we could only hit on the right signal.

We made up a series of simple questions for the Robot to answer, we had studied the legislation in depth and we knew that we could become an "Approved Premises" if we took one of three steps and so we framed the questions so that they could be answered by the computer in the Robot in a straight 0–1, or Yes–No, manner.

1) Accepting that the Ministry knew best and that according to their definition we were employing two too many "non productive" workers, we could dismiss two of our workers. We felt this would be a pity because we thought they were very productive and we needed them, but this would convert us to an "Approved Premise".

Please answer "Yes" or "No" (0–1).

If the circuits could not accept this logic try:

2) We could qualify for the Ministry's definition of an "Approved Premises" by moving our stock of spare castings which was in a "Non Productive Area" to another stores we owned about a mile away, this would make the ratio

$$\frac{\text{Productive Area}}{\text{Non Productive Area}}$$

admissable. (It would of course also ruin our production, but we knew this was admissable because one of the Robots had tentatively suggested this in London.)

Please answer "Yes" or "No" (0–1).

To make absolutely sure; you can see we were trying to be as helpful as possible; we threw in a third possible solution:

3) We could become an "Approved Premises" by taking on two more people and keep them standing about doing nothing, and provided they stood about in a "Productive Area" and did not wander into a "Non Productive Area" this would make the ratio

$$\frac{\text{Productive Workers}}{\text{Non Productive Workers}} \text{ correct.}$$

Please answer "Yes" or "No" (0–1).

Regrettably none of the Robots circuits were advanced enough to answer these simple questions and it kept repeating:

"These questions are inadmissable."

"These questions are inadmissable."

"These questions are . . ."

So we switched it off because some of its circuits were beginning to glow.

With a little poetic licence, this is a true story and now months later we still roar with laughter at the joke of 1975 "How anyone, or anything, in the Department of Industry could have the nerve to talk about anyone in our firm being 'non-productive'."

In the Millbank Tower ant heap there are more Civil Servants than the Victorians needed to rule India, or if that is too far off in time: at the present moment the D. of I. employs more people than the Common Market Commission needs to run the whole of Europe.

Since we wrote the above the Chief Robot became too much of an embarrassment to the Government because more and more people were noticing things, and he has been moved to another Department and "they" have told him not to be as conspicuous — but you have to watch these advanced Robots.

Note to Third Edition

When the above story was written, the then Labour Government was very antagonistic towards small firms and thought that "big was beautiful". Our heart rendering story was picked up by some Local and National Newspapers and given some publicity. "Cheshire Life" re-printed the article then sent a copy of the story to every member of Parliament and some laughter resulted in the Country's finest Club. It is possible that this story helped to change the attitude of Government, and the Department of Industry, towards small firms.

The first glimmer of hope came in October 1976 when we received a letter from Mr. N. S. Belam, Regional Director of the Department of Industry who was based in Piccadilly Plaza, Manchester. In his letter Mr Belam stated that as the Chief North Western Robot, he was sorry to learn of our problems and offered his help. He then signed his letter.

Yours automatically,

N S Belam
Regional Director

Since then we have had considerable help from the Department of Industry, under Labour and Conservative Governments, and attitudes have changed dramatically. The Department of Industry has changed enormously and is now very professional and knows what it is talking about. That being so, the reader may wonder why the story has not been deleted from the Third Edition. The reason it has been kept in is to serve as a warning to those who think that the State should be all powerful and we hope our readers will remember the lessons of the past.

As another writer said sometime before this book was written:

"The budget should be balanced, the treasury refilled, the public debt reduced. The arrogance of officialism should be tempered and controlled; assistance to foreign lands should be reduced less the State become bankrupt. The people should be forced to work and not depend on the Government for subsidence."

(Marcus Tullius Cicero—B.C. 43).

173

CHAPTER 10

Agencies

OUR AGENCIES

Heap & Partners Ltd represent:

Dunham Bush Ltd, Havant, Hants (1919)
Powerflex (Division of Senior TIFT), London (1922)
Saunders Valve Co Ltd, Cwmbran, S Wales (1933)
KSB Ltd, Northfleet & Loughborough (1947–1976, 1988)
Plenty & Sons Ltd, Newbury, Berkshire (1955)

CED Ltd, Marlow, Bucks. (1982)
Tomoe Saunders Ltd, Newport, Gwent (1986)
Aform Ltd, Thatcham, Berkshire (1991)

John Millar (UK) Ltd are Agents and Distributors for:

Hindle Cockburn Ltd, Leeds (1983)
Kinetrol Ltd, Farnham, Herts (1985)
Hytork Ltd, Gloucester (1989)

DUNHAM BUSH CO. LTD. (1919 to date)

Dunham Bush Ltd., European Headquarters, Havant, Hampshire.

Our oldest Agency is Dunham Bush Co. Ltd. formerly C. A. Dunham & Co. and ironically when we were first offered its Agency immediately after the First World War we declined to accept, because we thought it would be too small and we only accepted a few weeks later when Mr C. A. Dunham himself came into our Liverpool office and impressed A. H. Atkins and J. D. Crichton with its potential.

C. A. Dunham was an American engineer who worked for the National Heating Company of Marshaltown, Iowa, in 1895 and in his spare time he worked on the design of a new type of steam trap. Until that time the steam traps that were in use were rather crude and only worked well at the particular steam pressure and temperature they had been designed for, but they would not operate very well over a range of pressures and temperatures. Mr Dunham's idea was to have a thin wall metal capsule partially filled with a liquid which would boil at the required steam temperature, the pressure inside the capsule would then increase and expand the flexible capsule and this would close the orifice of the trap. This type of trap was very compact and had a much wider range of operating pressure than those in use at that time, because if the steam pressure increased, the external force exerted on the outside of the bellows increased and so balanced out some of the additional internal forces created by the boiling liquid inside the capsule. This was the first successful "self balancing" fluid-filled thermostatic steam trap which is now used throughout the world because the Patents have long since expired.

In 1905, Mr Dunham had not only perfected the design of the thermostatic trap, but also a complimentary range of other traps and so he decided that the time had come to go into business on his own, so he set up his own small factory for manufacturing steam traps in Marshaltown.

Mr Dunham worked hard and expanded his sales by appointing Agents and stockists in various parts of the U.S.A. and in a short space of time he bought another company called the Prior Valve Company which made a range of radiator valves of advanced design, both glanded and probably the first glandless design of valve employing bellows as seals made as a standard production item.

Soon a second company was purchased, the Young Pump Company, which made a combined condensate and vacuum return line and low pressure boiler feed pump, for use on steam central heating systems, enabling steam at less than 10 p.s.i. down to 1 p.s.i. to be used as the heating medium and the pumps maintained good circulation. The Prior glandless valves were of course, ideal for use with the vacuum return line system.

As the first multi-storey buildings started to go up in the U.S.A. the vacuum system became increasingly popular, because even in the tallest buildings there were no great static heads of water to worry about and circulation was quick and positive.

The demand for the new traps, valves and pumps was so good that by 1910 Mr Dunham decided to expand into Canada and so he set up C. A. Dunham (Canada) Ltd. and built a factory at Davenport, a downtown area of Toronto.

In Marshaltown, Mr Dunham had furnished his office with a mahogany roll top desk, plum coloured carpet, and hung the windows with heavy curtains decorated with tassles. When he built his Toronto office he made it an exact replica of his Marshaltown office, desk, carpet, curtains and even to the pictures on the walls.

Just before the first War when racial discrimination was still widely practiced all over the United States of America, Mr Dunham appointed a young Negro, Dave Crosthwait as a designer and within a short time had made him Chief Designer.

Dave Crosthwait was not only an M.Sc. and a brilliant engineer but had also qualified in law and was a Lawyer and Attorney.

One of the most advanced steam heating systems, if not the most advanced, ever produced was designed by Mr Crosthwait. This was the "Vari-Vac" system of sub-atmospheric pressure steam heating which employed steam for heating at a pressure of 1 p.s.i.g. max. down to 25" h.g. Even when the steam pressure was below atmospheric pressure, positive circulation from the steam line, through the trap and into the condensate line was maintained by a clever control system which always ensured that the vacuum in the condensate return line was lower, than the steam pressure. The condensate was extracted by the standard Dunham vacuum pump which pulled a vacuum, extracted the condensate, and any steam vapour, then increased the pressure through Venturi tubes and the same pump then pumped back to the hot well or directly into a low pressure steam boiler.

The advantage of the "Vari-Vac" system was that the response to the changing heat demands of the building was almost instantaneous compared with the sluggish hot water radiator schemes then being used.

The standard Dunham vacuum return line system was widely used for combined power and heating schemes because it could use exhaust steam at only 1 p.s.i. after the steam had done most of its useful work.

Dave Crosthwait was widely respected in the C. A. Dunham factories and white men were pleased to work under him, but in those early days at the end of the working day Mr Crosthwait would then have to board the back of the street car reserved for coloured people and was not allowed to travel in the main car with the white men who worked under him, but happily these days have long since gone.

We in Liverpool of course cannot feel superior over this story, because it is possible that Dave Crosthwait's ancestors were taken from Africa to America on a Liverpool ship, and most certainly they worked for a Plantation owner who had originated from the North of England, because like most American coloured people Mr Crosthwait has a British name—in this case a North of England name, taken from the name of the man who owned the plantation where they worked. Most of the plantation owners had British origins.

It was Mr Dunham's intention to use the Canadian Company to break into the U.K. market by taking advantage of Empire preferences, but the outbreak of the First World War interferred with these plans, but he was ready to go as soon as the Armistice was signed in November 1918.

We are not sure how Mr Dunham got hold of our name but he may have heard of us through our Canadian offices in Toronto and Montreal, because as we have already recounted at the beginning of the war we held almost the entire stocks of high speed steel in Canada and we were an important supplier of cutting tools to all engineering companies in Canada throughout the war.

Early in 1919, C. A. Dunham sent an Englishman, A. J. Assherton, who worked for him, to England to set up an office in London and also to establish a sales organisation. Mr Assherton offered us the Agency but A.H. and J.D. politely refused, but shortly afterwards Mr Dunham docked in Liverpool from New York and called in to see us in the Royal Liver Building and after talking to them they agreed to represent C. A. Dunham (Canada) Ltd. in the North West of England and to put in a stock of Dunham steam traps and valves in a basement room in the Royal Liver Building. At almost the same time C. A. Dunham opened an office in Regent Street, London.

Progress in the early days was comparatively slow because our sales were confined to steam traps and radiator valves, but early in the 1920's we broke into the marine business and in 1926 we managed to get the order for Dunham vacuum heating systems for the White Star liner S.S. "Laurentic" and this was followed by several Canadian Pacific ships being built by Cammell Laird and Harland & Wolf.

The first large land contract we secured for Dunham was the Edge Lane Tram Depot which

Dunham Vacuum Pumps, Liverpool Corporation Transport Depot, Edge Lane. These pumps were installed in 1926, ran until 1972 when they were taken out because at that time we could not supply a spare part. This made us decide to make spare parts ourselves in Hoylake.

Edge Lane Depot, Liverpool. Our first large land contract for C. A. Dunham in 1926.

was built for Liverpool Corporation in 1926 and opened in 1927. In those days the heating contractors in this country did not know very much about vacuum return line heating systems and so A. J. Assherton and L. C. Ashcroft were very closely involved in the design of the system. The duplicate vacuum pumps that were installed in 1926 ran continuously until 1972 when they were taken out because the works had stopped supplying spare parts. The tragedy is that shortly after they were scrapped we started making spares for these old vacuum pumps ourselves in Hoylake. The pity is that these superb pumps, that gave almost fifty years continuous service, with very little attention, could have been running still if we had been manufacturing spares then.

The first "Vari-Vac" system installed in the North West was in the "White Star" shipping line's building at Gladstone Dock, Liverpool, this system worked very well for a number of years until the "White Star" amalgamated with "Cunard" to form "Cunard White Star Line" and the

White Star Office, Gladstone Dock, Liverpool. First Vari-vac system in North West, 1929.

177

Dunham Vari-vac Pump and Controls. White Star Office, Gladstone Dock. Photographed 1930.

Gladstone Dock Building changed its use, and so the Dunham "Vari-Vac" system was taken out and installed at Upholland Catholic Teachers' Training College, where it was still running about fifteen years ago and may still be.

The last "Vari-Vac" system to be installed in the North West before the company stopped making the plant in this country was the steam heating systems for the large office blocks at Calder Hall Nuclear Power Station, where the consultant was Ernest Griffiths of Bromborough and where the steam is generated from the world's first nuclear power station.

DUNHAM VACUUM PUMPS IN THE POTTERIES

In Arnold Bennett's five towns of Tunstall, Burslem, Hanley, Stoke and Longton lies the world's greatest concentration of pottery manufacturers and the area is the home of some of the most illustrious names: Wedgewood, Doulton, Copeland, and a host of others. They made, and still do, some superb pottery but at one time the thermal efficiency of their plant was not striking, because they used to throw away their condensate and fuel efficiency was, in general, very poor.

Leonard Ashcroft in conjunction with a Hanley heating engineer, George S. Hall and others, was responsible for dozens of installations of properly trapped systems and Dunham vacuum return line systems, where a low pressure cast iron boiler with a steam drum generated steam at a pressure varying from 1 p.s.i. up to 10 p.s.i. maximum and then the steam was used for process and space heating and the vacuum pump returned the condensate into the boiler.

Eventually almost every single pottery was fitted with Dunham vacuum pumps and as one would imagine the new systems showed remarkable improvements in fuel efficiency over the old wasteful methods.

In some potteries we supplied combined power and heating schemes such as at Doultons where we installed two 300 kw compound steam engines and one 150 kw working with steam at 200 p.s.i. and exhausting at less than 10 p.s.i. into the process and space heating system.

SCHOOL HEATING

When World War II finished Britain had an enormous backlog of schools to be built and the post-war population bulge increased the problem. Before the war C. A. Dunham started manufacturing in Mordon a very quiet fan convector and after the war this was developed into a complete range of fan heaters that were ideal for the school building programme, because in general only one heater was needed per classroom and a cheap, effective temperature control was achieved by having a simple thermostat to switch the fan motor on and off to keep the temperature constant. The heaters were effective and site labour work was reduced when compared with the pre-war radiator schemes.

In the North West of England there was one period when every local authority used Dunham fan convectors and even today when competition is fiercer there are not many authorities that do not use Dunham heaters.

Over the last twenty years much thought has gone into ways of improving fan convectors and reducing their installed cost and it is interesting to note that the price of the fan convector

Doultons Pottery, Stoke-on-Trent. Combined Power & Heating Scheme. Two Belliss & Morcom Steam Engines exhausting at 5 psi into the process and space heating system using Dunham vacuum return line pumps.

Hulme Library, Manchester. 1965. Dunham Bush Fin Vector used for heating and also for a barrier rail. Through the windows the old terraced houses now demolished. Architect S. G. Besant Roberts, City Architect. Services designed by Manchester Corporation. Heating Contractor—Direct Works Department, Manchester Corporation.

is about the same now as it was years ago, but its appearance is vastly superior. This saving has been made possible by improved production methods and greater volume.

Photograph of the total workforce taken outside the works of C A Dunham Ltd., Lombard Road, Merton, London in 1936.
Front Row: 3rd from left Miss Thorne, Company Secretary. 4th from left A.J. Assheton, Managing Director. 5th from left L.C. Ashcroft, Heap & Partners Ltd. 1st from right Charles F. Assheton—Son of A.J. Assheton and later M.D. 2nd from right C.W. Naylor, Sales Director.
Middle Row: 1st from right E.R. Duprey—became Head Buyer. 5th from right Tom Nelson, Works Manager. 4th from right Freddie Button, Foreman. 2nd from right A.C. Patton, became Financial Director.
Back Row: 3rd from right Ron Quinton, became London Sales Manager.

Queen Elizabeth Law Courts,
Liverpool, 1984.
Architects, Farmer & Dark, London.
Consulting Engineers, J. Roger
Preston, London.
Main Contractor, Tysons Ltd.,
Liverpool.
Mechanical Service Contractors, Haden
Young, Warrington.

Queen Elizabeth Law Courts,
Liverpool. 1984.
Dunham Bush "Fin Vector" heaters
under the windows blend in well with
the agreeable architecture of the New
Courts. Queen Victoria in the square
outside looks much happier than she
did in May 1941
(see page 141).

Offices of Welsh Water—Bangor.
Dunham Bush Fin Vector Heating.

COOLING AND AIR CONDITIONING

In 1964 we were asked to start up a cooling and air conditioning section for Dunham Bush in the North West of England. At that time we did not think that there would be a great potential because of our temperate climate, but we nevertheless took up the offer. We had underestimated the increasing demand for more closely controlled temperatures, because this side of our business has made much more rapid progress than we ever envisaged.

Since the war, office and school temperatures have increased considerably until 68° F–69° F or 19° C is now quite normal, and if the temperature rises or falls only a few degrees above or below that figure people soon notice. In 1952 we supplied a vast quantity of heating equipment to the U.S. Air Base at Burtonwood, near Warrington and it was amazing at that time to find their offices heated to 70° F and to see men working in their shirt sleeves even in the depths of winter. At that time, we were in Empire Buildings and there were a few coal fires heating some of the rooms, and on very cold days in winter the temperature would fall to the low 50's and we had no complaints. Today we have full air conditioning in our Hoylake office and workshops and the temperature is maintained at 71° F summer and winter, we work in shirt sleeves in

Manchester University—Computer Building. Mechanical services consultants—Building Design Partnership, Manchester. Mechanical Services contractor—Matthew Hall Mechanical Services Ltd. Two Dunham Bush Packed Chillers used in the heat reclaim scheme waiting to be hoisted up into the building. Oxford Road has to be closed during the period of the lift.

Manchester University—lifting one of the Dunham Bush Packaged Chillers. (1972.)

winter and if the temperature moves a few degrees due to somebody altering the controls, it is soon noticed because we no longer dress as warmly for the office as we did in the old days.

We have supplied cooling and air conditioning equipment for a number of notable buildings in the North West of England and during the last few years we have supplied large tonnage packaged screw refrigeration compressors for several heat reclaim schemes. This is the type of scheme where surplus heat from occupants, lights, office machines, computors etc. is reclaimed for use elsewhere in the building and some recent schemes we have been involved in include the new B.B.C. studios in Manchester, the "Interim Building" of Lancashire C.C., Preston, Europa House, Manchester and the new head office for the Halifax Building Society in Halifax.

Two Dunham Bush packaged screw compressors (200 ton and 150 ton) installed on a heat reclaim scheme at C.E.G.B., Europa House, Stockport.
Architects: J. Gaytten & Associates.
Mechanical Services: Young, Austin & Young Ltd., Manchester.

Dunham Bush packaged Chillers supplied to Peboc Ltd., Anglesey.
Design and installation: Walkers Refrigeration Ltd., Liverpool. (1985).

By 1991 the Farlington home of Dunham Bush was getting rather long in the tooth and needed a substantial sum spending on its vast roof and so the site was sold and in May 1991 Dunham Bush moved its European Headquarters to a modern factory in nearby Havant, Hampshire and their progress continues.

POWERFLEX (DIVISION OF SENIOR TIFT), formerly POWERFLEXIBLE TUBING CO. LTD. (1922 to date)

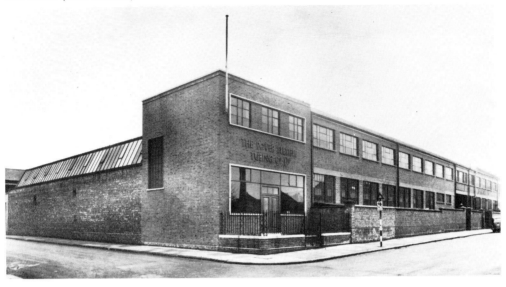

The Powerflexible Tubing Co., Ltd., Derby Works, Finsbury Park, London. (1952)

In January 1922 Eustace Baker went down to London to see a Mr Mann who had written to us asking if we were interested in being appointed his Agent in the North West of England for the sale of flexible metallic tubing.

Mr Baker found that Mr Mann who was of German extraction had built a small factory at Finsbury Park in London in 1914 and in 1922 employed about sixty hands, making good quality interlocked metallic flexible tubing. Eustace Baker put in a favourable report to A. H. Atkins and J. D. Crichton and they agreed to accept the Agency.

There was a complication, because there was already a small Agent in Manchester handling the tubing; his name was R. R. Smith and as well as looking after Powerflex he also represented Greenwood & Batley and the Yorkshire Electric Detonator Co. Mr Smith did a first class job in the Manchester area but his problem was that he was finding it very hard to keep going and so to solve the problem we bought him out and R. R. Smith became a wholly-owned subsidiary of Heap & Partners, and carried on doing excellent work for us in the Manchester area.

We handled the sales of Powerflex products in the rest of the area from our Liverpool office and up to 1939 we made steady progress.

In September 1939, when the Second World War was declared, the entire output of Powerflex's Derby Works was directed by the Ministry of Supply into Government projects and there was nothing for us to sell; but Mr Mann remembering the excellent work we had done for his firm throughout the slump of the twenties and thirties, and after, paid us an annual retainer throughout the war which we thought was a kindly and generous gesture.

After the war ended we again started selling Powerflex products and the introduction of corrugated bronze and stainless steel flexible tubing and also stainless steel bellows gave an additional impetus to our sales. The new products opened up new markets and we secured many important contracts for supplying stainless steel tubing and bellows for some notable aircraft including the Shackleton, Canberra, Lincoln and the Lightning supersonic fighter as well as large bellows for the Blue Streak Rocket which was scrapped by the Government. On all these projects our engineers had to advise the designers on the methods of using Powerflex products.

The British Aircraft Corporation "Lightning", Britain's first supersonic fighter. We supplied Powerflexible tubing, Stainless Steel Bellows and Flexible tubing for use on this aeroplane. September 1960.

Another post-war development was the production in 1949 by Powerflex of the first multi-ply, thin wall, stainless steel bellows type expansion joint which enabled much greater pipe line expansion movements to be catered for and our excellent connections with the heating trade enabled us to make good progress with selling Powerflex expansion joints, because they were well ahead of their competitors in the U.K. and Europe.

Again our engineers advised customers on the use of the bellows type expansion joint, but on occasions engineers overlook the fact that although they are a very simple product there are one or two technical points to watch, principally the anchor loads and the necessity for proper pipe guides—neglect these and trouble, sometimes a disaster, can occur.

As an example of the sort of responsibility engineers carry, there was the explosion at the Nypro Plant at Flixborough where a stainless steel bellows was inserted in a by-pass pipe without those doing the work realising the loads that were involved. The joints were not of Powerflex manufacture, but, as we are, our competitors are anxious to give technical advice free of charge if asked on the correct method of installing expansion joints and that is part of our work. When the load was applied to the large bellows at Flixborough it fractured and released a cloud of gas which exploded and killed eleven men and injured many others, millions of pounds worth of damage was caused to the plant and the surrounding property. Because they made most of the Capralactum in this country for "man made" fibres, the U.K. had to spend £60,000,000 in 1975 bringing in this material from abroad and this made a significant difference to our balance of payments.

We continued to make spectacular progress with selling Powerflex until 1967, when it was announced that there would be a change in their sales organisation. In 1949 Powerflexible Tubing Co. had been bought out by the United Flexible Tubing Co., their biggest competitors, but wisely they had decided to leave the two companies to operate independently and even to compete with each other; this worked admirably and the sales of both companies increased, but

A selection of "Powerflex" metallic expansion joints and flexible compensators.

"Elaflex" rubber bellows joints after being fitted with flanges in our workshops. (1982).

8 in and 6 in rubber "Elaflex" expansion joints on pump suction duties.

then the whole of the United Group of companies was bought out by Tube Investments and they decided that they would have to integrate their sales forces and on 1st March 1967 after forty-five years of almost continuous growth, our Agency was terminated, it was ironic that the previous year our sales had increased, by more than 20 per cent, to a new record.

Within a very short time, however, we were asked to carry on selling the Powerflexible Tubing range of stainless steel bellows type expansion joints, but the reorganisation led to the inevitable loss of sales and production. We could write the various stages of a takeover with ease, because at some time or another almost all our Principals have been taken over and time and again, the large companies doing the takeover all make the same mistakes, leading to dismissals, loss of morale and loss of sales. In the end they all start to pull back when they put right the mistakes they made in the first place, that is to let the small company operate under its own identity and to let the Management of the small firm take its own decisions and stand by them. So long as the big group tries to force the small company to change its image to that of the group, then they are treading the same path to disaster that the Nationalised industries followed and for the same reasons.

We are pleased to say that a few years ago the Powerflexible Tubing Co. was again allowed to trade under its own name and with its own Management team running things. We were encouraged to put in a stock of expansion joints in our stores and once again the business started to take off because again we were able to give good service.

A new product we were asked to stock is the Powerflex range of Elaflex rubber bellows type expansion joints, we take in the bellows and machine the flanges ourselves because they have to have a special contour in the bore and then we fit the flanges on to the bellows in our workshop.

In 1988 Tube Investments sold the Powerflexible Tubing Company to the Senior Group and it was re-christened Powerflex (A Division of Senior TIFT) and in 1990 the Powerflex division manufacturing bellows moved to a new factory in Waltham Cross which is conveniently placed for the M25 motorway network, and the metallic tubing production moved to Pheonix Flexible Tubes, Merthyr Tydfil, South Wales, also part of the Senior Group.

Powerflex is now responsible to the Group for its own affairs under Bernie Quinlan, Managing Director, and is making good progress.

Whereas under our original agreement we were only allowed to sell Powerflex Products in the N.W. of England, we are now free to sell all over the U.K. and we, and Powerflex, benefit accordingly.

Powerflex works at Waltham Cross (1991).

SAUNDERS VALVE CO. (1933 to date)

Assembling Saunders valves in Britannia House, Hoylake. (1982).

For years we represented one of the best centrifugal pump manufacturers in the country, the Rees Roturbo Pump Co. Ltd., Mr Rees was a fine engineer, but the trouble was that he tried to design a pump to suit every application. He designed the first self-regulating centrifugal pump impeller and we did extremely well for them at home and in Canada.

The development draughtsmen for Rees was a young man by the name of A. L. Trump and in 1933 there was another young man who had a small development bench and his name was P. K. Saunders.

In 1933, the bank became worried about Mr Rees and quite wrongly forced him into liquidation; the bank was wrong because he paid out twenty shillings in the pound and somebody made a wrong decision.

P. K. Saunders had been working in the Rand gold mines in South Africa and in 1929, while he was in the mines he became concerned about the enormous loss of compressed air through leaking glands and so he designed a rather crude valve, which had a piece of rubber, or diaphragm, stretched over the globe valve opening and to close the valve, the rubber was pushed down by turning a handwheel in the same way as a tap is shut off. Mr Saunders returned to England and joined Mr Rees in order to develop his "diaphragm valve".

It was September 1933 that the bank pulled the carpet from under the Rees Roturbo Pump Co. Ltd. and this caused problems for hundreds of people, for the employees who lost their jobs, for the thousands of customers who had Rees pumps installed all over the world, for P. K. Saunders who had lost a patron, for A. L. Trump who had lost his job and for Heap & Partners who had lost an excellent Agency.

P. K. Saunders decided that he would take the plunge and try to finish the development work himself and although he was very short of money he invited A. L. Trump to join him and they set to work. Mr Trump made the first drawings of the first Saunders diaphragm valve and it says much for the judgement of Mr Saunders and Mr Trump that their first designs have been copied all over the world, but nobody has ever improved on the original parameters. They hit on just the right height of "weir" and body shape for streamline flow and minimum stressing of the diaphragm and hence longest life. Since then there has been enormous development of diaphragm materials, valve linings and actuators, but nobody has yet improved on the first basic shape designed in Wolverhampton forty-three years ago.

P. K. Saunders wanted to set up a selling organisation and so he approached the best of the Rees Roturbo Pump Agents and asked them to be Agents for the new valve. Having secured

First Saunders Valves Sales Conference, Wolverhampton, September 1936.
Standing in doorway— left P. K. Saunders, right A. L. Trump.
Back row. First—J. T. Bainbridge originally our Saunders Valve sales engineer who we released to Saunders in 1936 so he could run their first
Northern Sales Office in Darlington.
Front row. First—John Crichton. 5th from left— E. E. Baker.

their assent he then persuaded some of them to help him financially because he was very short of capital.

One of the first company's he approached was Heap & Partners and Mr Atkins readily agreed to take on the new Agency, although in 1933, as now, there was no shortage of competition in the valve industry, but A.H. had enough shrewdness to see that the new valve did not suffer from the inherant problems of the traditional designs; leaking glands, corrosion and erosion. He was so impressed that he allowed P. K. Saunders to persuade him to buy some shares in the new company—A.H. was not a speculator, he was an investor.

Later when P.K.S. was again running short, he asked A.H. to buy more shares, but A.H. refused and instead paid for valves which we drew on over the next few months. History shows that A.H. was wrong; with the advantage of hind sight, he should have bought up P. K. Saunders, as he could easily have done. He had made perhaps the biggest mistake of his life.

Although A.H. could see the tremendous advantages of the new valve, this was by no means universal and we experienced considerable resistance from a number of engineers who ought to have known better. The first companies to try the new valves were those that employed the best educated engineers in 1933, the chemical industry. Lever Brothers, Joseph Crosfield, Sankey Sugar, Graesser Salycilates, Courtaulds and of course I.C.I. were all trying the new valve early in 1934 and we are delighted to say that today all these companies are still our customers; but they have been joined by thousands of others as well.

P. K. Saunders and A. L. Trump put up their first nameplate on the 16th September 1933 outside a small office at 5 Tattenhall Street, Wolverhampton and they stayed there until 1936 when they moved to Drayton Street.

For the first few years the only diaphragm that was available was pure rubber, but the initial size range was ambitious because it was from $\frac{1}{2}''$ up to 12'' bore. In 1936 the first oil resistant diaphragms became available and this gave a big boost to our Saunders valve business. We had first started stocking a few valves in India Buildings and when we moved to Georges Dock we enlarged our stock but it only comprised a few valves and some spare diaphragms and was but a fraction of the value of the Dunham steam traps and Securex fittings we also stocked.

Gradually a wider range of diaphragms was developed and new methods of closing the valve were designed, such as quick acting bonnet assemblies. The business grew so much that by 1938 Saunders decided to move to a larger works and to keep the Wolverhampton works for manufacturing the Safran centrifugal pumps that had been designed. A natural product for the ex-Rees men.

The inter-war slump had left huge areas of the country such as parts of Scotland, N.E. Coast, parts of Lancashire and South Wales in very bad shape with mass unemployment and declining industries. One man who was not only concerned but also prepared to take action was Lord Nuffield, who had made a fortune out of building up Morris Motors. He founded the "Nuffield Trust" which helped and encouraged expanding companies to move into the depressed areas and one area he concentrated on was Cwmbran in Monmouthshire, South Wales. The Saunders Valve Company were helped by the Nuffield Foundation and the Government to move to Cwmbran and so in 1938 they started to build a self-contained works and on the 1st March 1939, the new Cwmbran works opened, employing two hundred and fifty people.

The progress of the Saunders Valve Company since then has been remarkable, the original Patents for the diaphragm valve have run out long since and imitators in this country and practically every country abroad started to make diaphragm valves, but even today the Saunders Valve Company produces more diaphragm valves than all the rest of the world added together.

Any competent engineer can design a conventional valve or the metallic parts of the diaphragm valve, but the all-essential "know how" is in the diaphragms and this is where Saunders have spent years perfecting a wide range of diaphragms and now can probably handle a wider range of fluids more successfully than any other valve made anywhere in the world— U.S.A., Germany, Japan, Italy or U.S.S.R. There are now endless compounds of rubbers, additives and plastics that go into the Saunders range of diaphragms and even though a diaphragm for one type of valve say the "A" type with a weir, might have the same grade letter

190

The Saunders Valve Co., Cwmbran Works.

as the "KB" "straight through" type, the mixes can be quite different.

As we have already recounted, A.H. had a disagreement with Saunders in 1955 and as a result we had to decide whether or not to pull out or to fight to expand the business. Mr Atkins asked the writer what should be done to improve the business and so he was told that we had already made a good start by carrying the largest stocks of Saunders valves in the country, but if we wanted a dramatic improvement we should need a large increase, because we thought that availability would help to stimulate demand. Accordingly he authorised another £10,000 of stock which then meant that we had six months supply in stock—a situation which was not likely to appeal to our Accountants.

After another year had gone by we reviewed the position and found that the position, far from improving, had actually deteriorated further. We told A.H. that we were still sure that our analysis was correct but we had not gone far enough and that we were like an aeroplane that had not reached take off speed, we felt that we should invest another £15,000 and then we should be carrying a year's supply of valves. At that time A.H. was in his seventies and at a time of life when few men would be willing to stake substantial sums on backing theories that, to say the least, had not showed much sign of success up until then, and that even if they were successful would take some years to mature, but he took a few slow puffs on his pipe and then said, "Well you had better get on with it".

We took over another large basement stores in Empire Buildings and placed substantial orders for valves and then we all set to work without worrying at all about success or failure. That was really the turning point and from then on our turnover started to increase dramatically, as it has every year for the last twenty years, except one when it remained stationary. Although inflation automatically pushes up turnover figures, we have had real growth over the years, because the standard of living of our people is directly proportional to the flow of liquids, and those who assist industry to control these fluids must do well providing that their product does the job efficiently; that their prices are competitive and, last but not least, that they can deliver the goods in a reasonable time. For over twenty years we, and the

191

A Saunders A2½″ valve installed 1938 in the basement at Saunders Valve Co., Ltd., Cwmbran and removed in 1974. This valve has been in continuous use controlling mains water to a header tank on the roof.

Saunders Valve Company, had satisfied the first two requirements but not the third.

Within a couple of years good relations were once again restored with the Saunders Valve Company and eventually we were restored as their Agents once again.

Over the years we have ploughed back our profits into the company and we steadily increased our stocks in Empire Buildings, by taking over room after room until eventually we occupied the whole basement floor, then we blanked-off the large basement hall at one end by constructing a stores counter and this gave us more space.

W. S. Durkin in Empire Building store about 1963. Note the conveyor in the background.

192

B. Aves and part of our basement stores in Empire Buildings 1967.

In 1966, to celebrate our Centenary we had planned to have a celebration dinner, but sadly Mrs Atkins died a few months before and so this was cancelled. To mark the event, however, we built a test bench to improve our facilities for testing Saunders Valves and with help from the Saunders Valve Company who provided us with their drawings, we built a dip tank for testing valves under water and we installed spark testing equipment for checking glass and rubber lined valves. The test bench we built in 1966 was an important step forward because it enabled

The test bench we built in 1966 to celebrate our centenary. Although simple in design it was a milestone because it enabled us to start building advanced and sophisticated control valves.

Some of the Control Valves our new Test Bench enabled us to build. Empire Buildings, 1968.

193

us to start building much more sophisticated control valves and at the same time we improved our productivity by installing air driven tools and simple jigs.

STORES IN EMPIRE BUILDINGS

Empire Buildings was situated just off Old Hall Street in the business quarter of Liverpool and by the late sixties we were carrying in the basement of Empire Buildings the largest stocks of diaphragm valves in the world—a most improbable and unsuitable setting. When we first started our expansion, all deliveries had to be made down a wooden slide into the basement, but as the weight of the valves increased, we had to buy a mechanical conveyor and the whole time we were in Empire Buildings, every casting that was delivered and every valve that was despatched had to be off-loaded by hand, and then put on the conveyor. The weight of valves we carried in the basement was so enormous that we quite expected to arrive at the office one fine morning to discover that the whole of Empire Buildings had dropped through to the Mersey Tunnel below.

The size of valves we were building steadily increased, particularly when we began building control valves and we reached the point when we would build a large and sophisticated valve in the basement and test it. Then because it was too heavy for the conveyor, we had to strip it down and take the pieces up to street level, manhandle the valve components on to the lorry, rebuild it and then run air lines from the test bench out to the valve and retest. Not ideal, but the astonishing thing is how well our people coped with these difficulties and even then we were building more diaphragm valves than many industrialised countries were.

It was a great blessing in disguise when we found that Empire Buildings was to be demolished, because after we had found Britannia House, Hoylake we planned it so that we could handle large tonnages with ease, but while the building was being converted we faced a very difficult twelve months, because all the other tenants had moved out and the contractors building the Royal Insurance Company's new headquarters frequently caused big problems by blocking access to the stores. They did their best to minimise these, but it did not make life easier when a load of say 20 tons of components arrived, only to find that they could not get near the entrance to our stores because somebody had dug up the road outside. After we moved

Alan Close assembling the largest valve we ever built in the basement of Empire Buildings.

W. S. Durking testing the largest valve built in Empire Buildings. After testing it had to be dismantled, the pieces taken up to street level by our conveyor, the various bits and pieces had to be manhandled onto the waiting lorry, the valve reassembled and finally re-tested on the vehicle. We had to make the best of our facilities.

The largest and most sophisticated Diaphragm Valves built anywhere in the world in 1970. The control mechanisms on top were designed and built in our Hoylake workshops. Today the valves would only be a fraction of the size and small microprocessors would be used for control.

E. J. Howell showing a Saunders Valve to the Indian High Commissioner who was visiting the "Industry Advances Exhibition" Liverpool 1964.

Paul Tattum examines a 20 in bore Saunders diaphragm valve—the largest diaphragm valve in the world. The valve is installed 30 feet below ground level in Hong Kong Sewage Works and we fitted gear boxes and made the extended spindles for operating the valves from ground level. (1984).

to Hoylake our output improved because we were on one level, we had the luxury of fork lift trucks, mobile crane, radial arm drill and lathe and we were able to carry out much of the work we had previously sub-contracted.

APPROACH BY THE SAUNDERS VALVE COMPANY (June 1971)

In the 1950's and 1960's the Saunders Valve Company had opened two or three stores in various parts of the country, but they were proving to be very expensive to run and were not achieving the required results. In view of this the Saunders Board decided to revert back to their old, successful, policy of selling exclusively through Agents and Distributors.

In June 1971 we were approached and were asked to prepare a presentation for the Directors of Saunders Valve Company telling how we would handle a greatly enlarged sales area, embracing our old area plus the whole of the Midlands. This we did and our plans were favourably received; but before the new scheme could be put into operation there was a dramatic change of course in the fortunes of the Saunders Valve Company that was to rock the very foundations of that company and which almost led to the deliberate, and quite unnecessary, destruction of Heap & Partners.

TAKEOVER OF SAUNDERS (August 1971)

In August 1971 we received a telephone call from one of the Directors of the Saunders Valve Company to say that there would be a press announcement the following day stating that the Gallagher Tobacco Group had bought the Saunders Valve Company; but that we were not to worry because the business was to be run as before, on its old profitable lines.

The old board of the Saunders Valve Company had done a magnificent job in developing the diaphragm and ball valves and in building up the company, but they had made one serious mistake, in that they did not train up some of their bright young men to follow on as future Managers and Directors of the Company. The result of this lack of foresight was that within a year of the takeover, almost the entire Saunders team of senior and middle management retired; leaving a gaping hole in Management skills.

Gallaghers had no choice but to bring in a new team to run, what was then a well run, profitable company. On paper, the new men looked good, but they soon made it obvious that they had very different ideas from the old management and the first policy to be scrapped was the idea of selling more through Agents and Distributors.

DIFFICULTIES AND DANGERS (1972–1978)

The new Managing Director had a strong personality and was a very pleasant, affable, Cambridge educated lawyer. The new Sales Director who was not so pleasant; had been in the valve industry for some years and during the war had been an officer in the R.A.F. He had a rather curt manner and in our opinion whilst he may have been an officer, we suspected he was not a gentleman.

The new men visited us after they had settled down and they told us that they valued the work we were doing, but felt that they would like to open even more of their own offices and stores all over the country in order to give customers a wider choice of supply. In return we were to be freed from the restriction of only being allowed to sell in the North West and would be free to sell Saunders Valves anywhere in the U.K. We enthusiastically agreed to the new proposals because we firmly believe in competition and we were quite sure that we could compete with anybody.

In the first three years everything went well and we established a good working relationship with the local Sales office of the Saunders Valve Company and our business prospered and expanded.

Early in 1975 however there was dramatic change in the attitude of the Saunders Valve Company towards us. The local management was changed and the Saunders representatives started to exert great pressure on customers to persuade, threaten or bully them to stop placing orders with us and instead switch orders to their own stores. In spite of this campaign however our Saunders business continued to expand.

During the next two years things went from bad to worse until eventually a whispering campaign started; spreading rumours to the effect that we were in deep financial trouble, which was completely untrue.

We had, of course, not been sitting back and doing nothing while this campaign had been going on and we made numerous complaints and had made several visits to Cwmbran to speak to the Sales Director about these very worrying events. He told us several times that we must be imagining things because the Saunders Valve Company had no intention of dispensing with our services and said that they had no desire to see customers switching business from us to them. It was simply a matter of giving customers more choice.

We remained unconvinced and the campaign against us continued unabated until eventually in 1977 we undertook an investigation to try to discover if there had been any secret change of policy in 1975, which was the beginning of our troubles.

In the meantime we were not the only ones to suffer; customers suffered, because changes were made in production control resulting in long delays in delivering valves. Saunders own employees suffered because some of the best men were moved or dismissed. The company's profits suffered; initially they dropped and then vanished and Saunders started to make losses.

THE FINAL SOLUTION (1975)

Our investigation discovered the existence of a secret document typed in 1975 and marked "Strictly Confidential" which was the minutes of a secret meeting that had taken place at an hotel well away from Cwmbran and at which only top Management were present. The document was entitled *Elimination of U.K. Distributors*.

The document then detailed how the Saunders Valve Board had decided to eliminate their U.K. Distributors because Saunders own depots were not doing very well.

Saunders proposed treating their Scottish Distributors quite well because the Sales Director felt that if they did not, then there might be a tartan backlash from their Scottish customers. It was intended to take over stocks in Scotland for a reasonable price and they would also consider taking over staff and premises.

We were considered to be the most successful, and able, of their Distributors, but because of our loyalty to the Saunders Valve Company we were also considered to be the most vulnerable because we did not, at that time, sell any valves other than Saunders, and a high percentage of our business was accounted for by Saunders.

The intention so far as we were concerned was that Saunders would build up their Eccles stores and organisation and then; when they were ready; would simply cut us off by offering us impossible terms. The document detailed the advantages and disadvantages of the proposed course of action. The advantage from Saunders point of view was that they would take over our business at no cost to themselves. The advantages listed for Heap & Partners was a very bleak and chilling: NONE.

We were stunned at the shocking deception and at the callous way we, and our staff, were to be treated after 45 years of completely loyal service to the Saunders Valve Company. The document was quite right however in assessing our vulnerability because we had always refused offers from other valve manufacturers and we had sunk millions of pounds into the Saunders business. If Saunders carried out their FINAL SOLUTION then we should be forced out of business and we should have been compelled to dismiss our staff. Incredible to think that we were to be killed off, after more than a century, not because we could not do our job properly, but because we were too successful; and the weapon to be used against us was our own loyalty to Saunders.

We have never subscribed to the idea of giving in without a fight and so with the FINAL SOLUTION document tucked away in our briefcase we went to Cwmbran and saw the Sales Director. Over the preceding couple of years, his manner had deteriorated from curt to rudely arrogant, but we were prepared to be courteous to him.

We said that he would appreciate that we had been very concerned at the series of attacks that had been made on us by his men over the last few years, and we felt that, in view of our long association, if the Saunders Valve Company had changed its previously stated policy of running its own offices in parallel with Distributors, then we should discuss the implementation of such changes so that change could be brought about without harming either company. We added, innocently, that if there were any sudden, or violent, change of policy then we were in a very vulnerable position because of the vast amount of capital we had invested in the Saunders business.

The Sales Director was quite arrogant in denying that they had, or ever had, any wish, or intention, of dispensing with our services and again stated that they did not mind whether customers ordered from us or them.

In view of the document signed by him, sitting in our briefcase it confirmed our suspicions that we were not dealing with a gentleman. However we accepted his assurances without revealing that we had proof of his duplicity.

Our reader will find it hard to believe that even at this stage we were still naive enough to give him the benefit of the doubt; feeling that there might have been another change of plan in our favour. Later we discovered that there had been no change from the FINAL SOLUTION but the Saunders Board kept postponing action against us because it was taking longer to weaken us than they had originally thought, and they wanted to be absolutely sure that when they moved we would be killed off quickly and without a struggle.

In the meantime the Saunders Valve Company was running deeper and deeper into trouble. Money and effort was being pushed into fighting us, instead of the competition at home and abroad. A huge new stores was built in Cwmbran costing over one million pounds in an endeavour to improve their service to customers. Unhappily the new stores was not without its own problems and soon it was christened "The Bermuda Triangle"; the joke being that once a valve entered the huge cathedral like building, it was never seen again.

Stocks costing millions were poured into their own stores all over the country, but invariably they had the wrong items in stock and they discovered that it is one thing to manufacture valves, but quite a different matter to try and distribute as well. Henry Ford could have told them that sixty years earlier.

Eventually on the 1st November 1978 after recording another gigantic loss the Saunders Board decided to apply the FINAL SOLUTION so far as we were concerned. We had gone to Cwmbran to discuss a new £50,000 expansion of our test facilities. The Sales Manager was late for our meeting and when he arrived he was rather agitated because he said he had just come from a meeting with his Directors and had been told that, once again, their results were dreadful and so he was to tell us that our already meager margin was to be cut to an even lower level! We replied that it would be impossible for us to operate at such a figure, but all we received in reply was a letter thrust at us confirming the terms and we were told to sign our acceptance!

We declined, adding that we obviously wanted to do everything possible to help the company, so we put forward a scheme that would help them without putting us out of business; but there was no interest in our plan.

We returned to Hoylake and confirmed our discussions to the Sales Manager, who by then had been appointed hatchet man to do the Director's dirty work. He replied stating that we must withdraw our letter—or else! We declined.

Shortly afterwards we were exhibiting at the "Interflow" exhibition in Harrogate and the Sales Manager visited our stand and said that if we did not withdraw our letter and accept their terms; impossible though they were; then we were fired!

So we were faced with a choice—acquiesce and walk into the gas ovens; or fight. We chose the latter and invited the Sales Manager to confirm his threat in writing.

As already related the then Managing Director was a Cambridge trained lawyer whereas we have never had a law lesson in our lives. We did however, have a reasonable working knowledge of the law and we felt that the Saunders Board had broken the law by secretly plotting our destruction whilst giving us numerous assurances that they wanted our relationship to continue, and this amounted to a conspiracy.

We made further investigations and discovered that in 1975 the Sales Director had organised secret War Games against us with his top Management team. Being an ex officer he would of course. Various scenarios were presented giving all possible courses of action we might take once the fatal blow had been delivered. We obtained a copy of this "War Game" and were amused to note that the "Singapore" mentality of the military mind was alive and well, because firstly it was taken for granted that they would not make any mistakes and secondly they had pointed all their guns in the wrong direction.

Naive we might have been, but not so naive that we had not kept a careful note of everything that the "Dirty Tricks" brigade had done; nor so naive that we had not confirmed all our discussions in writing.

We resolved to sue the Saunders Valve Company for deliberately conspiring to destroy our business; although we were well aware that the law has absolutely nothing to do with justice. Further we also knew that most barristers charge so much for their services that they should be compelled to wear black masks as well as their wigs; but we felt that we had nothing to lose and that we stood a fair chance of being awarded the millions of pounds that we intended to claim.

Fate however had other plans. Our reader will recall that the Scots Distributors were to be treated in a civilized fashion, because a tartan backlash was feared. In our case no customer backlash was even considered because the tolerant, too tolerant, English generally avoid trouble if they can, and do no seek it out. Thankfully however not all are so passive and we suddenly received most welcome help from our largest customer, I.C.I.

We had kept our troubles to ourselves but word reached our largest customer via Saunders that change was in the air. We were asked to go to London and we were gently quizzed about possible changes and although our answers were guarded, they were bright people and they knew the score, without us telling them.

Shortly afterwards they invited the then Managing Director of Saunders to visit them in order to discuss what they considered to be disturbing rumours about plans to eliminate us as Distributors. If true they said that they would be rather upset because we had given excellent service and if there were any interruption in supplies it could affect their production. They asked if the rumours were true? The Managing Director looked very uncomfortable and then said, unconvincingly, "No".

"Good" they replied.

Shortly afterwards the Managing Director of Saunders came to see us; large; hearty; friendly; and said that he heard some unbelievable rumours concerning reputed, ridiculous, plans to eliminate us as their Distributor. Could we throw any light on these absurd rumours?

We told him we were puzzled because we had been dismissed by his Sales Manager.

"You must have badly misunderstood what he said" he earnestly replied.

We said that it was hard to misunderstand the words "You are fired".

"Goodness me, he didn't really say that did he? You see how difficult it is to run a large company when one is surrounded by such people? You can take it from me that it has all been a big misunderstanding and you must carry on as before" he concluded.

We said we were pleased it had all been a misunderstanding and agreed to carry on as before.

This story illustrates the excellent relationship that frequently exists between giant British companies and their smaller suppliers. Whilst we were by no means defenseless against the savage attacks being waged against us, we greatly appreciated, and still appreciate, the help given to us by Imperial Chemical Industries.

NEW MANAGEMENT

Not long afterwards Gallagher made changes and they brought in Richard Miles as Managing Director. Again Cambridge educated, but this time an engineer and excellent business man. He immediately saw what was wrong and started to make improvements. The old Managing Director had departed and he was soon joined by the Sales Director. New younger, bright, Directors were appointed and given responsibility and the old arrogance went and the new men listened to their customers.

Turning a very large business round is a very difficult, often painful and agonisingly slow business. A bit like riding a large log on a fast flowing Canadian river and trying to make it go in a different direction. One painful matter that had to be tackled almost immediately was overmanning and this meant that a number of employees had to be declared redundant.

Another problem was production. In common with many other British companies at that time, not enough investment had been made in new, advanced, machine tools and there were numerous bottlenecks.

Many engineers think of the Saunders valve as being a very simple product and they are right. It is however one of the most difficult valves to produce in the range offered by Saunders because of its great variety of materials, shapes and operating mechanisms. The various permutations make up millions of combinations and a shortage of only one component can cause problems.

Ian Garnish was made Production Director and was given the horrific job of sorting out the production difficulties. New machines were bought and installed and old machines were thrown out. Working practices were improved and pressure was exerted on outside suppliers to improve their quality, prices and delivery dates. Quality Assurance was introduced throughout the factory and quality and production soon started to improve.

The company's finances were entrusted to John Cadman who is almost unique in that he is a qualified engineer as well as being a qualified Accountant. He applied better financial control and introduced systems producing better Management Information for his colleagues.

Sales and Distributors were reorganised by Richard Miles and almost immediately, he closed all their own Distribution depots, except one, and appointed new Distributors to join us.

John Lever and Stephen Curtis were given the job of reorganising the new sales and Distribution network and this they tackled with energy and enthusiasm. The new distributors put in large stocks all over the country and service to customers slowly started to improve.

Overseas sales were re-organised and Doug Eaton rejoined the Company to strengthen the Sales Management and he spent much time overseas improving their sales networks. Ron Evans, a tough Lancastrian, and an old friend and sparring partner, went out to Singapore and then to Melbourne and tackled the task of supporting their Distributors in Australia and has made a splendid job of increasing sales in that part of the World.

The one section at Saunders that came through the troubled years with their enormous reputation completely unsullied was the Technical Services Section. Vic Street and Ken Marshall, were unquestionably the World's greatest authorities on diaphragm valves. During the troubles they received slights, and were not well treated, but their work was not interfered with, largely because the old Management couldn't understand what they were doing anyway; and they gave superb service and kept alive Saunders proud reputation of being not only the inventors of the diaphragm, but, half a century later, still manufacturers of the best diaphragm valves in the World.

Slowly the company pulled round and with everybody working as a team the haemorrhage of financial losses was staunched and within a couple of years the company moved back into profit, and now that the business is on a firm footing, is taking on more people to handle the greater volume of business.

Once it was clear that the Company was on the right course Richard Miles departed for new challenges. Ian Garnish was made Managing Director; Roger Staite came in as Production Director and Peter Sulley became Technical Director continuing the excellent work of his predecessors.

A sequel to the Saunders story is that in 1986 P.K. Saunders came back to England from the U.S.A where he has lived for many years to visit the factory he had founded over sixty years before. Although then over 87 years of age he showed a lively interest in the production of the diaphragm valve which he had invented so many years earlier. Philip Saunders has led a varied and fascinating life and has had many adventures; from being a young midshipman on HMS Canada at the Battle of Jutland in 1916; to creating a new golf course from scratch in the West Indies; but probably the one creation of which he is most proud is his invention of a new type of valve and his early struggle to get his company established between the years 1931 to 1939.

An underwater trench cutting machine built by Land & Marine of Merseyside, for laying the cross Channel cable linking the French with the British Electricity Distribution System. We supplied actuator operated Saunders valves for controlling the ballast tanks, and so the buoyancy, of the robot. (1983).

Some export orders awaiting despatch. The Saunders valves in the foreground had been given a special finish in our workshops as they were for use on oil rigs in the North Sea. (1981).
Over the last few years we have exported to 64 countries.

Philip Saunders who invented the diaphragm valve almost 60 years earlier examines a stainless steel body. Ian Garnish, Managing Director, Saunders Valve Company, points out that the shape of the valve body has not changed since it was first invented in 1930. (1986)

Philip Saunders, then 87 years old, visited his old works in Cwmbran in 1986 and is seen here with the Board of Saunders Valve Company.
L to R. John Cadman, Financial Director Saunders Valve Company, Stephen Curtis, Sales & Marketing Director, Mrs Saunders, P. K. Saunders, inventor of the diaphragm valve and Ian Garnish, Managing Director of Saunders Valve Company.

PLENTY & SON LTD., NEWBURY (1955 to date)

Plenty & Son Ltd., Newbury.

In age, we are a struggling youngster compared with Plenty, because when William Heap and Thomas Arkle set up in business in 1866, Plenty & Son had already been in existence for seventy-six years and even then had an honourable list of achievements behind them.

William Plenty was born in Southampton and went to Newbury in 1790 and started up his own business in Cheap Street as a millwright and agricultural machinery maker. He made a variety of simple implements for the farm, including pig troughs and in 1800 he Patented a new type of plough.

In 1817, William Plenty became concerned about the loss of life at sea and so he designed, and made, a lifeboat made of cork and launched it on the nearby River Kennet. This design was adopted by the Admiralty and was the first standard lifeboat ever made and a number were ordered and made in Newbury.

In 1832 William Plenty died and the business passed to his two sons James and Edward Pellem, they were an enterprising pair and in 1851 they entered a competition for a new design of lifeboat sponsored by the Duke of Northumberland and out of two hundred and eighty entries the Plenty lifeboat came third; the model they made was exhibited at the Great Exhibition of 1851.

The two brothers were responsible for the gradual transition of a family business based on agriculture to one centred on engineering. In 1864 they built a combined boiler and steam engine which comprised a horizontal boiler with a single cylinder vertical engine bolted on the end. It was a very compact design and was an early example of factory "packaging" to cut down site labour and to speed up installation.

In 1866, the Plenty brothers designed and built a steel launch into which they installed a boiler and steam engine and they entered this craft for the first race ever organised by the Royal Yacht Club for steam yachts. A number of well known engineers entered the competition including Maudsley, Penn and Rennie but the Plenty yacht beat all comers. Plenty and Son had entered the marine engineering business. From that time on, Plenty & Son concentrated on marine engines and were one of the many British Companies that built engines that powered the ships and factories of the world in the reign of Queen Victoria.

A Plenty "Constant Pressure" CPC Pump on a lubricating oil line feeding can filling machines. Burmah Castrol Co., Ltd., Ellesmere Port.

A Plenty variable output "Varipak" pump. Mobil Oil Co. Ltd., Birkenhead.

In 1876 a vicar, the Rev. Garrett designed the first submarine called "Resurgan" which he offered to the Admiralty. It was a crude wooden, iron clad boat and the machinery comprised a coal fired steam boiler and it had a retractable smoke stack. This submarine was 35 feet long and had a crew of one, this brave fellow had to extinguish the fire when he wanted to submerge, retract the chimney and then flood the tanks. The Royal Navy tested the new boat, but rejected its use because it was not very practical.

Nine years later, in 1885, Mr T. H. Nordenfelt designed a much larger version of the "Resurgan" which was 100 feet long. Again the boiler was coal fired but the Nordenfelt chimney had to be unshipped after the fire had been put out, and the opening sealed off. A novel feature of the new submarine was that there were two horizontal propellers on deck that assisted the flooding of the tanks in speeding descent. The armourment comprised two machine guns mounted on deck.

Plenty worked with Mr Nordenfelt in the design of the submarine and supplied all the machinery. One was sold to the Turkish Navy, and then to preserve the balance of power, another was sold to the Greek Navy. A third submarine fitted with 1,000 hp engines took part in the Spithead Review of 1887, but was not purchased by the Admiralty because they still felt that the method of submerging was too clumsy and so she was sold to the Russian Navy, but was wrecked after running aground on her way to Russia.

The very latest British Nuclear Submarines are all fitted with Plenty filters and Plenty maintain their marine connection by supplying pumps and filters to the Admiralty for Royal Navy vessels.

Another interesting engine built by Plenty was the Plenty–Still engine which was a combined diesel and steam engine, the chamber above the piston being the diesel part and the underneath was the steam cylinder; they were no toys because they ranged in power from 150–900 hp.

The Plenty range of marine engines was developed until at the outbreak of the Second World War, they were building 1,500-hp engines and during the war they made engines up to 2,000 hp for minesweepers and other naval ships and the last engine to be built by Plenty was about twenty-five years ago.

In 1935, Plenty were approached by a Mr Cox who at one time was in the Insurance business; he had the idea of a novel sliding vane pump that had unique features, because with a standard speed drive it could be made to have a variable output and was reversible—all by turning a handwheel mounted on top of the pump. Mr Plenty was impressed with the idea and he took over the manufacture and they developed the germ of an idea into a practical working range of pumps.

They found that the new pump was ideal for handling viscous fluids and they were supplied to many different industries for pumping a wide range of fluids such as fuel oil, lubricating oil, soap, fats, grease and even chewing gum.

Later the variable output feature was developed by controlling the eccentricity of the pump by means of a piston and a spring or dead weight accumulator. This enabled the pump to deliver at a constant pressure irrespective of the flow. This is valuable in systems such as can filling, where the pressure in the pipeline feeding the machines should be maintained constant for good can filling, irrespective of how many machines are drawing from the pipeline at any one moment.

Another development was to fit the pump with an air motor on the top, or an electrically operated activator, so that a remote signal could be sent to the pump to increase, or decrease its output.

In 1939, about the outbreak of the Second World War the last of the Plenty's to run the firm died and so after almost one hundred and fifty years, control passed from one family to another; from the Plenty's to the Shoosmiths, but Mrs Plenty remained on the Board until the middle 1950's, when we were appointed Plenty Agents.

In September 1955, when we were made Agents of Plenty & Son, the works was still in Cheap Street and the Managing Director was G. T. Shoosmith who had joined the company a couple of years earlier and had taken over from his father. He recruited a number of bright young engineers from Cambridge and the old traditional business was about to be transformed, because the reign of the steam engine had just about come to an end and new products had to be developed to supplement the pump production.

In 1955 when we took over the Plenty Agency for the North West of England and North Wales they were having some difficulty in getting supplies of good, reliable, filters for use with their pumps and so G.T. Shoosmith decided that they would overcome the problem by making their

4 in Plenty filters on a fuel oil distribution system at a Shell refinery.

own. Not only did they do this, but they improved on the designs then current by fitting quick access covers so that the filters could be cleaned easily. The new filters became so popular with customers that orders started to roll in for filters and so the range was extended. This created new demands for the Plenty filter so that eventually a Filter Department had to be set up to cope with the demand.

The filters are in use by every major oil company throughout the world, as well as by the chemical industry, general industry and the food industry.

When the gas fields were discovered in the North Sea, off the East Coast, it was a great boon to the British Economy because the gas fields were not too difficult to exploit but as soon as it started to flow into the grid of gas mains in our towns and cities, trouble was experienced because the new gas was dry, whereas the old coal gas was somewhat wet. Over the decades a lining had formed inside the gas pipes, but, after it had been dried out by North Sea gas, pieces would crumble away and a dust storm would rage through the system, causing the sensitive gas governors to clog up and fail.

Plenty & Son set to work and designed new elements to fit into the standard filter body which would filter out the very fine powder in the gas. They followed up this work by designing a range of large high pressure gas filters for the National Gas Grid, and it is true to say that today there is scarcely a town, village or community served by North Sea gas that does not have Plenty gas filters fitted.

When oil was discovered in the North Sea, Plenty again developed new equipment and have supplied gas separators and very fine filters for the rigs. When oil is tapped, most of it can be extracted by its own pressure but after a while this falls and the remainder of the crude oil is

A 10″ Plenty filter on the 30 mile pipeline supplying Shell Carrington from the Ellesmere Port Refiners of Shell (UK) Ltd.

extracted by pumping high pressure water into the porous rock and so pressurising the oil to the point when it will flow up the rising main. The pores in the rock holding the oil are so fine that the water has to be filtered to a very fine degree so that the pores will not block and these special filters were developed and made by Plenty & Son.

We started stocking Plenty filters in 1967 and started off with the Simplex range in cast iron up to 4″ bore, but this has been steadily increased until now we stock Simplex and Duplex filters in cast iron, cast steel and stainless steel with a wide range of baskets and inserts. Some filters we stock undrilled and then we drill the flanges ourselves to suit our customers requirements.

Until 1990 we could only sell Plenty Filters in the North West of England, but in 1990 changes in EEC law meant that we could sell Plenty Filters all over the country and we are continuing to make good progress.

Plenty automatic backflushing fuel oil filter installations supplied to Shell (UK) plc, Stanlow. (1987).

KSB CO LTD (1947–1974, 1989 to date)

As previously mentioned our association with KSB started in 1947, just after World War II when we received orders from water companies in the North West of England for submersible borehole pumps which we placed with KSB Manufacturing Co. of 6 Broad Street Place, London EC2. They were the Agents for KSB Germany but during the war they had also started making their own submersible pumps in Northfleet, Kent.

Over the years we have been involved in a number of interesting pumping schemes with KSB and we give below an outline of a few of them.

Highest Pressure Boiler Feed Pumps in Britain

In 1959 we received a piece of paper about six inches square from Simon Carves Co. Ltd. of Stockport, that was the order for two K.S.B. barrel casing boiler feed pumps for the "Super Critical" Benson Boiler at the Margham works of the Steel Company of Wales. This was the first "Super Critical" boiler to be built in Britain and although this was many years ago we believe that there are still only two in the U.K., the other being the G.E.G.B. station at Drakelow "C" where we think the pumps run at a slightly lower pressure.

The pump duty was difficult because the capacity of the boiler was small compared with the pressure. This was an interesting project for us because one pump is turbine driven through epicyclic gears while the other is motor driven, again through epicyclic gears. If one pump shuts down through a fault then the standby pump automatically starts and has to be up to full load in 30 seconds, which presented some interesting engineering problems.

The operating conditions of the Marghan "B" pump are:
Temperature—118 C
Capacity—253,000 p.p.h. = 115 tons/hr.
Pressure—4,700 p.s.i.g. = 331 Bar.
Pump speed—4,500 r.p.m.
H.P.—2,500

These pumps have now been running superbly for over fifteen years without trouble and so far as we are aware are still the highest pressure boiler feed pumps in Britain.

Glandless Pumps for Nuclear Power Stations

Again in 1959 we were successful in securing the order for twenty-four 80 kw and twenty-four 22 kw glandless circulating pumps for the Latina Nuclear Power Station, the first Nuclear Power Station to be built in Italy. This was designed by the Nuclear Power Group of Knutsford.

Widnes Sewage Pumping Station—Ditton

In general we do not install plant nor equipment but occasionally if no other company can do it then we help out and one of these was the supply and installation of the sewage pumps in the Ditton Sewage Station where the following K.S.B. pump were installed in 1975:
6—240-hp Foul Water Pumps
2—180-hp Storm Water Pumps

The two KSB boiler feed pumps installed at Margham Works, Steel Company of Wales. The highest pressure boiler feed pumps in the U.K.

The motor driven 4,700 p.s.i.g. KSB boiler feed pump, Margham Works, Steel Company of Wales.

Ditton Sewage Pumping Station, Widnes. Consulting Engineers—John Taylor & Sons, London and Liverpool

Five of the six KSB sewage pumps installed at Ditton Pumping Station, Widnes in 1975. Consulting Engineers— John Taylor & Sons, London and Liverpool.

West Kirby Pumping Station

Another scheme where we assisted in the installation of the pumps was the West Kirby Pumping Station, where we supplied and helped install three large storm water pumps and five sewage pumps.

Offloading the KSB pumps for the West Kirby Pumping Station at Britannia House, Hoylake, 1972.

Tony Smith & Brian Rice working on the five sewage pumps that cleaned up the West Kirby beaches. Consulting Engineers—John Taylor & Sons, London and Liverpool.

Over a century ago when Thomas Brassey spent a pleasant afternoon on the beach at West Kirby, he sat on golden sands. The total population of Wirral was then quite small, but as the population grew outfalls were built and crude sewage was discharged only a few hundred yards off shore into the Dee estuary. This disgusting state of affairs grew until in 1970 it was decided to build a new pumping station in West Kirby to pump the effluent to another station in Meols which then pumped it three miles out to sea where it was discharged into a deep, fast-flowing tidal current which carried it out to sea. It would have been better if they had built a full treatment works at Meols in the first place, but the politicians got busy and spent so long arguing that in the end they could not afford it.

We supplied and installed the following K.S.B. pump at West Kirby.

3—125-hp Storm Water Pumps
3—20-hp Sewage Pumps
2—25-hp Sewage Pumps

Since the new pumping station was finished and commissioned there has been a noticeable improvement in the condition of the beaches in West Kirby and Hoylake and golden sand is now to be seen, where formerly there was only foul mud and this project has given us particular pleasure.

In 1974 we parted company with KSB because KSB Germany offered a job to a German Sales Engineer and told him he would be on our staff, but regrettably they forgot to mention it to us and to ask if we agreed. We, and the Sales Engineer found ourselves at cross purposes when he reported to us for duty when we knew nothing about it, so we agreed to part company with KSB because we like to decide who joins our staff, not others.

In August 1989 KSB once again asked us to represent them and we are delighted to be selling their excellent range of pumps.

In the last two years we have secured a number of important contracts including:

Welsh Water—Barmouth Outfall Pumping Station
Metropolitan Borough of Wirral—Bromborough Sewer
N.W. Water—Rivington—Clean Water Plant
Ellesmere Port Land Reclamation Pumps

West Kirby Pumping Station, West Kirby, Wirral. Consulting Engineers—John Taylor & Sons, London and Liverpool.

Yorkshire Water, Dewsbury Road Clean Water Plant
City of Carlisle—Line Street Refurbishment Scheme
Thames Water, Swansea Sewage Works
Northumbrian Water—Sunderland Sewage Interceptor Scheme
BNFL Effluent Treatment
Pumps for the Chemical Industry

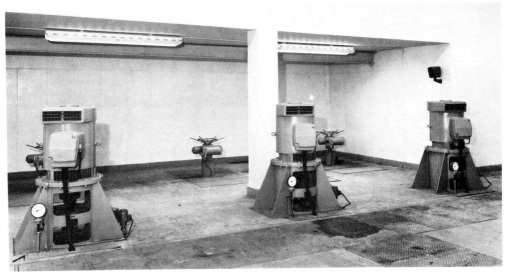

West Kirby Pumping Station. The three 125-hp Storm Water Pumps.

Three KSB-PNT submersible motor pumps with mixed flow impellers handling clean and slightly contaminated liquids.

An installation of KSB-CPK chemical pumps with water cooled glands.

CHAPTER 11

the 1980's

THE 1980's – A DECADE OF CHALLENGE, OPPORTUNITY AND DEVELOPMENT

When the first edition of this book was published in 1976 the country was in a mess because it had suffered from poor Government for years. Industry was overmanned, badly equipped and in poor shape. Management moaned that the Trade Unions were running the show; the Unions disagreed and felt that their only job was to disrupt. The Prime Minister couldn't move without sending for the Tammany Hall bosses, who strutted into Downing Street for beer and sandwiches but could not deliver the promises they made because real union power rested with the militants on the shop floor. All this meant that when the World recession hit us at the end of 70's Britain was in very poor shape to cope with it.

The winter of discontent in 1979, when the unions went mad and left the streets full of rubbish, refused to bury the dead and toppled the Labour Government, brought Margaret Thatcher to power. Once again when it was in a desperate situation Britain was fortunate to find a remarkable individual to lead it out of trouble.

The 1980's were not easy, for even if we had not had gross overmanning in many industries, and uncompetitive companies, there would have been millions thrown out of work. Look at Germany which had been ruled sensibly since the war; with a better educated work force and more intelligent union leaders than we had – they too suffered and in 1988 had 2.5 million people unemployed and soon will have more unemployed than we have in spite of being able to send back home some millions of foreign "Gastarbeiter" – guest workers.

Perhaps only a very remarkable woman could have carried out the enormous tasks that have been tackled over the last decade, but although many will disagree, she has brought wise Government to a sorely pressed land. There is much to do, but at long last the country is moving ahead and all our people will benefit from the improvements she has brought about and indeed they already have.

Although there were severe problems for many of us in the 1980's the standard of living of most people improved during the decade. Indeed in preparing the third edition of this book and changing the staff photographs taken in the 1970's and even in the middle of the 1980's, it was quite startling to note the enormous improvement in appearance, style and dress that had taken place in that period.

Today our young people do not give a second thought about taking their holidays all over the World; the Caribbean, U.S.A., Egypt, Far East and of course Europe. Hard for them to believe that until Margaret Thatcher came to power in 1979 the Labour Government rationed the amount of money people could take abroad and so in effect they controlled where individuals could take their holidays "The Socialist State Knows Best."

It was obvious to us when Margaret Thatcher came to power that difficult times lay ahead. For one thing inflation would be brought under control and that, no doubt to the surprise of some, would make life much more difficult for us. Under Labour and roaring inflation, companies such as ours could hardly help making a profit. As we carry millions of pounds worth of stock the value of our stock was automatically increased, as were our profits, as inflation raged out of control. That is why so many Company Directors did not welcome the coming to power of Margaret Thatcher, because they knew that in the real world of stable finance their deficiencies would be cruelly exposed whereas Labour propped up old fashioned, inefficient industry at the cost of the sick and the elderly.

Memories are short, but history shows that those who suffered under socialist inflation were the pensioners on fixed incomes; the sick, because there was no real increase in investment in the National Health Service and the unemployed because inflation priced us out of so many markets. If anyone doubts the truth of these comments they should look up the facts.

So we entered the 1980's knowing that we, and the country, were in for a tough time, but still we welcomed this new decade because we prefer honest money, efficient industry and growing wealth for our country. We thought that there would be opportunities as well as dangers and difficulties and so it proved. In spite of all the problems we made progress during the 1980's and in spite of all the rhetoric to the contrary, so did the country.

IBM COMPUTER (1982 to date)

As related elsewhere we bought our first computer in 1969 and as it was an early machine it was very simple and rather crude. In 1982 we decided to buy a new machine as our old one was then well out of date. After investigating various model we chose an IBM System 34 with nineteen screens that were to be spread throughout our Hoylake and Manchester offices. Three years later this was sold and a more powerful System 36 was bought.

As IBM did not have a suitable software package to suit our needs they suggested that we should work with a young Scot, Bob Locke, who only lived about five miles from our office in Gayton Hall, Gayton, Wirral, and who ran a software house, Motis Systems (UK) Ltd.

Bob came to see us and then set up a meeting in Gayton Hall which in those days he used for his business as well as being his home, and in that beautiful hall, which used to be the home of the ancient Glegg family, Bob had set aside certain rooms that were full of computers for his business.

Gayton Hall has an interesting history because in 1689 King William III left Kensington Palace with an army of 10,000 men en route for Ireland, and the King, the Prince of Denmark and other members of the Quality, arrived in Chester on Tuesday 10 June and stayed the night in that beautiful city. The next day the Royal Party arrived at Gayton Hall where they stayed as the guests of William Glegg. The huge army marched on to Hoylake where they encamped between Meols and Hoylake, just about where our Hoylake office is now, and there they stayed for a week.

The King and his party stayed at Gayton Hall and when he was leaving on Wednesday 11 June 1689, the King was so impressed by the hospitality he had received from William Glegg that he bid him "Kneel" and touching both shoulders with his sword said, "Arise Sir William". Having knighted William Glegg, William of Orange then sailed from Hoylake for Ireland, the Battle of Boyne, and history.

However, we digress, back to computers. The problem with our business from a computer viewpoint is that we have a fast moving business and need to have fast answers about thousands of components that are usually in stock, but which can be built up to millions of different assemblies. We also have a manufacturing organisation and need the capability of any of our offices being able to interrogate our stocks of components and then be able to prepare the factory order sheets and have the paperwork printed at the particular location where the assembly and manufacture is to be carried out.

Over a period of several years, Bob Locke has worked with John Keith Millar and they have developed a superb system that is very powerful, but simple to use. Now we have a computer system that is the envy of much larger companies and it is all thanks to our work with the brilliant, young, dark haired, slightly built, Glaswegian.

In return, Bob Locke has benefitted from the work he has done for us because this particular package has now been adopted by such companies as Rolls Royce, Cummins Diesels, Audi-Volkswagen, and others, and he richly deserves his success.

Sales Office, Britannia House, Hoylake, showing some of our staff and some of the I.B.M. System 36 V.D.U.'s.

As well as the I.B.M. System 36 computer we also have half a dozen P.C. computers for doing technical work. here Steven Low is using a control valve selection programme he wrote. (1988).

FORMATION OF JOHN MILLAR (UK) LTD., ENGINEERS (1981)

After our traumatic experiences in the period 1975–1978 when we were almost put out of business by ruthless individuals we resolved to widen our base and to develop new business and our own products, so that in the future, we should not be at the mercy of any Sadists we might encounter. However, Heap & Partners did not have the capacity, nor the space, to handle more new products and so we decided to form a new company which would handle new products, and developments, and we decided to build a new factory and offices for the new business.

On 24 June 1981, in spite of the then current recession, a new company, John Millar (UK) Ltd was formed and work started on a 10,000 square foot factory with office block. The new factory was finished in October 1981. We believe that too many companies take too short a view of expansion and we are pleased that we took prudent steps to expand in the middle of a recession.

We now had a new company, and empty factory, no staff, but we did have a few ideas and we were reasonably confident that we could make the new venture a success.

In November 1981 Paul Tattum, who had been working in the Marketing Department of Unilever, was taken on as Manager of the new company and in due course he, Dorothy Millar, John Keith Millar and David Millar were made Directors of the new company and Ann Tattum was appointed Company Secretary. Staff were gradually recruited and by the end of November 1981 we were in business.

Rallim House, Carr Lane Industrial Estate, Hoylake. Head Office of John Millar (UK) Ltd. (1985).

HINDLE COCKBURNS LTD (1983 to date)

The first Agency the new company took on was the old established Leeds valve manufacturer, Hindle Cockburn.

The Hindle Cockburns works in the centre of Leeds. About 100 yards from the original works founded in 1880.

The industrial revolution started in the North of England and soon factories, cotton and woollen mills, dye works and steelworks started to spring up all over the North of England, Scotland and Northern Ireland. Industrial development depends upon the flow of fluids and soon factories and foundries making valves or controlling the fluids were spawned all over the country, but nowhere with a greater concentration than in England's largest county, Yorkshire.

With the growing pace of industrial activity, more and more men with experience started to produce valves. One such man was Joshua Hindle a Victorian engineer who set up in business in the centre of Leeds in 1880, not a hundred yards from where the present works is.

In the early days the company produced a range of valves, locks and pipeline fittings in its own foundry where they cast iron, and brass, and carried out the machining of the castings. During World War I, Joshua Hindle produced their range of valves in increasing numbers but they also made a significant contribution to the war effort by making munitions.

In the 1930's Joshua Hindle engaged a young man by the name of William Gomersall. This young man was quite small but what he lacked in inches he made up for in drive and ability and in 1937 at the remarkably young age of 22 years he was made Managing Director.

Two years later World War II started and once again Hindle geared up for war production. In 1940 a second foundry was opened and two years later a new works was opened in Neville Street, Leeds, within a few hundred yards of the original works.

At the time the foundries were producing castings made of bronze, aluminium bronze, white metal, aluminium, nickel alloys but not stainless steel nor monel.

In 1946 after the war ended peace time production resumed and the Neville Street Works made valves, fire fighting nozzles, swivelling nozzle holders for fire engine ladders, standpipes and even firemen's helmets. They even had a section selling plumbers fittings and refrigeration equipment. The original works and foundry were closed as it was then over sixty years old and production was concentrated on the new site. The first row of machines were moved to the new site in 1948 and in 1954 a second bay was added.

In June 1967 there was a dramatic change in the fortunes of Joshua Hindle because the Hindle family sold their 75% share of the equity to the Thomas Tilling Group, but Bill Gomersall held on to his 25% holding.

An early decision after the takeover was to close Neville Street works and to build a new office block on the present site. The third foundry was also closed because it was proving difficult to make it pay. A not uncommon phenomena over the last twenty years so far as foundries were concerned.

Next door to Hindle's Neville Street works was another valve manufacturer making a similar range of products. Relations between this valve maker, Sarah Dixon, and Joshua Hindle were always, well: "competitive", but that may be an understatement; perhaps open warfare may be more accurate. They fought over markets, products and men; the advantage first going to one firm and then swinging back to the other.

Eventually, however, in the early 1950's one of the Sarah Dixon Directors had a disagreement with his company; resigned, and then joined Joshua Hindle next door. This event was really a watershed, because gradually other people drifted away from Sarah Dixon and then joined Hindle. Eventually in 1968 Hindle were employing 230 people and Sarah Dixon 120 and the Directors of Sarah Dixon called it a day and sold out to Joshua Hindle. Today, twenty years later there are still some of the Sarah Dixon men employed by Hindles.

In October 1972 after only five years of ownership Thomas Tilling sold their 75% of the Hindle shares to Lake and Elliot, the steel founders of Braintree in Essex. Bill Gomersall also sold his 25% of the stock and then gave a party for 100 members of his staff. At that time Hindles employed 330 people including two grandsons of Joshua Hindle, David and his cousin, Keith Hindle.

There followed several difficult years for the company with many management changes. Then in 1974 they introduced a very tall man as joint Managing Director with the diminutive, bespectacled, pipe smoking, able, firebrand—Bill Gomersall. It was asking for trouble and they got it. Within a short period Bill Gomersall resigned as did the Financial Director and the Company Secretary. It was the end of an era.

Between the years 1974 and 1979 there were several new Managing Directors and the only management consistency was provided by Brian Varley who was then the Works Director and Stan Borgen who was Sales Director.

Part of the Hindle Machine Shop in the 1960's. Now replaced by modern machining centres.

Brian Varley had worked all his life with Hindles, starting in the drawing office at the age of 16 years. A man of ability he was made Chief Draughtsman at the tender age of 23 years; became Works Manager at 27 years and Works Director at 33. In 1980 Lake & Elliot had the good sense to see that while they had been busy bringing all kinds of outsiders to run Joshua Hindle, they had, in Brian Varley, the right man for the job. He was knowledgeable about designs and production, tough but popular, and he had the necessary foresight to carry the company forward through what was to be one of the most difficult decades in our industrial history. Ten years in which the country had to transform its industry from the ways of the past to setting itself on the road to a bright new future.

In the meantime up in Glasgow another old Victorian engineering company, Cockburns Ltd, was also struggling to survive in a rapidly changing industrial world. At the turn of the last century David Cockburn was in business as a boilermaker in McNeil Street, Glasgow. His son George had set up business in Sussex Street, Glasgow, making his own invention, the Cockburn steam safety valve.

The Test Area of Cockburns Glasgow works in 1972. Typical of the old fashioned, untidy, out of date, state of many British industries in the 70's.

In 1900 the two works amalgamated and father and son produced safety valves, made boilers and were regarded as excellent marine steam specialists.

After World War II Cockburn took out a licence from Rockwell of U.S.A. for the manufacture of their standard range of butterfly valves. Over the next ten years the sales of butterfly valves gradually increased and with the decline of British, and Continental, shipbuilding, the sale of safety valves gradually diminished.

In 1968 Lake & Elliot bought Cockburns Ltd and as already related four years later they bought Joshua Hindle. In 1978 the Cockburns works in Scotland was closed and the production transferred to Leeds. The small Cockburns marine valve repair works in North Shields was kept going for another ten years but on 1 January 1988 this too was closed and the work transferred to Leeds.

One of the first things Brian Varley did on becoming Managing Director was to take a hard look at their design of ball valves. Hindles had been making ball valves through a subsidiary company, Spensall Machining Company, in Leeds for twenty years. Brian Varley set to and had a vastly improved two piece ball valve designed and then they manufactured this new valve in stainless steel and cast steel. This was a most important piece of work because the new valve, christened the "Ultraseal", became the launch pad to project Hindle Cockburns into a prosperous future.

The valve was launched in 1981 and sales were encouraging but in 1983, Rod Whitehouse the young Sales Director, persuaded his Board to change their sales outlets from selling exclusively through their own sales force to a Distribution organisation.

In 1983 John Millar (UK) Ltd were one of those companies appointed as distributors for the "Ultraseal" ball valve and in 1987 we became distributors for the whole of the United Kingdom for the Hindle Cockburns range of stainless steel, globe, gate, float and check valves.

The change to a distribution system of selling the "Ultraseal" had a dramatic effect on sales and this in turn enabled modern machining centres to be gradually installed, replacing older, less efficient, machine tools.

In 1985 the Suter Group, led by David Abell, who had been the youngest Main Board Member of British Leyland, bought Hindle Cockburns from Lake & Elliot and they injected more capital to enable the modernisation to continue. In 1987 a 26,000 square foot machine shop exten-

The Hindle range of stainless steel globe, gate, float and check valves stocked in Hoylake.

Hindle ball valves fitted with extended spindle to clear pipe lagging. This modification was carried out in our own workshops.

A Hindle cast steel ball valve fitted with Heap & Partners switchbox.

A Hindle stainless steel ball valve fitted with an electric actuator in our Hoylake workshops.

Hindles' new 26,000 square foot machine shop extension in 1987. Clean, modern, efficient.

sion was opened which now houses eight large machining centres, including the half a million pound Schiess machine tool.

The story of the transformation and modernisation of Joshua Hindle of Leeds and Cockburns of Glasgow is really the story of British industry over the last ten years or so. A transformation, often painful, from old, outdated, workshops and work practices to modern products produced in clean, efficient, workshops.

CED PROJECTS LTD, MARLOW, BUCKS (1980)

The industrial turmoil of the 1980's when industry had to slim down, adopt healthier working practices and become much fitter, meant that inevitably some companies had to pull out of certain types of manufacture in order to concentrate their resources on their core business.

One such company was Plenty & Son Ltd of Newbury who closed down their Bescon division which had manufactured packaged plant systems and an agreement was reached that CED (Chemical Engineering Development) then of Windsor would take over this role. As we were the North West Agents for Plenty & Son we were asked by Ted Sulley, one of CED's Directors if we would represent them and in 1980 we visited their delightfully situated offices on the banks of the Thames at Windsor and reached agreement.

CED was formed as an engineering consultancy in 1972 as part of the Mitchell Cotts organisation and became independent in 1975 when Doug Bradley, Ted Sulley and Ken Sutherland bought the company in a Management Buyout and in 1984, Don France, formerly Bescon's Contract Manager, joined the CED team.

Work was carried out for A.E.R.E., Harwell and for Kuhni of Switzerland and Bronswerk of Utrecht, Holland.

CED now provide a wide range of plant for many different industries including the oil industry, power generation, chemical, food, pharmaceutical and the water industry.

Since 1980 we have been instrumental in securing a wide range of plants included a large water filtration plant for B.N.F.L.; solvent filtering and pumping systems, thermal oil control systems for vacuum dryers, drum ovens and a large condensate return package.

Industry will continue to demand complete plant packages, works tested and approved to cut down costly uncertain and lengthy site assembly work and the future for CED looks bright.

CED's offices at Marlow, Bucks.

KINETROL LTD., FARNHAM, SURREY (1985 to date)

Britain is a fortunate country in many respects, particularly in the number of people with inventive minds who live here. It is difficult to know why so many original ideas spring from this land but possibly it has something to do with our pride in being individuals rather than members of a group.

In 1985 Japan's Ministry of International Trade and Industry became concerned at the lack of new inventions originating in Japan and so they carried out an investigation to discover which countries had made the greatest contributions to what they termed "significant" inventions since World War II.

They found, as they suspected, that Japan is non too inventive; for its contribution was only 6%; Germany and France were somewhat better and the U.S.A. was in second place and had contributed 22%. The Japanese Ministry were surprised to find that the U.K. had invented no less than 55% of the World's "significant" inventions—more than the rest of the World added together.

Possibly some of those "significant" inventions were designed by the remarkable Barnes Wallis and his team at Vickers Aviation; who produced many new inventions including the bouncing bomb and the first swing wing aircraft. During the war his Chief Scientific Officer at Vickers was A.R.B Nash.

In 1958 Alan Nash decided to set up in business on his own and, with an assistant and a boy, he formed his new company called Kinetrol. He derived the name from two words "Kinetic Energy" and "Control" because he intended his new company to be control engineers.

The first two products that the new company made were a fine wire feeder that could satisfactorily feed very fine wires used in some coils and the second was a range of rotary dashpots.

Alan Nash had worked on rotary dashpots at Vickers because he had found a need for rotary precision damping device but at Kinetrol he perfected the Kinetrol rotary dashpots.

The company no longer manufactures fine wire feeders because the technology has changed but it still produces dashpots.

After Kinetrol had been in business for some time they were approached by Quaker Oats who had run into a problem in the production of their famous product "Puffed Wheat". The puffed wheat was produced in steam heated ovens and the steam was controlled by a manually operated valve. This was rather unsatisfactory as it depended on production staff remembering to open, or close, the valve and the result was very wasteful.

To overcome the problem Kinetrol designed a quarter turn vane type automatic actuator operating a bronze quarter turn steam valve and this new actuator operated valve was spectacularly successful. This first actuator set Kinetrol on the road to being one of the leading actuator manufacturers.

Using the sealing knowledge gained from work on rotary dashpots the Kinetrol vane type actuators have been very successful. They have been copied in the U.S.A. but the transatlantic version suffered from sealing problems, because they were unable to copy the Kinetrol sealing mechanisms.

Today Kinetrol actuators are used all over the world and they are made in four manufacturing sites in Farnham covering some 50,000 square feet and where 160 people are employed.

Although we have used Kinetrol actuators in a small way since the early 1970's we were asked to start stocking the Kinetrol range of quarter turn actuators in 1985 and since then the growth in the stock business has been quite remarkable. We are able to select the right actuator for a particular valve by using our computer programme and then we can fit the actuator to the valve, test and despatch, in a matter of hours. So giving industry the fast service it needs.

Another product made by Kinetrol in Farnham is rather surprisingly, a range of small aircraft! As already recounted Alan Nash spent 25 years of his working life in the aircraft industry before founding Kinetrol. In 1979 he was approached by a man who had started a project at Lasham airfield near Farnham building a light aircraft that would be suitable for acting as a glider tug. Funds had run out before the project could be completed and after examining the plans Alan Nash agreed to take it over and he formed Nash Aircraft Ltd to run it.

A batch of Kinetrol actuators fitted to Saunders 'M' type ball valves outside our workshops in Hoylake. (1987).

Kinetrol actuators fitted to Hindle ball valves in a chemical plant. (1986).

226

Kinetrol actuators fitted to Audco 3-way plug valves. (1988).

The plane, named the "Petrel", has the potential to be used as a conventional two seater aircraft as well as a glider tug. Modifications to the frame design were necessary before the prototype could be produced, but then a programme of test flying was started to get the full C.A.A. certification.

Although a professional test pilot was employed, Alan Nash spent many hours in the air in the second seat making observations, and his eldest son, Richard Nash, a qualified pilot, has also flown the plane.

The prototype was shown at the Farnborough Air Show in 1984 and a batch of five aircraft were then started. Unhappily shortly after these decisions were taken Ian Nash had to undergo major heart surgery from which he did not recover for two or three years. This inevitably caused delays in production but it is hoped that, with a design update, that a fully aerobatic aeroplane will be finished in the near future.

The future of Kinetrol is very promising because working under Alan Nash are his two sons, Richard, now Managing Director and John, is Technical Director and they have an excellent support team.

It is interesting to see how men of enterprise and ability push ahead with new, innovative products in a free Society. We are very lucky to live in such a fortunate country.

TOMOE SAUNDERS LTD. (1986)

In the 1960's the Saunders Valve Co. designed an excellent range of general purpose butterfly valves to compliment their range of diaphragm valves, and then in the 1970's they introduced a range of hygienic butterfly valves, but they needed new designs to compliment their range because since the 1970's the butterfly valve has been one of the most rapidly growing types throughout Europe.

In 1982 John Lever, then Sales Director of the Saunders Valve Company approached the Tomoe Valve Company of Osaka, Japan with a view to reaching an agreement for a joint venture in the UK.

For those who think that this is another example of "know how" flowing from Japan to the UK, we would mention that Saunders export millions of pounds worth of diaphragm valves to Japan in the other direction.

Tomoe Saunders
UK Headquarters,
Newport, Gwent,
South Wales.

Again we must mention that Britain still exports per head of population about 1.5 times the figure for Japan—if we don't tell the facts who will? Certainly not the media who are contracted to only tell bad news about the UK.

The Tomoe Valve Company was founded in 1963 in Osaka, Japan by Mr I Yamamoto a graduate engineer. Initially Tomoe manufactured gate valves for the shipping industry but about that time the big advantages in weight and space saving of the butterfly valve over the gate valve was being realised, and so Mr Yamamoto decided to manufacture nothing but butterfly valves and he made an excellent job of the transformation.

In October 1986 a new company jointly owned by Tomoe Valve Company and the Saunders Valve Company was incorporated and a new factory was built in Newport, Gwent. The Managing Director of Tomoe Saunders, as the new company is called, is, John Waite who had formerly been Commercial Manager of the Saunders Valve Company, Cwmbran and Mike Perkins of Saunders Technical Department also joined the new company.

The new company incorporated the Saunders General Purpose butterfly valve and the Tomoe range with some valves being built in Cwmbran and some in Osaka. Eventually most of the valves will be produced in South Wales.

The growth of the Tomoe Saunders business has been very gratifying over the last few years and we expect this growth to continue in the future.

A Tomoe Saunders 700G butterfly valve, white epoxy coated fitted with a PVC coated Hytork actuator and switch box in our Hoylake workshop.

HYTORK (1989)

In 1989 we were asked to become the distributor for Hytork actuators to compliment the Kinetrol range of quarter turn actuators.

Ross Stewart the MD of Hytork took a Masters Degree at Cranfield Institute of Technology in Bedford and joined the Worcester Valve Company in the UK. In 1973 Ross left Worcester and moved to Tetbury in Gloucestershire and started Hytork in an old Woollen Mill building in Stroud.

In 1975 Rod Duncan who Ross had met at Cranfield joined Hytork and development of the Hytork range continued apace.

In 1977 Serck took over Hytork to operate as the actuation company for Serk and they injected significant investment into increasing Hytork's manufacturing capacity but in 1981

Two stage shut off valves built in our Hoylake workshops based on Hytork actuators and including limit switchboxes, filter regulators and twin pilot solenoid valves with built in L.E.D.'s. (1990).

Serck in turn were taken over by the BTR Group who had also bought Worcester. Big fish gobbling up smaller fish.

The Monopolies and Merger Commission were not happy about BTR's acquisitions in the valve field and so in 1982 Ross Stewart and Rod Duncan bought Hytork back from BTR and once more they were independent.

Since then Hytork have bought a 23,000 square foot factory in Gloucester and in 1987 set up Hytork Control Inc. in Florida, U.S.A. and are going from strength to strength.

A 4 in and a 2 in Hindle stainless steel ball valve with Hytork actuator and pneumatic air switches built in our Hoylake workshops. (1990).

AFORM LTD, THATCHAM, BERKSHIRE (1991)

In the section dealing with Plenty & Sons Ltd earlier in this book (page 206) mention was made of the group of bright young Cambridge educated engineers that Guy Shoosmith recruited in the 1950's. One of those Cambridge graduates was John Hall Craggs who was largely responsible for pushing forward the Plenty Filter and Plenty Mixer in their early days when others were not quite so enthusiastic. John eventually became Managing Director of Plenty & Son but left in the early 1980's to set up his own company of Management Consultants and in due course he became Chairman of Aform UK of Thatcham, Berkshire.

Aform was founded in1970 and made fibreglass mouldings for various industries including covers for Mercedes vans to enable the van to have greater height. Another imaginative piece of work they did was to make the fibreglass Archemedes screws for a well known pump manufacturer and for this they were awarded the Dardalus Award for Innovation in the plastics industry.

Eventually, however, they developed, with the aid of computers, a range of self-supporting fibreglass covers for tanks up to 30 m in diameter as well as channel flumes, GRP weirs and other products widely used in the water industry.

Although at first sight the products are simple, the reality is that the design of the covers is most complex and the production employs many different types of fibreglass matt depending on the stresses at any particular point.

Although the works is not very large it has a tremendous output and in 1991 we were appointed as North West Agents for Aform by John Hall Craggs and his colleague, Tim Williams.

John Hall Craggs and Tim Williams are quite remarkable because although they are both extremely hardworking businessmen they also have hobbies that in themselves could be the subjects for two books.

When John Hall Craggs was a child his Father, who was also an engineer built up a most impressive model railway for his son. In turn John not only took over the model railway but he has built an astonishing miniature railway in the grounds of his delightful house in Berkshire. This miniature railway is no toy because it covers several acres and has cuttings, tunnels, full scale signals, signal boxes, ticket offices and workshops and a range of working locomotives that include a scaled down "Rocket" up to powerful locomotives more than 4 feet long with boilers working at 100 psi and capable of pulling along trains loaded with passengers.

John's railway is not called a model railway but is referred to as "the railway" because that is what it is and it must be one of the finest in Europe.

Tim William's hobby is also in transport but this time in the air because Tim owns, and flies, a 1930 de Havilland Puss Moth G-AAZP. In 1932 this remarkable little aircraft made the first ever commercial flight in Egypt and she then operated as an air taxi in Egypt until 1936 when she was bought and flown back to England.

In 1934 the greatest air race of all time took place, this was the McRobertson Air Race from Mildenhall in Sussex to Melbourne, Australia, and second in the Handicap was a de Havilland Puss Moth.

1984 was the 50th Anniversary of this great race and so Tim Williams and Henry Labouchere decided to fly G-AAZP from Mildenhall to Melbourne following the original route as near as possible and so they set about the formidable task of overhauling the plane, gaining sponsorships, seeking permission from the countries on the route and arranging for additional petrol tanks to be fitted and the numerous supplies they would need for the journey.

Weight had to be kept down to a minimum and so all non essentials were cut down to a minimum and they ended up with 10kg of clothes each, but 15kg of maps.

Today Mildenhall is a USAF base and with typical American enthusiasm they entered into the spirit of the thing and organised an eve of departure dance in one of the hangars for two thousand five hundred people with 1930's music being provided by Joe Loss and his band.

En route the pair of aviators were treated Royally, sometimes figuratively speaking, sometimes actually, for in Amman the King of Jordan, himself an aviator, gave them a superb welcome and great hospitality. On through the Gulf, Karachi, India, Burmah, Singapore, Indonesia and finally across the dangerous Sea of Timor to Darwen, Australia; then across Australia flying just above the bush to Melbourne where they arrived dead on time at 3.00pm Saturday, 8 December 1984.

At 54 years old, de Havilland Puss Moth G-AAZP, was the oldest aircraft ever to have flown from England to Australia.

A great adventure, and a worthy memorial to the aviation pioneers of half a century earlier.

A form self supporting fibreglass covers on 15mm diameter boiling acetic acid tanks at Warwick Chemicals, Mostyn, N. Wales.

One of seven self supporting covers installed over 20m diameter sludge holding tanks at Wigan S.T.W.

THE RETIREMENT OF E. J. HOWELL (Director 1955–1981)

Jimmy Howell's maternal Grandfather was James Kindler who in the 1860's was a plumber who resided at 146 High Street, Stockton on Tees, and it was here, on 18 January 1981 that Jim's Mother, Florence was born.

The plumbing business prospered and in 1887 James Kindler was elected Mayor of Stockton on Tees. In that year, the six year old Florence Kindler, was invited to name a new Merryweather fire engine at a public ceremony in High Street, Stockton. This, the grave little girl did and named the engine 'Florence'.

In 1883 the family fortunes had improved so much that the Kindlers bought a new house called Eden Lodge in the very pleasant village of Hutton Rudby which is about two miles from our office on Stockton on Tees Industrial Estate. The house is still there and it, and the village, are completely unspoiled and are very desirable places to live.

Unhappily, a decade later, James Kindler's business ran into trouble and in 1893 he had to sell up, and he, and his family, moved to Birmingham to be near his daughter Caroline.

In 1906 Florence Kindler married John Edward Howell who was an engineer working for Belliss & Morcom Ltd of Birmingham. In 1908 a daughter Francis was born and in 1916 Edward James Howell was born.

Francis was a very bright girl and in due course attended King Edward School for Girls in Birmingham and when she was seventeen won an open scholarship in Mathematics to Newnham College, Cambridge. She could not go however because of home circumstances, and instead she went to Birmingham University were she graduated with 1st Class Honours in Mathematics. Later she studied at Liverpool University and was awarded M.Sc. in Mathematics. Francis Howell chose teaching for her career and eventually she became Deputy Head Mistress of Oldershaw Grammar School, Wallasey.

Jimmy Howell too was bright but he was not as interested in academic study as his sister. After taking a School Certificate at Oldbury High School he matriculated and in November 1933 he started as an Indentured Apprentice with his father's employers, Belliss & Morcom Ltd of Birmingham.

The Howell family in 1931. L to R. Florence Howell (nee Kindler), Jim Howell (age 15 years), Frances Howell, John Edward Howell.

234

John Howell had been made Manager of the Outside Erection Department of Belliss & Morcom in 1914; a position he was to hold until he retired in 1948 after 52 years with the company. In those days Belliss & Morcom were one of the World's leading manufacturers of steam engines, steam turbines, diesel engines and air compressors and it was commonly stated that "One never leaves Bellis & Morcom, one merely graduates to another job."

After completing his apprenticeship in 1937 Jim Howell worked in the Erection Department building testing all kinds of engines and when World War II came he was sent out on outside erection all over the United Kingdom installing steam engines, alternators, steam turbines and compressors.

The years between 1943 and 1949 were spent installing Bellis and Morcom engines abroad. His first visit overseas was to West Africa when he sailed in a wartime convoy from the U.K. to Freetown in Sierra Leone. In 1944 he returned to that country again but this time he flew in a Dakota. It was slow and primitive, and the flight, with stop-overs, took three days and when they were flying at 7,000 feet it was so cold that the passengers were issued with flying suits and fur lined flying boots. Other work was undertaken in Gibraltar, Portugal, Spain, Grenada and St Vincent in the British West Indies.

Working alone in another country installing heavy machinery calls for skill and ingenuity and Jim Howell possessed these and other qualities. He was an excellent practical engineer and although he was very quiet he was quite determined and possessed a gentle sense of humour.

In 1949 Jimmy Howell joined Heap & Partners working on Bellis & Morcom plant under H. H. Gwillam and when Mr Gwillam departed suddenly early in 1952 after a row with A.H. Atkins, Jim Howell took control of the eight B & M fitters we ran.

In 1955 E.J. Howell was made a Director of Heap & Partners Ltd and continued working mainly on B & M work until 1962 when an unexpected blow fell.

The story of Bellis & Morcom was typical of too many British engineering companies at that time. They were developed by enterprising Victorians and until the first war they made great progress. In between the wars, however, they did not develop their products, nor methods of production, and although World War II gave them a great boost in work, they entered the post war era with outdated designs. They were still making steam engines long after it was obvious that its days were numbered. They had been making diesels from the earliest days but their designs were pre-war and they had been overtaken by more enterprising British and foreign manufacturers. Their air compressors were of a very robust design but they badly needed a modern design and finally their Management skills had declined to dangerous levels.

The Directors, being unable to sort out the mess themselves, called in Consultants who added to their problems by creating a new "Production Control" department which grew with amazing speed until it employed 200 people; all busy passing slips of paper to each other working the marvellous new system.

It could not last, and in 1962 the axe fell and the bank stepped in. Most of the old Management, including Directors, had to go, hundreds of workers lost their jobs and the business contracted and one complete factory was sold. The price was being paid for Management not doing it's job properly in it's latter years.

Bellis & Morcom just survived by gradually introducing new designs but in 1962 they had to divest themselves of all their outside sales team and so we had to part company with them after representing them for over 50 years.

Jimmy Howell was very upset because he and his father before him, had spent their entire working lives with B & M, but there was no point in moping about the changes and we had to find work for Jimmy Howell.

Jim was so shy and diffident that in the face of it he was not likely to make a good sales engineer, but in fact he became one of the most successful sales engineers we have ever had. He was quite incapable of "selling" anybody anything—but that is not our style in any event. He was an excellent engineer, very conscientious, completely honest and customers liked, and trusted, him.

About that time we started to do more work fitting actuators to Saunders valves and when Alan Caldwell joined us from I.C.I. in 1967 he suggested that we should stock some Serck

Glocon actuators because deliveries were very long and we could gain some business by fitting these more advanced actuators. This proved to be an important turning point in our history and although Alan Caldwell returned to I.C.I. after a couple of years we have benefitted from his suggestion ever since.

To celebrate our Centenary in 1966 we built our first test bench in the basement of Empire Buildings, Liverpool, and gradually Jimmy Howell started to accumulate knowledge about the actuation of valves and then he started to train our younger men in the art.

We moved to Hoylake in 1970 and our new facilities enabled us to develop more sophisticated valves and switches and soon it was clear that the loss of the B & M Agency was a blessing in disguise because we had never made much money out of the Agency and it had grown out of date, whereas we were now in a new advancing business and Jimmy Howell played a key role in it.

Jim Howell was very interested in engineering and in 1980 one job he took responsibility for was the manufacture of four sets of sliding valve mechanisms for the S.S. Great Britain, now undergoing restoration in Bristol after returning from the Falklands Islands in 1970 after a century's neglect.

The S.S. Great Britain was designed by Isambard Kingdom Brunel and was built in Bristol and our involvement came about because she was Liverpool owned and she sailed for most of her life Liverpool–New York; Liverpool–Melbourne; and so when an appeal was made for engineering companies to make and donate components for a replica engine for the ship we offered our assistance as a contribution from her home port.

Our young men, under the guidance of Jim Howell, and our Workshop Manager, Brian Makinson, made four sliding valve mechanisms for the engines. Although made of aluminium for lightness, instead of the original cast iron, Jim Howell insisted that the valve gear should be made as near as possible to Brunel's original design, even to the extent of making the nuts to the original Brunel, non standard, dimension.

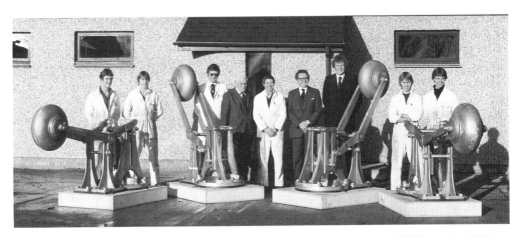

The valve mechanisms for the "S.S. Great Britain", December 1981 L to R. Gerard Williams, Paul Miller, Brian Aves, Jim Howell, Brian Makinson, John Millar, John Keith Millar, Mark Swann, Adrian Baker.

In 1981 Jim Howell was 65 years old and decided to retire. Six months earlier when we knew he would be leaving we had taken on a man in his early fifties to replace Jim and he spent six months training with Jim Howell, but a couple of days before he was due to take over he told us that he could not stay because he knew that he could not do the job! This posed a problem for us, but Ann Millar suggested that, although he was very young, we should try Oundle educated J.K. Millar, who was then working in our Manchester office. There was no time for training for takeover and he was pitched into the deep end; but fortunately he learned to swim very quickly.

Jim Howell retired in March 1981 and spent his two years of retirement travelling and enjoying himself, but unhappily he died on 24 May 1983.

Today we have carved out a rather special niche in providing industry with some of the most advanced valves in the World.

Jimmy Howell would be quietly pleased and amused if he could see the results of his earlier work, because he dug and laid the foundations of our present good future.

E. J. Howell (Director 1955–81).
Two years before his retirement (1981).

CHAPTER 12

New Products and Facilities

THE "INTELLIGENT" VALVE—THE VALVE OF THE 21 st CENTURY
(1980 to date)

In November 1979 we were invited to attend a seminar at Port Sunlight where the Department of Trade and Industry were giving a presentation to local companies about microprocessors, in the hope that local industrialists might be able to see a possible application in their own products or production.

We do not know what success others had but so far as we were concerned it did set us thinking. (See how the D.T.I. changed in the 1980's?)

For years we had supplied valves fitted with switches that would indicate whether a valve was open or closed, but having had a glimpse of what microprocessors could do we wondered if anybody was interested in what happened in between "open" and "closed". So we decided to build a valve fitted with a microprocessor circuit so that we could instruct the valve to go to a certain position and give a required flow.

A new invention, the World's first, but there was one small snag. We knew nothing about electronics, and for that matter the writer is still in that unhappy state of ignorance.

One great advantage we have in this area is the close proximity to the great University of Liverpool so we sought the University's help in developing our idea, and we appointed Dr Ray Gibson and Dr Robert Holmes of the Department of Electrical Engineering and Electronics as Consulting Engineers. In three months they had produced our Mark I device which could control a valve and gave a numeric indication of the position of the valve and also the flow through the valve.

The next stage was the development of a controller that was a little more sophisticated and which could give messages; this was the Mark II model and this was made within a year.

So far so good but we really wanted to be able to convert any standard valve into an "intelligent" valve by adding a microprocessor device and so be able to tell a valve what to do and then have the valve report back giving details of its opening position, an accurate indication of flow through the valve when handling a wide range of viscosities, as well as giving various reports about any problems there might be with the valve. Some more work was undertaken and eventually we arrived at our Mark III "intelligent" valve—the World's first.

Before publicising the new device we decided to patent it and it was patented throughout the industrial World, but at a cost in excess of £40,000 over several years.

Having built our first truly intelligent valve we wanted to have it tested and so we approached the British Standards Laboratory for the measurement of liquid and gas flow—the National Engineering Laboratory at East Kilbride. In 1983 the first intelligent valve was tested at East Kilbride and passed its tests with flying colours.

Since then we have carried out further development and extension tests on the "Intelligent Valve" and now we can convert almost any valve into an intelligent valve by adding a microprocessor on to the valve and then imprinting the particular "personality" of the valve on to the micro chips.

In future it is possible that oil rigs out in the fierce North Sea or in remote parts of the World such as the Artic or the Amazon Basin will be manless and control will be exercised from, say the U.K. Intelligent valves will be used to control the flow of fluids and will also be able to give progress reports of their state of health so that maintenance crews will know when they need to visit the rig to carry out maintenance work.

So the Intelligent Valve was born in the improbable setting of the backstreets of Hoylake, Wirral, and to identify this type of valve we designed the high tech symbol "

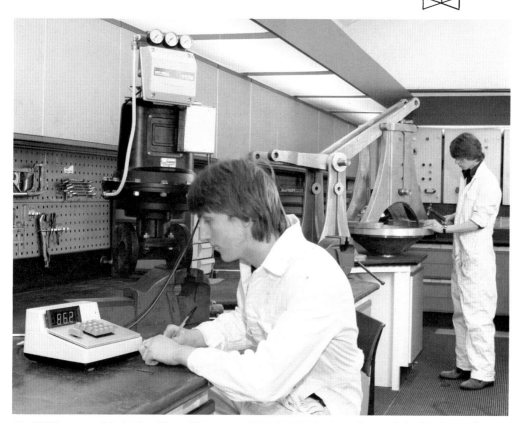

Paul Miller tests a Mark I Intelligent Valve control (1980) while in the background Joe Hughes works on one of the valve mechanisms for Isambard Kingdom Brunel's "S.S. Great Britain" designed in 1839. A photograph that encapsulates our span of engineering history. (1980).

Brian Rice (Heap & Partners) and Mr Kenneth Baker, Minister for Information Technology, with a Mark I Intelligent Valve on the Department of Industry's exhibition train that toured the country in 1981.

Roy Wrigley using a Mark II Intelligent Valve Control. (1981).

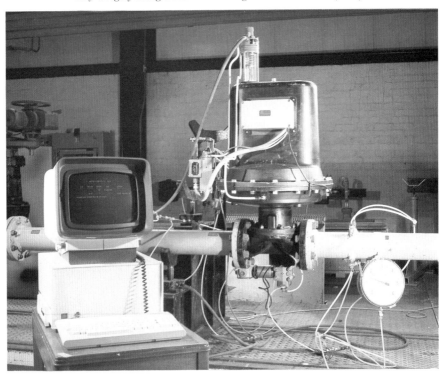

The World's first "Intelligent" valve on test at the National Engineering Laboratory, East Kilbride. (1983).

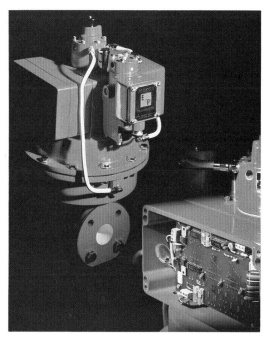

An early Mark III "Intelligent" valve. (1980).

A display of "Intelligent" valves incorporating JM (UK) EP50 electronic positioners at The Control & Instrumentation Exhibition, NEC, Birmingham, (1991).

241

FLOW TEST RIG (1985)

The National Engineering Laboratory provides a superb service to industry, but so far as we were concerned they took several months to carry out the test on the intelligent valve because of pressure of other work and also one test alone cost about £2,000 and we wanted to carry out dozens of tests on different valves, and that would be prohibitively expensive.

We approached other test houses but we found that they were even slower, and just as expensive, and time was passing; so in the end we decided to build our own flow rig.

In 1984 we were asked to give some training to Steven Low, a young graduate engineer from Birmingham University. After training, we gave Steven the job of designing and making our new flow test rig. Quite a challenge for a young engineer, but one that we were quite sure he could accomplish with some help and guidance.

We were offered help by the Department of Industry but were were reluctant to accept because of our frustrating, if comical, experiences under the Labour Party madhouse in the middle 1970's.

Eventually, however, we agreed to let them see what we were doing; but what a difference ten years had made to the Department of Industry.

Instead of sending bureaucrats who could not begin to understand what we were doing, the D.T.I. sent along a Dr Fleming, a bright young Scot who had been seconded to the D.T.I. for a year from our friends N.E.L., East Kilbride and he was an expert on microprocessors and was able to assess in a short space of time what we were aiming for and its likely value to the U.K. and mankind in general.

The D.T.I. made an offer of a substantial grant and we gratefully accepted.

Several months later the flow rig was finished complete with a computer control system developed by the University of Liverpool. Steven Low did practically all the work himself having subcontracted some of the larger fabrications, and when it was finished it worked like a dream.

We use the rig for testing intelligent valves and for calibrating valves made by other manufacturers as well as testing systems designed by some of our customers.

Steven Low left us at the end of 1989 to go back to his birthplace, Canada. In the five years Steven was with us he had made a significant contribution to our advancement and Britain's loss was Canada's gain.

The flow test rig we built in Hoylake for testing "Intelligent Valves". There are twelve Intelligent Valves used on this rig. (1985).

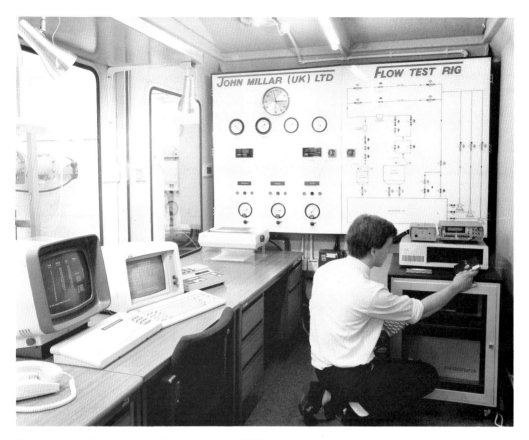

Steven Low in the control room for our flow rig. (1986).

QUALITY ASSURANCE

In 1982 John Keith Millar said that he thought we should improve our Quality Assurance Programme because the new Conservative Government was anxious to improve quality throughout British industry, and it was obvious that our high tech customers, B.N.F.L., I.C.I., Shell, Associated Octel, and others would soon be demanding Q.A. to BS5750.

The writer has to admit that he was not very enthusiastic because he could see that it would be a very time consuming and expensive programme to comply with. We were right in assessing the cost in time, and capital, but wrong in lacking enthusiasm because today we could not handle many of the sophisticated orders we manufacture with the Q.A. approval and systems.

Alan Swann our Inspector checking a gauge that had just been calibrated. In the background Mark Swann (standing) and Wayne Marigold are testing valves on test rigs at Rallim House, Hoylake. (1985). The black "Heap & Partners" nameplate above the clock is from our first test panel built in 1966 to celebrate our centenary. (See page 193).

The Quality Assurance handbook we all work to.

Initially B.N.F.L. were instrumental in encouraging us to gain approved Quality Assurance and they were very helpful in going through our systems and manufacturing methods and with their help we were approved to BS5750 (Part II) in 1983.

In 1991 we were assessed by Lloyds Register and we upgraded Heap & Partners Ltd and John Millar (UK) Ltd to BS5750 Part I, the European Standard IS9001 and have Lloyds Register Quality Assurance (LRQA) approval.

It is an expensive programme to comply with for we have spent almost half a million pounds in installing test equipment and we have to rigorously check and test at all stages of assembly and manufacture and keep a full time Inspector busy. We do however provide products that can carry deadly chemicals, or alternatively maybe used in life saving pharmaceutical plants, and we must do everything we can to ensure that the products we supply perform their design function without trouble. We like to sleep at nights.

NEW MACHINE SHOP (1985)

Late in 1984 we concluded that the demand for special control valves and control devices was likely to grow in the next few years and as our machining capacity was limited we decided to

Brian Makinson, Workshop Manager, at the Inspector's desk, Britannia House. Chris Docherty and Roy Wrigley standing. (1977).

Richard Strode at the marking out bench, Britannia House, Hoylake. (1987).

Chris Docherty operating a Colchester 2000 lathe. (1987).

Brian Makinson operating our Colchester 1600 lathe. (1987).

build a new machine shop with financial help from Andre Winter of 3i's Liverpool office. Once again we decided to expand during a recession, knowing that recessions do not last forever and that when the upturn in trade came we should be ready to cope with more work.

We appointed Carl Thompson as the Architect but as the tender prices were too high we decided to act as main contractors ourselves and one of our Sales Engineers, Peter Bolt,

Roy Wrigley operating our Ajax milling machine. (1987).

changed roles and became Main Contractor and we hired skills and labour as required. The result was an excellent building at considerably less cost than the original quotations we had received.

The new shops were just finished in time because just as the new machines were being installed we were awarded a contact for over 200 actuators, switches and nuclear shields for the Thorpe Project of B.N.F.L. at Sellafield and later this order was more than doubled in size and kept our new machines going flat out six days a week for over a year.

Steven Atkinson (left) and Dave Askew (right) in the "Clean Build and Test Area", Britannia House, Hoylake. (1991).

Test and Inspection Area, Britannia House, Hoylake. (1987).

A consignment of Saunders actuators complete with Heap & Partners Mk4 switchboxes, pilot solenoid valves and Heap & Partners special yokes fitted to cast steel globe valves for a nuclear installation. (1989).

A few of the 450 modified Saunders ESC actuators we supplied for operating bellows sealed valves for BNFL's Thorpe reprocessing plant. The actuators are fitted with our switchboxes and limit switches and have pilot solenoid valves. The yokes for marrying up the actuators, valves and parts of the nuclear shield were also made in our workshops. (1987–8).
Back Row—L to R. Paul Miller; Brian Makinson, Workshop Manager; Chris Docherty; Joe Hughes; Steve Devon; Dave Venables and Alan Swann, Inspector.

247

NEW DESIGN OF CONDENSATION PUMP AND RECEIVER SETS (1987 to date)

Since the early 1930's we had sold Dunham Bush condensation pump and receiver sets but early in 1987 Dunham Bush decided that, as the business had declined, they were going to pull out of this field in the U.K. This was a blow to us because we started to rebuild our steam trap business and the condensation pump sets, were a complimentary product.

After talking with Dunhams we decided to design a new range of set which we would manufacture in our own workshops and market under our own name.

Within a matter of six weeks we had developed a modern range of packaged, automatic, pump sets with a choice of advanced control systems and which were fitted with our own design of electronic switches.

In the first year of manufacture we sold and delivered in the North West of England alone five times the average sales of the old design of set and with exactly the same sales effort.

Our plans for the immediate future is to expand the sale of these sets in the rest of the U.K. and Europe.

Steven Low testing the first packaged condensation pump and receiver set built in Hoylake. The new range was designed by Steven Low and the first unit built in 6 weeks from deciding to go ahead with the new venture.

Peter Doleman building three condensate return sets in our Hoylake workshops. These were exported to a soap factory in Indonesia and had specially protected circuits because of the climate. (1990).

Christ Docherty standing by one of the largest and most complex condensation pump sets ever built. There are four separate circuits in this package and it is installed in a nuclear plant in the U.K. (1989).

TRAINING (1980–1991)

In 1980 we built a training room in Britannia House for use by our own staff and for training staff employed by our customers. Since then we have built similar rooms at Rallim House, Hoylake, Empire Buildings, Thornaby, Victoria House, Eccles and Royal Victor Place, London. The rapid changes in design and business methods that have taken place since 1980 mean that all our people have to have periodic updates in training to keep abreast of times.

Paul Tattum using a video for a training session at Rallim House, Hoylake. (1986).

John K. Millar takes a training course in Britannia House, Hoylake. (1988).

Training Room, Royal Victor Place, London. (1991)
L to R: Julie Geary, David Millar, Eddie Warren, and Claire Ryan.

EMPIRE BUILDINGS, THORNABY, CLEVELAND (1987)

In April 1987 we were asked by Ray Beever of Armstrong Machine Works to consider opening a branch in Teesside to service industry on the North East coast. After considering the matter we decided to go ahead with the new venture and John Millar (UK) Ltd bought a 6,500 square foot factory and offices on a very pleasant industrial estate in Thornaby, Cleveland, and as a link with the offices we occupied in Liverpool from 1945 to 1971 we called it "Empire Buildings". Ian Nisbit joined us the same month and was responsible for outside sales.

The new offices are linked to our Hoylake computer and it is self sufficient in that it has stocks, assembly facilities and test equipment with approved Quality Assurance to BS5750

*Empire Buildings,
Thornaby,
Cleveland. (1988).*

*Julie McGeeney in our Teeside
Office.*

(Part 1). It is also part of our E.D.I. links with industry in the North East and elsewhere in the country.

The office is staffed by Ian Nisbit, Stuart Laverick and Julie McGeeney and is supervised by a Director and we hope to expand the staff in the near future.

It was expected that we would lose money on the new venture for three years but we were delighted when the new office broke even in its second year and then made a small profit in its third year and in future it is expected that it will make a significant contribution to the company's profit and so we shall be able to continue our investment in the North East.

Stuart Laverick in the assembly and test area, Empire Buildings, Thornaby, Cleveland. (1988).

Sales office, Empire Buildings, Thornaby, Cleveland Ian Nisbit (R). (1988).

ELECTRONICS LABORATORY AND NEW PRODUCTS (1987–1991)

In parallel with our work on the Intelligent Valve we also designed a number of new products in the 1980's.

Steve Atkinson checking the electronic circuits of a JM (UK) switchbox. (1991).

EC66 SWITCHBOX (1989–1990)

The Saunders Valve Company introduced an excellent new design of compact actuator for small valves called the EC for valves 8mm bore upwards, and they also made a switchbox. Although we were enthusiastic about the actuator we did not like the new switchbox because in our opinion it was too flimsy and the switches that could be incorporated were too restricted. Therefore we designed our own switchboxes known as the EC66 which could incorporate many different types of switch and permutations of switch in a standard box. This product has been extremely successful.

After work done in developing the Intelligent Valve and the flow test rig it was obvious that in addition to the work being done for us by Liverpool University that we should have to build our own electronics laboratory and take on an electronics engineer. So in August 1987 Chris Marsland who had just graduated with a First Class Honours degree in electronics from the University of Liverpool joined us to work on new electronic products.

The first product Chris designed for us was electronic level control for our condensation pump and receiver sets. These level controls we now manufacture at a fraction of the cost of the old fashioned float control switches that used to be used and they are much more reliable.

EP50 VALVE POSITIONER

The second product was a new design of electronic valve positioner which was much smaller and cheaper to make than the old designs of I/P convertors and positioners. We had wanted to build these new devices for some years but lacked the "in house" capacity until our new lab was built. This we call the EP50 and it is now in production.

PROJECTS

One of the first projects to be developed and built was an order for fifty automatic control valves for British Rail, Crewe, together with a sophisticated computer control panel. The new

253

system automatically sets all the appropriate valves in their correct position to enable fuel oil, lubricating oil, water, etc., to be supplied to the various types of diesel electric locomotives used by BR. This order was built and installed by us in six weeks from receipt of the order and has been followed by further contracts.

ICS55 INTELLIGENT CONTROLLER

Our Intelligent Valve market research revealed that there was a demand for a controller which would control a small plant; switching on boilers, start and stop pumps and take charge of a complete process; but it had to be easy to programme and use.

The ICS55 intelligent control system was developed by Christ Marsland to satisfy the needs of small plants, breweries, dairies, etc.

We are sure that electronic control of valves will continue to develop in the future and we are pleased to have laid the foundations for future growth.

An ICS55 installed on a plant. (1991).

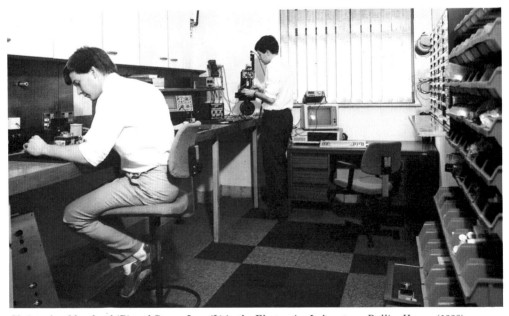

Christopher Marsland (R) and Steven Low (L) in the Electronics Laboratory, Rallim House. (1988).

*The computer panel for controlling
the static engine test beds at British
Rail, Crewe. Designed by us, built,
programmed, installed and working
6 weeks after receiving the order.
(1988).*

*EC66 switchboxes
fitted to Saunders EC
actuators. In front
are some of the
different types of
switches that can be
fitted in the standard
box. (1989–90).*

Steven Atkinson assembling EC66 switchboxes in our new Electronics Assembly Room. (1991).

The electronic circuit boards of the JM (UK) EP50 electronic-pneumatic valve positioner. (1991).

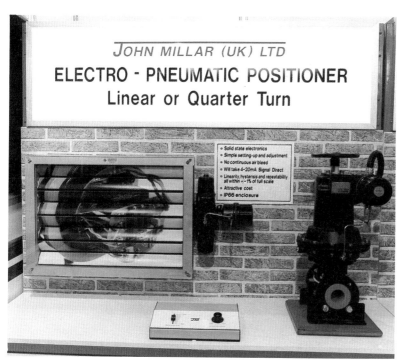

A display of the EP50 positioner in Rallim House. (1991).

A display of the JM (UK) ICS55 Intelligent Control Systems. (1991).

RETIREMENT OF JOHN MOTTERSHEAD (1989)

John Mottershead joined Heap & Partners in 1957 after serving an apprenticeship with Metropolitan Vickers Electrical Co. Ltd. of Trafford Park, Manchester and he proved to be a very useful member of the company, because in those days we were staffed by mechanical engineers and John had served an electrical apprenticeship and then worked on high vacuum plant and products and so brought skills that were badly needed.

In those days Metropolitan Vickers was one of the most important training grounds for engineers in the World. At the end of World War II there were 23,000 people employed in Trafford Park including no less than 3,000 apprentices. Young men and women came from all over the U.K. and the rest of the World to train at M.V. This great works produced; turbines, alternators, switchgear, meters and instruments, jet engines, aircraft, rocket launchers, high vacuum pumps and plant, scientific equipment and had great engineering expertise in many different fields. All backed by a superb Research Department.

Today the works is owned by GEC and there are only about 3,000 people in total working there. It is one thing to cut out overmanning and to make a company more efficient and profitable, but that is quite different from wholesale butchery in order to build a cash mountain. GEC Trafford Park still does some excellent work, but is but a shadow of its former self and we engineers who were trained by Metropolitan Vickers are not amused at what has been done to a great factory and training ground.

In 1960 we decided to open our Manchester Office and John Mottershead became Manager of our office in Royal London House, Deansgate, Manchester and later became a Director and when the office moved to Victoria House, Eccles in 1972 he was in charge of the Manchester area.

In the 1960's we represented General Engineering of Radcliffe and their subsidiary company, Genevac, both of whom made high vacuum plant and products and John recruited Roy Wrigley and Harold Turner and successfully ran the Agency in the North West of England until both companies went out of business some years ago.

Another responsibility of John Mottershead's was to run Dunham Bush in the Manchester area and their cooling division throughout the North West. He was responsible for a number of important schemes including some of the earliest heat reclaim schemes to be installed in Europe. A heat reclaim scheme is one where unwanted heat from the air in a building is extracted and put into domestic hot water. For example, in the Manchester T.V. Studios of the B.B.C. the studio arc lights generate vast quantities of heat but the Dunham Bush packaged screw refrigeration plant we supplied takes out the unwanted heat from the studios and puts it into the hot water system.

Other schemes John was responsible for included Manchester University Computer rooms, Halifax Building Society and many others. At one point we had eleven large heat reclaim schemes in the North West of England at a time when there were probably only about fifty in the whole of North America.

In small companies people have to be versatile and John Mottershead illustrated this when he designed the rotary turntable in the grounds of Victoria House, Manchester, which we use for turning commercial vehicles round after they have driven into the yard. This has worked splendidly and has been in continuous use since 1972. A far cry from electrical engineering, high vacuum plant and refrigeration, but that is engineering versatility.

In February 1989 John Mottershead decided to take early retirement so that he could spend more time travelling, gardening, fishing, enjoying golf and serving the Community by being Chairman of the Parish Council in Over Peover, Cheshire; Governor of the village school and Vice President of the village cricket club. A successful retirement is really a happy exchange of jobs.

John Mottershead, Director. (1957–89).

NEW BUSINESS TECHNOLOGY AND CONTROLS (1989)

The period 1970 when we moved to Hoylake from Liverpool until 1990 saw the company grow from employing just over twenty people to almost seventy and in that period the capital employed had grown from a couple of hundred thousand pounds to a few million. We had changed from a very small company to a small/medium size one and it was necessary to improve our Management Systems to keep tight control of the growing company. Flying the company by the seat of our pants was no longer good enough.

In 1987 David Millar joined us as Director to help with our transitions. He had taken an Honours degree in Business Studies at Portsmouth Polytechnic and had spent some time with us and the Avon Rubber Company as part of his training.

When times were easier we could manage without monthly accounts, budget control and costing analysis, but the last few years have been so difficult that only the efficient survived.

COMPUTER AIDED DESIGN (CAD) (1991)

In 1991 the demand for drawings had reached a point where we felt that we could no longer postpone moving over from traditional methods of producing drawings to C.A.D.

In July 1991 Howard Sanders who had worked for us in his long VACS, graduated with an Honours Degree in computer aided design and he joined us in our design office and he and David Millar are responsible for changing over to computer aided design.

Howard Sanders (left) and David Millar (right) using our CAD system. (1991).

E.D.I. (ELECTRONIC DATA INTERCHANGE) 1991

In 1990 our largest customer, I.C.I., said that the cost of handling comparatively small orders was so high that they wanted to link their computer to ours so that the computers could talk to each other and orders could be typed on our printers at the instruction of the I.C.I. machine.

It sounded a good idea but our computer speaks a different language to the giant I.C.I. machine and so we had to train our little fellow to translate from the I.C.I. language to ours, so that an I.C.I. employee could call up an item using their codes and this would be converted into our codes by our machine and then the paperwork could be printed on our machine.

The system went live in April 1991 and involves the printing of orders, works instructions and acknowledgement. The next phase involving invoicing is ready to go at time of writing and the final stage will follow. Then an operator on the shop floor will be able to tell the system what he requires and the computer takes care of the rest and almost instantaneously the order instructions and works manufacturing sheets are printed in our premises.

Justine Rylance in the computer Room at Britannia House. The stained glass sign was the original sign of Hoylake Laundry which occupied our Britannia House site from 1900 to 1970. It is kept as a memento of the past.

LONDON OFFICE (1991)

The changes in the EEC law in the 1980's meant that companies could no longer have an exclusive sales area and so companies from other parts of the country started to move into the North West to compete with us. We believe in competition because it stimulates ideas, improves service and gives the customer better value for money, but we do not like losing business.

The growing competition in the North West meant that we had to take advantage of our freedom to sell in other parts of the UK, Europe and the rest of the World.

Our expertise in manufacturing advanced control valves and other products enabled us to create new markets for ourselves in the South of England and so in 1989 we decided to open a London Office to help consolidate our trade in the South and to facilitate our growing export business, for London is probably the World's most important centre for developing and handling exports.

Some people say that the British Empire is dead and gone but do not believe it. Walk through the streets of any of our major cities and Empire is all around you; so are the many benefits of

No. 9, Royal Victor Place, Tower Hamlets, London. (1991).

262

Empire including London's superb connections with the countries of the Commonwealth, Europe and many other Nations.

After a search we found just what we wanted in the East End of London; an area undergoing rapid change. The premises comprised an office with a self contained flat above, but there was one small snag, however, and that was that the price of commercial property in London had rocketed over the previous three or four years and we could not afford the asking price; so we waited.

The recession of 1990 had an impact on property prices and by the end of 1990 the asking price of the premises had dropped to a reasonable figure and so we took advantage of the recession, stepped in and in January 1991 bought number 9 Royal Victor Place, Tower Hamlets, a few yards from Victoria Park, which is a magnificent park given to the citizens of the East End, in perpetuity, by Queen Victoria and only two miles from the Tower of London.

Matt Brown who had joined us in 1985 moved to London from Hoylake working on outside sales covering the process industries and we engaged two bright young 'A' Level school leavers, Claire Ryan and Julie Geary for inside work and Eddie Warren who had previously worked for Powerflex joined us to cover the Building Service Industries.

Our London office, like Manchester and Thornaby is linked to Hoylake by computer modems, dedicated telephone lines and fax.

This means that the excellent communications enable us to handle business speedily and efficiently and we have high hopes from our new venture.

General Office, Royal Victor Place. (1991). L to R. David Millar, Eddie Warren, Claire Ryan.

BUSINESS STANDARDS

Under this heading in 1976 we wrote that, if our experience was anything to go by then business standards in the UK were still very high indeed; that there had always been some corruption but it was negligible. We mentioned that we had a turnover of millions of pounds and had been awarded large contracts by Government Bodies, large companies, small companies and Local Authorities, but in over one hundred and ten years we had never offered, nor given, a bribe, nor any other form of corrupt inducement and what was more we had never been asked for one.

Unhappily we have to report that since 1976 we have been offered a substantial order, with more to follow if we co-operated, but on a very corrupt basis. The offer was made to the writer in London and will confirm the sceptic's worst suspicions that business standards in the capital have fallen.

The good news is that the unlikely venue for the corrupt offer was made in the Offices of the Trade Delegation of the USSR which are located in Highgate, London.

The offer was made some years ago by one of those mysterious East European "Iron Curtain Trade Specialists" in the presence of, and with the approval of, a mainly silent Russian Buyer, who was apparently quite happy that we should overcharge his country providing he, and the "Trade Specialist" were given a substantial cut.

We declined the offer, although it was made clear to us that if we did not accept we were unlikely to get orders in the future from them—since proved true.

We mentioned to them that we had heard that in Moscow they had an establishment called the Lubyanka, and we added that in Liverpool we had a similar place of residence, called Walton Jail. The writer had been in Walton Jail on one occasion, but only to sort out some technical problems with a condensate pump set we had supplied, and whilst he had found the inmates and warders quite pleasant, even amiable, we had no wish to take up residence there.

We left without our order, but we have no regrets. There are reports that under Mr Gorbachev a big clean up of corruption is going on in the USSR at the present time, so who knows, one day we may be able to supply goods to the Soviet Union without lowering our standards.

LINCOLN DECALOG

We ended the First Edition of this book with the Lincoln Decalog and we believe that the words are still as wise and relevant today as they were when they were first spoken—about the time our company was founded.

The Great Emancipator said:

1 You cannot bring about prosperity by discouraging thrift.
2 You cannot strengthen the weak by weakening the strong.
3 You cannot help strong men by tearing down big men.
4 You cannot help the wage earner by pulling down the wage payer.
5 You cannot help the brotherhood of man by encouraging class hatred.
6 You cannot help the poor by destroying the rich.
7 You cannot establish sound security on borrowed money.
8 You cannot keep out of trouble by spending more than you earn.
9 You cannot build character by taking away man's initiative and independence.
10 You cannot help men permanently by doing for them what they could and should do for themselves.

HEAP & PARTNERS LIMITED

Britannia House
Newton Road
Hoylake
Wirral
Cheshire
L47 3DG

Empire Buildings
Dukesway
Teesside Industrial Estate
Thornaby
Cleveland

Victoria House
Albert Street
Eccles
Manchester
M30 0NR

9 Royal Victor
Place
Old Ford Road
Tower Hamlets
London E3 5SS

DIRECTORS
John Millar (Chairman & Managing Director)
John Keith Millar
Paul M. Tattum
David P. Millar

COMPANY SECRETARY
Raymond P. Vine

SHAREHOLDERS
John Millar
Dorothy Dean Millar
Ann Dean Tattum
John Keith Millar
David Paul Millar

BANKERS TO HEAP & PARTNERS LTD
Midland Bank plc
City Office
4 Dale Street
Liverpool
L69 2BZ

ACCOUNTANTS
Sloan & Company
19/21 Stanley Street
Liverpool
L1 6AA

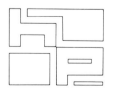

265

JOHN MILLAR (UK) LTD

Rallim House
Carham Road
Carr Lane Industrial Estate
Hoylake
Wirral
Cheshire
L47 4FF

Empire Buildings
Dukesway
Teesside Industrial Estate
Thornaby
Cleveland

9 Royal Victor Place
Old Ford Road
Tower Hamlets
London
E3 5SS

DIRECTORS
John Millar (Chairman & Managing Director)
Dorothy Millar
John Keith Millar
Paul M. Tattum
David P. Millar

COMPANY SECRETARY
Ann D. Tattum

SHAREHOLDERS
John K. Millar
Ann D. Tattum
David P. Millar
Dorothy D. Millar
John Millar

BANKERS TO JOHN MILLAR (UK) LTD
Barclays Bank plc
22 Grange Road
West Kirby
Wirral

ACCOUNTANTS
Sloan & Company
19/21 Stanley Street
Liverpool
L1 6AA

Although we no longer have commercial links with Heap Noseworthy we keep in touch and for historical interest and we give their Directors and Offices.

Heap Noseworthy Ltd
Head Office
87 O'Leary Avenue
St John's
Newfoundland
Canada

DIRECTORS AND OFFICERS
David A. Cook, Phar., President
Elizabeth S. Parke, Secretary
Peter P. Cook, Director
Norval R. Blair, Director
Chesley Penney, Director
John B. Angel, B. Eng., Ph.D., Director
Angus Angel, Director
Roger F. Angel, B.Eng., Director
Verne J. Somers, C. A., Director

SHAREHOLDERS
T. McMurdo & Co., Ltd. (Established 1823)
The Angel Family

Bibliography

The Life and Labours of Mr Brassey, by Arthur Helps. G. Bell & Sons Ltd, London 1872.

The Lives of George and Robert Stephenson, by Samuel Smiles. John Murray, London 1857.

Thomas Brassey, Railway Builder, by Charles Walker. Frederick Muller, 1969.

Isambard Kingdom Brunel, by L. T. C. Rolt. Longmans Green, London 1957.

The Grand Trunk Railway of Canada by A. W. Currie. University of Toronto Press, Toronto 1957.

The Railway Navvies by T. Coleman. Hutchinson, London 1965.

Birkenhead and its Surroundings by H. K. Aspinall. The Liverpool Booksellers Co. Ltd., 1903.

The Britannia and Conway Tubular Bridges by Edwin Clark. Day and Son, Gate St., London, 1850.

The Newfoundland Railway (Book of Newfoundland) by Alfred R. Penny. St John's, Newfoundland.

The Construction of the Great Victoria Bridge by James Hodges. John Weale, London 1860.

The Contribution of Sir William Fairbairn to the Advancement of Mechanical Engineering by A. I. Smith. Institute of Mechanical Engineers, London 1975.

The Civil Engineers' and Architects Journal (page 224, 1848). (Description of the Roberts Jacquard Press.)

The Great Northern Railway of Ireland by E. M. Patterson. The Oakwood Press, 1962.

Ireland Vol. I and II Railway History by Alan McCutcheon. David & Charles.

Collected Letters of Sir Lawrence Bragg. The Royal Society, London 1975.

The Battle for the Mediterranean by Donald Macintyre. B.T. Batsford Ltd., London 1964.

A Talent for Trouble by Captain Sir Ranulph Twistleton-Wykeham-Fiennes. Hodder & Stoughton Ltd., London 1970.

Engineering Heritage edited by E. G. Semler. Institution of Mechanical Engineers.

The Boyne Viaduct by K. A. Murray. Irish Railway Record Society, 1947–49.

Seven Golden Miles by Kathleen Eyre. 1961.

OUR STAFF

A company is made up of people, and it is as good, or as bad as they are. We think we are very fortunate in the quality of our staff and they are as good today as ever they were, perhaps better. It is not possible to mention them all in the text of our story, but here they are together with the date they joined the firm.

John Millar (1952)

Peter Bolt (1963)

Brian Aves (1963)

Raymond Vine (1964)

Alan Close (1966)

Susan Boswell (1968)

May Garrity (1968)

Graham Gould (1969)

Leslie Allen (1970)

Antony Smith (1970)

Ann Smith (1972)

Lynne Bottomley (1974)

Denise Willey(1975)

Joe Hughes (1976)

John K Millar (1977)

Mark Swann (1977)

Peter Doleman (1978)

Gerard Williams (1978)

Steven Devon (1978)

Brian Makinson (1979)

David Venables (1979)

Ann Tattum (1979)

Valerie Fulton (1979)

Dorothy Millar (1980)

David Kehoe (1980)

Douglas Macey (1980)

David Askew (1981)

Paul Tattum (1981)

Denise White (1982)

Brian Sutton (1982)

Christine Hamilton (1982)

Kathleen Watts (1982)

Richard Gibson (1982)

Alan Hayes (1982)

Alan Swann (1983)

David Shiells (1983)

Christopher Hall (1984)

Valerie Ward (1985)

Matthew Brown (1985)

Susan Lunt (1986)

Ian Nisbet (1987)

Brian Fulton (1987)

Christopher Marsland (1987)

Stephen Atkinson (1987)

Mark Furlong (1987)

Susan Hughes (1987)

Stuart Laverick (1987)

Craig Fulton (1988)

Sally Ann Smith (1988)

Neil Hart (1988)

Ian Youd (1988)

Katherine Caswell (1988)

John Rayner (1989)

Geoffrey Hamilton (1989)

Debbie Sherlock (1989)

Jason Richards (1989)

Brian Stott (1989)

Rupert Owen (1989)

Sarah Patterson (1989)

David Millar (1989)

Julie McGeeney (1989)

Mark Lomas (1989)

Melanie Tucker (1990)

Claire Lamey (1990)

Andrew Hartley (1990)

James Neal (1990)

Howard Sanders (1991)

Claire Ryan (1991)

Julie Geary (1991)

Eddie Warren (1991)

INDEX

Britannia House at dusk. (1981). (Photograph by Roger Sanders)